300 best
Chocolate
recipes

D1021872

300 best
Chocolate
recipes

Julie Hasson

Robert
ROSE

For complete cataloging information, see page 368.

Disclaimer
The recipes in this book have been carefully tested by our kitchen and our tasters. To the best of our knowledge, they are safe and nutritious for ordinary use and users. For those people with food or other allergies, or who have special food requirements or health issues, please read the suggested contents of each recipe carefully and determine whether or not they may create a problem for you. All recipes are used at the risk of the consumer.

We cannot be responsible for any hazards, loss or damage that may occur as a result of any recipe use.

For those with special needs, allergies, requirements or health problems, in the event of any doubt, please contact your medical adviser prior to the use of any recipe.

Design & Production: PageWave Graphics Inc.
Editor: Sue Sumeraj
Recipe Tester: Jennifer MacKenzie
Proofreader: Sheila Wawanash
Indexer: Gillian Watts
Photography: Mark T. Shapiro
Food Styling: Kate Bush
Prop Styling: Charlene Erricson

Cover image: Chocolate Potato Cake (page 102)

We acknowledge the financial support of the Government of Canada through the Book Publishing Industry Development Program (BPIDP) for our publishing activities.

Published by Robert Rose Inc.
120 Eglinton Avenue East, Suite 800, Toronto, Ontario, Canada M4P 1E2
Tel: (416) 322-6552 Fax: (416) 322-6936

Printed in Canada
1 2 3 4 5 6 7 8 9 FP 14 13 12 11 10 09 08 07 06

To Jay, my soulmate

Contents

Acknowledgments *8*

Introduction *9*

Common Ingredients *10*

Tools and Equipment for Perfect Desserts *17*

Kitchen Tips *22*

Breakfasts *25*

Breads, Sandwiches and Scones *37*

Muffins *59*

Cakes *81*

Cupcakes *131*

Pies, Tarts and Pastries *149*

Cookies, Bars and Squares *175*

Candies, Snacks and Other Treats *237*

Puddings and Mousses *263*

Frozen Desserts *285*

Sauces, Syrups, Frostings and Spreads *317*

Beverages *343*

Sources *369*

Index *371*

Acknowledgments

You've heard the expression "It takes a village to raise a child." Well, it takes an army to produce a cookbook. A legion of people were involved in putting this book together, and I would like to express my heartfelt thanks to all of you:

- Lisa Ekus, for being my über-agent.
- Bob Dees at Robert Rose: it's always a pleasure working with you.
- Carol Sherman and Sue Sumeraj, for your great editing and for making everything come together so beautifully.
- Jennifer MacKenzie, for your excellent recipe testing and recommendations.
- Mark Shapiro, for your fine photography, and Kate Bush and Charlene Erricson, for your great food and props styling.
- Andrew Smith, Kevin Cockburn, Daniella Zanchetta and everyone at PageWave Graphics.
- Everyone at Robert Rose for working so hard on this book and doing such a great job!
- My incredible husband, Jay, for your awesome support, humor and love. I couldn't do it without you. You truly are the best!
- My beautiful children, Sydney and Noah, for tasting thousands of recipes, even when you thought that you couldn't possibly taste another bite. You are incredible kids!
- Mom, for sharing your love of great food with me. Thanks for starting me on this delicious journey.
- Jon, for all of your support and great culinary input.
- Louie, for your love and support.

Introduction

I adore chocolate in any shape or form. Whether it's bittersweet, semisweet, milk or white, I love them all. One day, while I was contemplating the wonderful virtues of chocolate, my publisher approached me with the idea of writing a cookbook on chocolate. I thought, "What a timely idea." I have mountains of it in my kitchen, and I bake with it almost daily. To be honest, I wouldn't dream of showing up to a meeting or dinner party without some chocolate goodie in hand. The topic of chocolate was kismet. Before I could say yes, my imagination was already off concocting recipes.

Over the past 17 years, I have worked as a pastry chef, caterer, recipe developer and writer. Life has taken me down many interesting paths, juggling work, family, business and other responsibilities along the way. But through it all, food has always been the focus. Although I have a great reputation for my cooking, my desserts take on a life all their own.

After cooking school, I worked in several restaurants and bakeries in Los Angeles. When I was ready to branch out on my own, my husband, Jay, and I opened a bakery in Los Angeles called Baby Cakes. At that time, the coffeehouse boom had just started, and we supplied coffeehouses and restaurants with biscotti, cakes, cookies and specialty desserts. Jay and I also owned and operated a catering and baking company in Boise, Idaho, for six years. I regularly teach cooking classes and contribute articles and recipes to several popular food magazines. I have included a few of the recipes from these articles in this book, as well as many of the most-requested recipes and best-selling items from my bakery.

From years of commercial baking, I have learned to streamline my recipes. Without sacrificing taste or flavor, I take them to their basic form, eliminating the intimidation factor. Because I have simplified the techniques, the preparation time is decreased significantly. Most of these recipes are designed for maximum impression with minimum fuss, and they can be thrown together in a matter of minutes.

Take some time to acquaint yourself with the list of ingredients, tools and equipment on the following pages. Make a list of all the things you'll need to round out your cabinets and pantry, then go shopping. That way, whenever the spirit moves you, you can pull out the cooking paraphernalia and go to town.

Last, but not least, invite children into the kitchen. They will become your greatest fans. And who knows — with any luck, one day *they* may cook for you. Have fun!

— Julie Hasson

Common Ingredients

I have included a list of common ingredients used in this book. I recommend stocking your pantry with many of these items, as it will make baking a snap. If you have to run to the store every time you want to bake a cake or whip up a batch of cookies, you will think twice about baking. My trick is to always have certain items on hand so that at any given moment I can whip together a recipe. With items such as chocolate chips, flour, oats, sugar, butter, eggs, milk and nuts in your pantry or fridge, you can throw together scones, cookies, ice creams, puddings, cakes and other treats in mere minutes.

CHOCOLATE

Bittersweet, semisweet and unsweetened chocolates vary depending on the percentage of chocolate liquor (a by-product of the manufacturing of the cocoa beans into chocolate) and sugar they contain. By law, bittersweet and semisweet chocolates must contain at least 35% chocolate liquor.

> **Tip**
>
> Store chocolate in a cool, dry place for up to one year. Chocolate will sometimes develop a white "bloom," or coating, when it gets too warm, causing the cocoa butter to separate. The chocolate is still fine to use in recipes or for melting.

Readily available store brands include Ghirardelli, Nestlé, Hershey's, Baker's and President's Choice. Some of the premium brands include Callebaut, Valrhona, Scharffen Berger and El Rey. Although these premium chocolates will often give you superior results, you don't always have to use them to make delicious desserts. In some baked goods, the distinguishing flavors of the premium chocolates can be lost to some extent. You can save these chocolates for dipping, candies and sauces, where you want the distinct chocolate flavor to shine through.

Dark chocolate: Many dark chocolate bars now come with a percentage on the package. The percentage represents the amount of cacao (cocoa butter, cocoa powder and cocoa mass) by weight in the bar. The remaining percentage is sugar and a small amount of vanilla, and often soy lecithin. The higher the percentage of cacao, the deeper the chocolate flavor will be.

Bittersweet chocolate: This is a dark chocolate that contains less sugar than semisweet chocolate, with an intense flavor.

Semisweet chocolate: Semisweet chocolate is slightly sweeter, with a somewhat less intense chocolate flavor. Often, but not always, this chocolate can be used interchangeably with bittersweet chocolate.

Milk chocolate: This mild chocolate contains dry or condensed whole milk, which produces a creamy chocolate flavor. Milk chocolate must contain a minimum of 10% chocolate liquor and 12% milk solids.

Unsweetened chocolate: I like to use unsweetened chocolate in tandem with chocolate chips as it can deepen and enhance the chocolate flavor. Baking chocolate and bittersweet chocolate cannot be substituted for the unsweetened chocolate in these recipes.

Semisweet and bittersweet chocolate bars: I like to keep a few on hand because if you are out of chocolate chips, they make a very tasty stand-in. Coarsely chop the bars with a sharp chef's knife and use, measure for measure, as you would chocolate chips. Valrhona and Scharffen Berger are two very good brands. They are becoming more readily available at better grocery and health food stores.

Chocolate chips: When using chocolate chips in these recipes, use good-quality, real semisweet chocolate chips. The better the quality, the better the taste of the final product. I recommend keeping a big bag of chocolate chips in the pantry at all times so that you can be ready to go with any of these recipes. Large bags of chocolate chips are available at club stores in most cities.

White chocolate: White chocolate is technically not chocolate, as it contains none of the cocoa solids that give chocolate its flavor. It is often made of cocoa butter, milk and sugar, but can contain hydrogenated fats instead of cocoa butter. North American store brands tend to be somewhat sweeter than European or premium brands.

Tip

Cocoa powder needs to be sifted before use because it can be very lumpy, which makes it difficult to incorporate. Use a fine-meshed sieve to remove any lumps before adding cocoa powder to other dry ingredients.

Unsweetened cocoa powder: I use unsweetened Dutch-process cocoa powder in my baking. It is a dark, rich cocoa powder that has been processed with alkali, which neutralizes its natural acidity. Pernigotti, Van Leer, Droste and Guittard are all excellent brands of Dutch-process cocoa powder.

COFFEE

Ground coffee: The recipes in this book were tested using finely ground French-roast coffee beans. To make strong-brewed coffee, use a ratio of 2 tbsp (25 mL) finely ground coffee per 6 oz (175 mL) water. This ratio will yield a strong yet flavorful brewed coffee.

Instant coffee granules: This is an easy way to add coffee flavor without brewing coffee. The crystals dissolve instantly in hot liquid.

DAIRY

Butter: I recommend using unsalted butter unless otherwise specified in the recipe. The quality is better, the flavor purer, and you can control the saltiness of your recipe. If you only have salted butter in the house, you can substitute it in most cases; just be sure to omit all other salt called for in the recipe. Unless otherwise noted in a recipe, margarine cannot always be substituted for butter, as it can drastically affect the final product.

Tip

To bring cold butter to room temperature in a hurry, use a microwave oven. I usually set it on Medium (50%) for 10 to 20 seconds, making sure not to melt the butter.

Buttermilk: Buttermilk is made from low-fat or nonfat milk that has had a bacterial culture added (somewhat like yogurt), creating a slightly tangy, creamy product. It gives baked goods a delicious flavor and moist texture.

Tip

If you are out of buttermilk, you can make your own sour milk: Pour 1 tbsp (15 mL) lemon juice or white vinegar into a measuring cup. Add enough milk to make 1 cup (250 mL). Let stand for about 5 minutes before using.

Milk: The recipes in this book were tested using whole milk, but 2% is also acceptable. Do not substitute nonfat or low-fat varieties, as this can affect the outcome of a recipe.

Cream: Look for whipping (35%) cream, or heavy whipping cream, as well as half-and-half (10%) cream. They will keep, refrigerated, for quite a while. For better flavor, look for brands from organic dairies. I always have cream on hand, as it is perfect for last-minute desserts, from ice cream to truffles.

Cream cheese: Cream cheese is a fresh cheese made from cow's milk. For quality and consistency, you are better off sticking with name brands and avoiding the "spreadable" nonfat or low-fat varieties in baking.

Sour cream: The addition of sour cream, a high-fat version of buttermilk, helps produce rich and tender results. Light, low-fat and nonfat varieties are not interchangeable with regular sour cream in these recipes.

Sweetened condensed milk: Sweetened condensed milk is made from sweetened nonfat or whole milk with all of the water removed. It is not the same as evaporated milk and cannot be used interchangeably.

DRIED FRUIT

Dried fruit is great to keep on hand for baking. Certain fruits, such as dried cherries, cranberries and apricots, go especially well with chocolate.

EGGS

The recipes in this book were tested using large eggs. I generally suggest bringing your eggs to room temperature for baking, but in most of these recipes you can use chilled eggs if need be. Store your eggs in the refrigerator.

EXTRACTS AND FLAVORINGS

Always use pure extracts in your baking, as they are superior in quality and flavor to artificial flavorings. Imitation vanilla is made from synthetic substances, which imitate only part of the natural vanilla smell and flavor.

Lemon oil: This is a fabulous flavoring that I prefer to lemon extract. It is made from pressed fresh lemons and is 100% pure, with a bright lemon flavor. It is also available in lime and orange. Look for the Boyajian brand (see Sources, page 369).

FLAVORED BAKING CHIPS

Some of the recipes in this book call for flavored chips, such as mint, butterscotch, milk or white baking chips. Do not substitute these chips for semisweet chocolate chips.

FLOUR

All of the recipes in this book were tested using unbleached all-purpose flour, which I feel is a healthier alternative. Bleached flour has been chemically treated and bromated; I prefer not to use it. You can, however, substitute bleached flour for unbleached flour in these recipes.

LIQUEURS

I love to keep a stash of flavored liqueurs and spirits on hand for cooking and baking. Some key ones are rum, orange liqueur (such as Triple Sec), kirsch (cherry brandy), coffee liqueur and brandy. Airline-size bottles work great in a pinch if you don't have full-size bottles on hand.

Tip

To make your own nonstick pan release, whip together $1/3$ cup (75 mL) vegetable or canola oil, $1/3$ cup (75 mL) vegetable shortening and $1/3$ cup (75 mL) all-purpose flour. (I use a mini food processor for this.) Store in an airtight container in the refrigerator (it will last several months).

NONSTICK COOKING SPRAY

This is a great time saver in the dessert kitchen. Nonstick cooking spray is a quick way to grease your pans and can be more reliable than butter or oil. Choose a spray that is unflavored. Use a pastry brush to "paint" or coat the inside of baking pans.

Tip

To toast nuts: Preheat oven to 350°F (180°C). Spread nuts on a foil- or parchment-lined baking sheet and bake for 5 to 10 minutes, stirring occasionally, or until lightly browned and fragrant.

NUTS

The recipes in this book use a variety of nuts, such as almonds, walnuts and pecans. Store nuts in the freezer to keep them fresh, as they can become rancid very quickly. Toast them for the fullest flavor (see Tip, at left).

OATS

Oats are a whole grain that are usually purchased "rolled." Buy quick-cooking and old-fashioned varieties to use in cookies, bars, cakes and granola. They are not interchangeable.

OIL

The recipes in this book call for vegetable oil. I prefer canola oil, but you can substitute another vegetable oil should you desire. You will want to use a light, flavorless oil, which is why olive oil is not a good choice.

SALT

All of the recipes in this book were tested with plain table salt. Although I like kosher or sea salt on my food, I prefer to use table salt for baking.

SHORTENING

When the recipe calls for shortening, always use solid white vegetable shortening. Do not substitute margarine or butter.

SPICES

Certain spices, such as ground cinnamon, ground ginger, ground allspice, ground cloves and ground cardamom, are a must-have in the dessert kitchen. Ground spices tend to go stale quickly, so discard them if they are no longer fragrant.

SUGAR

Granulated sugar: A highly refined sugar that comes from sugar beets or sugar cane.

Confectioner's (icing) sugar: Sugar that has been "powdered" or pulverized and mixed with a small amount of cornstarch.

Brown sugar: Granulated sugar mixed with molasses. When a recipe calls for "packed brown sugar" (without specifying light or dark), medium, golden or light brown sugar can be used. Medium brown sugar, a blend of light and dark brown sugars, can be found in large bags at club stores. I have used it with great success in many of the recipes in this book.

Tip

If you cannot find superfine sugar in your local grocery store, you can make your own: Process granulated sugar in a food processor until very finely ground.

Superfine or baker's sugar: Ultra-fine granulated sugar that dissolves very quickly in liquid.

Corn syrup: This thick, sweet syrup is made from cornstarch. Corn syrup can be purchased in both light and dark varieties.

Honey: Bees make honey from flower nectar. When using honey as a sweetener, the darker the honey, the stronger the flavor. A light honey is preferable when you don't want to overwhelm the flavors of a dessert. Do not substitute honey for sugar unless called for in a specific recipe.

Molasses: The liquid left after pure sugar has been extracted from sugar cane or sugar beets. There are several varieties of molasses: sulphured and unsulphured, fancy, cooking and blackstrap. The recipes in this book were tested with light unsulphured or fancy molasses.

Tools and Equipment for Perfect Desserts

In the grand world of kitchen equipment, there are definitely items that make baking a breeze. You can certainly make do with a large mixing bowl, a wooden spoon and a sturdy baking sheet, and in some cases I believe simplicity is better. But drawing on my experience in professional kitchens and my obsession with kitchen equipment, here's a list of equipment I believe will make everyone a professional in the kitchen.

MEASURING EQUIPMENT

Liquid measuring cups: The most accurate way to measure liquid ingredients is in glass or plastic liquid measuring cups with a lip or spout. I keep a variety of sizes in my kitchen. Glass measuring cups are also perfect for melting chocolate and chocolate chips in the microwave (see Tip, page 21). Oxo makes some brilliant plastic measuring cups that make it easy to read the measurements from both the side and the top. (Don't use the plastic measuring cups in a microwave oven, though!)

Dry measuring cups: These are the most accurate way (with the exception of a digital scale) to measure dry ingredients. I like to use a good-quality set of metal nesting measuring cups, which come in a variety of measurements.

Tip
When measuring, always remember to spoon your dry ingredients into the cup and level the top by scraping across it with the flat side of a knife or skewer. This will give you an accurate measurement.

Measuring spoons: These are the most accurate way to measure small amounts of both liquid and dry ingredients. Look for a metal set that ranges from $\frac{1}{8}$ tsp (0.5 mL) to 1 tbsp (15 mL).

Mixing bowls: A nesting set (or two or three) of mixing bowls is a must in the dessert kitchen. I like to use both stainless steel and ceramic, depending on the mixing job. Stainless steel works better for whipping cream, ceramic for mixing cookie or cake batters.

Cookie/ice cream scoops: Available in a variety of sizes, these are a blessing in the kitchen. Use scoops to measure batter and dough evenly so that every cookie and muffin will turn out the same size. Plus, using a scoop will save you quite a bit of time.

HAND TOOLS

Heat-safe rubber spatulas: The new silicone spatulas are heatproof to 600°F (300°C). They are a boon to bakers, as they will scrape a bowl clean with ease. They are dishwasher-safe and can be used for stove-top cooking as well.

Microplane® zester/grater: This tool makes quick work of removing and grating citrus zest. Just rub it over the surface of oranges, lemons and limes, carefully removing the colored peel.

Sifter or strainer: This is an important tool for sifting dry ingredients or dusting a dessert with confectioner's (icing) sugar.

Whisk: The most important tool for cream, eggs, batter and anything else that requires whisking.

BAKING EQUIPMENT

Baking pans: You will need a variety of pans to make the desserts in this book. Always invest in heavier, quality pans, as they conduct heat more efficiently. Here's a list of the basic pan sizes I use frequently:

- 9- by 5-inch (2 L) metal loaf pan
- 8-inch (2 L) square metal pan
- 13- by 9-inch (3 L) baking pan
- muffin tins
- madeleine tins
- rimmed baking sheets (also known as jelly-roll pans)
- 10-inch (3 L) Bundt pan
- 9-inch (23 cm) springform pan
- 9-inch (23 cm) tart pan

Silicone baking pans: These are the baking pans of the future. Like Silpat® pan liners (see below), they are made with food-safe silicone and can withstand temperatures from −40°F (−40°C) to 480°F (248°C). My favorite are Flexipans® from Demarle. They require no greasing and are totally nonstick, making your baked goods look like they came from a French bakery.

Baking sheets: These are key pieces of equipment in the dessert kitchen. Look for good-quality, heavy-duty construction and feel. You can often purchase them bundled in groups of two or three at large warehouse stores. A good-quality pan is definitely worth the small investment.

Nonstick saucepans and skillets: There really are big differences in quality with nonstick pans. I personally like a saucepan that has a nice heavy feel to it yet releases food with ease. You will love making custards, puddings and sauces in nonstick saucepans. They're not a must, but they certainly make cooking (and cleanup) easy.

Parchment paper: This grease- and heat-resistant paper is used to line baking pans. It keeps your cookies and cakes from sticking and burning (unless you overbake them) and makes cleanup a breeze. This is the number one item on my list of baking equipment. It is sometimes labeled "baking paper" and is stocked with other food wraps or in the baking section in the grocery store.

Silpat® pan liners: Fabulous nonstick baking mats that fit on top of your baking sheet. Used in place of parchment paper, they are heat resistant up to 480°F (248°C), making any baking sheet nonstick. Silpat® pan liners are made of woven glass coated with food-safe silicone.

Cooling rack: A wire cooling rack elevates baking pans or baked goods so that air can circulate around them.

ELECTRIC EQUIPMENT

Stand mixer: This isn't a must for all recipes, but it sure makes life a lot easier. I recommend a heavy, sturdy stand mixer, such as a KitchenAid®. It will last you for years (and comes in some beautiful colors). A stand mixer is your best bet for mixing batters, whipping cream or beating eggs.

Hand mixer: This is a great tool for quickly whipping cream or egg whites.

Blender: This is a must for smoothies and milkshakes. Try to find a blender that has an ice-crushing button, which works well for frozen fruit or chocolate bits.

Immersion/stick blender: I love immersion/stick blenders. They blend quickly with a minimum of mess, making them ideal for sauces, dressings and whipped cream.

Food processor: This machine is essential for chopping nuts, chocolate chips, dried fruit and cookies, and for making the most delectable scones imaginable! I recommend the Cuisinart® and KitchenAid® brands. They will last forever and do a more consistent job than less expensive brands.

Chocolate tempering machine: Designed for home use, this machine takes the labor and guesswork out of tempering chocolate. It heats the chocolate to a precise temperature, cools it slightly, then reheats and mixes it. When tempered chocolate cools, it will be evenly colored, shiny and crisp, yet will melt to a smooth, creamy consistency. If you enjoy making chocolate candies at home, this is a fantastic tool. I've been using a ChocoVision® for tempering chocolate, and it's an impressive machine.

Ice cream maker: Not only are these machines fun to use, but homemade ice cream and sorbets are nothing short of ethereal! There are several kinds of ice cream makers on the market — from those that use a frozen insulated bowl to those that have a built-in compressor — and a lot of them are reasonably priced. I tested the ice cream recipes in this book on several models of Cuisinart® machines, and I absolutely loved them.

Microwave oven: A microwave oven is definitely a plus in the dessert kitchen. I use mine extensively to melt chocolate, heat cream and soften butter. (You can also use a double boiler to melt chocolate.) I have tested the recipes in this book using a 1,000-watt microwave oven.

Tip

To melt chocolate in a microwave oven: In a large microwave-safe bowl (preferably a large glass measuring cup), melt chocolate or chocolate chips (and shortening, cream or butter, if using) on High, uncovered, for 30-second intervals, stopping the microwave and stirring every 30 seconds, until chocolate is shiny and almost melted. Stir until smooth. Be careful not to overheat or cook the chocolate too long, as it burns easily.

Oven: It really doesn't matter whether you use a gas or electric oven for baking. But do make sure the oven is calibrated (precisely adjusted) so that it bakes evenly and at the required temperature. A great way to make sure your oven is baking at the correct temperature is to use an oven thermometer. Leave it in your oven at all times, as it can withstand high temperatures. Before placing your items in the oven to bake, check the thermometer to make sure the oven is at the correct temperature.

Kitchen Tips

Here are a few tips to help make you a professional in the kitchen.

- Remember that cooking and baking are fun! I like to look at them as a spiritual retreat from the chaos and stress of our everyday lives.
- Read through the entire recipe before starting. That way, you know both the steps and the ingredients in the recipe before you start.
- Place your baking racks as close to the center of the oven as possible.
- Make sure your oven is fully preheated before baking. It will likely take between 15 and 20 minutes to preheat, depending on your oven.
- Line your baking sheets with parchment paper for blissful baking. It will keep your baked goods from sticking, making cleanup a snap.
- When measuring dry ingredients, always spoon them into dry measuring cups or spoons, then level the top by scraping across it with the flat side of a knife or skewer.
- Use a cookie scoop for both consistency and a professional appearance. Your scones, cookies and muffins will bake more evenly if they are all the same size.
- Make sure your cookies and scones are evenly spaced on the pan to allow room for spreading and rising. Place them 2 to 3 inches (5 to 7.5 cm) apart.
- Let your baking pans cool thoroughly before reusing for your next batch.
- If baking more than one pan at a time, rotate the pans halfway through baking. Baking will take slightly longer. Adjust your baking time accordingly, relying on visual signs of doneness; generally, you will need to bake about 5 minutes longer.
- Store chocolate at room temperature for up to 1 year. Wrap it in a large resealable bag or several layers of plastic wrap and store away from strong-smelling foods.

Breakfasts

Chocolate Chip Cherry Granola *26*

Cinnamon Toast with Milk Chocolate *27*

Chocolate Chip Cherry Breakfast Biscuits *28*

Chocolate Chip Oat Breakfast Biscuits *29*

Maple-Glazed Chocolate Walnut Breakfast Biscuits *30*

Chocolate Chip Hotcakes *32*

Chocolate Chip Pecan Waffles *33*

Chocolate Orange French Toast *34*

Raspberry Dutch Baby with Chocolate Chips *35*

Chocolate Chip Cherry Granola

This is definitely the breakfast of champions. It is also delicious as an afternoon or midnight snack, sprinkled over vanilla ice cream or just eaten out of the hand like a trail mix.

TIPS

Kitchen shears are a great way to slice dried apricots (or any dried fruit, for that matter).

This granola can be stored in an airtight container for several weeks.

Preheat oven to 350°F (180°C)
Rimmed baking sheet, lined with foil

4 cups	old-fashioned rolled oats	1 L
1 cup	almonds, sliced, slivered or chopped	250 mL
1/2 cup	packed light brown sugar	125 mL
2 tsp	ground cinnamon	10 mL
1/2 cup	unsalted butter, melted	125 mL
1/4 cup	liquid honey	50 mL
1 cup	semisweet chocolate chips	250 mL
1 cup	dried sour cherries	250 mL
1/2 cup	dried apricots, snipped into thin strips (see Tip, at left)	125 mL

1. In a large bowl, toss together oats, almonds, brown sugar and cinnamon.

2. Whisk together melted butter and honey. Pour over oat mixture, mixing well until all the oats are coated.

3. Spread mixture onto prepared baking sheet. Bake in preheated oven, stirring occasionally, for 25 to 30 minutes or until golden brown. Remove from oven and let cool.

4. Place cooled oat mixture in a large bowl and toss with chocolate chips, dried cherries and dried apricots.

Variations

Substitute dried cranberries for the cherries or vegetable oil for the butter. If you use oil instead of butter, the texture will be the same, but the granola will not have a buttery taste.

Cinnamon Toast with Milk Chocolate

SERVES 4

This recipe usually serves four, but when I made it, it served only one. My daughter ate this up with gusto. Sometimes siblings show no mercy when it comes to sharing. In our house, if you snooze, you lose.

2 tbsp	unsalted butter	25 mL
$1/4$ cup	packed light brown sugar	50 mL
$1/2$ tsp	ground cinnamon	2 mL
3 oz	milk chocolate	90 g
4	slices buttermilk or egg bread	4

1. In a food processor fitted with a metal blade, pulse butter, brown sugar, cinnamon and chocolate until well mixed and chunky.

2. Toast bread. Sprinkle chocolate mixture evenly over warm toast and spread with a knife. Serve immediately.

Variation
Substitute bittersweet chocolate for the milk chocolate.

Chocolate Chip Cherry Breakfast Biscuits

These are amazingly delicious biscuits. I wanted to create a recipe for a cream-style biscuit that you could eat for breakfast, studded with dried cherries and chocolate chips. This recipe is it.

TIPS

This recipe can be doubled.

The biscuits will stay fresh for several days if stored in an airtight container.

Ragged dough looks moistened but doesn't form a ball.

Preheat oven to 400°F (200°C)
Baking sheet, lined with parchment paper

2 1/4 cups	all-purpose flour	550 mL
1/3 cup	dried sour cherries	75 mL
1/3 cup	semisweet chocolate chips	75 mL
1/4 cup	granulated sugar	50 mL
1 tbsp	baking powder	15 mL
1/4 tsp	salt	1 mL
1 1/4 cups	whipping (35%) cream	300 mL

Topping

2 tbsp	whipping (35%) cream	25 mL
	Confectioner's (icing) sugar, for dusting	

1. In a large bowl, mix together flour, cherries, chocolate chips, sugar, baking powder and salt.

2. Pour in cream, stirring just until dough is soft and ragged (see Tip, at left).

3. Turn out dough onto a lightly floured work surface and gently shape into an 8- by 6-inch (20 by 15 cm) rectangle. Using a sharp knife, cut into 8 pieces. Transfer biscuits to prepared baking sheet, making sure they do not touch or overlap.

4. *Topping:* Lightly brush tops with cream. Bake in preheated oven for about 20 minutes or until crisp and golden brown. Transfer biscuits to a rack to cool. Dust lightly with confectioner's sugar before serving.

Variation

Substitute 1/2 cup (125 mL) dried cranberries and 1 tsp (5 mL) grated orange zest for the dried cherries.

Chocolate Chip Oat Breakfast Biscuits

**MAKES
8 BISCUITS**

This is a great-tasting way to get your oatmeal in the morning, as well as your chocolate fix. If you like scones, you will love these cream breakfast biscuits.

TIPS

This recipe can be doubled.

The biscuits can also be patted out into a circle and cut into pie-shaped wedges or cut into hearts or circles with biscuit or cookie cutters.

Preheat oven to 400°F (200°C)
Baking sheet, lined with parchment paper

1 1/2 cups	all-purpose flour	375 mL
3/4 cup	old-fashioned rolled oats	175 mL
1/2 cup	semisweet chocolate chips	125 mL
1/4 cup	granulated sugar	50 mL
1 tbsp	baking powder	15 mL
1/4 tsp	salt	1 mL
1 1/4 cups	whipping (35%) cream	300 mL

Topping (optional)

2 tbsp	whipping (35%) cream	25 mL

Glaze

3/4 cup	confectioner's (icing) sugar, sifted	175 mL
4 tsp	orange juice	20 mL

1. In a large bowl, mix together flour, oats, chocolate chips, sugar, baking powder and salt.

2. Stir in cream, mixing just until dough is soft and ragged (see Tip, page 28).

3. Turn out dough onto a lightly floured work surface and gently shape into an 8- by 6-inch (20 by 15 cm) rectangle. Using a sharp knife, cut into 8 pieces. Transfer biscuits to prepared baking sheet, making sure they do not touch or overlap.

4. *Topping:* Lightly brush the tops with cream. Bake in preheated oven for about 20 minutes or until crisp and golden brown. Transfer biscuits to a rack to cool.

5. *Glaze:* In a medium bowl, whisk together confectioner's sugar and orange juice until smooth. Dip tops of cooled biscuits in glaze or drizzle glaze over top. Let biscuits stand on a rack until glaze hardens.

Maple-Glazed Chocolate Walnut Breakfast Biscuits

I love the flavor combination of maple, walnuts and chocolate chips. These breakfast biscuits are my favorite way to start the day.

TIPS

I love parchment paper! It's a grease- and heat-resistant paper used to line baking pans. It keeps your baked goods from sticking and burning and makes cleanup a breeze.

Ragged dough looks moistened but doesn't form a ball.

Preheat oven to 400°F (200°C)
Baking sheet, lined with parchment paper

2 1/4 cups	all-purpose flour	550 mL
1/3 cup	coarsely chopped walnuts	75 mL
1/3 cup	semisweet chocolate chips	75 mL
1/4 cup	granulated sugar	50 mL
1 tbsp	baking powder	15 mL
1/4 tsp	salt	1 mL
1 1/4 cups	whipping (35%) cream	300 mL

Topping (optional)

2 tbsp	whipping (35%) cream	25 mL

Glaze

3/4 cup	confectioner's (icing) sugar, sifted	175 mL
4 tsp	milk	20 mL
1/4 tsp	maple extract	1 mL

1. In a large bowl, mix together flour, walnuts, chocolate chips, sugar, baking powder and salt. Stir cream into flour mixture just until dough is soft and ragged (see Tip, at left).

2. Turn out dough onto a lightly floured work surface and gently shape into an 8-inch (20 cm) circle. Using a sharp knife, cut circle into 8 wedges. Transfer wedges to prepared baking sheet, making sure they do not touch or overlap.

TIPS

This recipe can be doubled.

The biscuits are best served the day they are made.

The biscuits can also be patted out and cut into hearts or circles with biscuit or cookie cutters.

3. *Topping:* Lightly brush tops with cream. Bake in preheated oven for 19 minutes or until crisp and golden brown. Transfer biscuits to a rack to cool.

4. *Glaze:* In a medium bowl, whisk together confectioner's sugar, milk and maple extract until smooth. Dip tops of cooled biscuits in glaze. Let biscuits stand on a rack until glaze hardens.

> **Variation**
> Substitute lightly toasted pecans for the walnuts.

Chocolate Chip Hotcakes

**MAKES
18 PANCAKES**

Who wouldn't like a sprinkling of chocolate chips on their pancakes? When I tested this recipe on my children and their friends, my kitchen became eerily silent. Then, once the pancakes were devoured, they uttered three words: "More pancakes, please!"

TIPS

These pancakes are wonderful served with maple or berry syrup.

This recipe can be halved for a smaller batch.

2 cups	all-purpose flour	500 mL
3 tbsp	granulated sugar	45 mL
2 tsp	baking powder	10 mL
1 tsp	baking soda	5 mL
$\frac{1}{4}$ tsp	salt	1 mL
2	eggs	2
2 cups	buttermilk	500 mL
2 tsp	vanilla	10 mL
	Unsalted butter, as needed	
$\frac{2}{3}$ cup	semisweet chocolate chips	150 mL

1. In a large bowl, combine flour, sugar, baking powder, baking soda and salt.

2. In a separate bowl, whisk together eggs, buttermilk and vanilla. Add buttermilk mixture to flour mixture, stirring just until combined. (The batter will have small lumps.)

3. Heat a griddle or skillet over medium-high heat and lightly grease with butter. Scooping batter with a $\frac{1}{4}$-cup (50 mL) measure, pour onto hot griddle or skillet. Sprinkle each pancake with about $\frac{1}{2}$ tbsp (7 mL) of the chocolate chips. Cook until bubbles appear on surface, bottom is golden and edges look firm, about 2 minutes. Flip pancakes and cook until golden, about 1 minute.

Variations

To make banana chocolate chip pancakes, sprinkle 1 cup (250 mL) banana slices on top of the pancakes along with the chocolate chips.

To make cinnamon chocolate pancakes, lightly dust with ground cinnamon after sprinkling with chocolate chips.

Chocolate Chip Pecan Waffles

My children know that it's a special occasion if I'm making waffles for breakfast. I don't know why waffles seem so daunting, because the batter goes together pretty quickly. Maybe it has more to do with where I store my waffle iron, usually in the back of the cupboard behind every other appliance I own.

TIP

To serve these waffles as a dessert, drizzle with maple syrup and top with freshly whipped cream and toasted chopped pecans.

Waffle iron

2 cups	all-purpose flour	500 mL
$1/3$ cup	chopped pecans	75 mL
$1/2$ cup	semisweet chocolate chips, coarsely chopped	125 mL
2 tbsp	granulated sugar	25 mL
$1 1/2$ tsp	baking powder	7 mL
$1/2$ tsp	baking soda	2 mL
$1/4$ tsp	salt	1 mL
3	eggs, separated	3
2 cups	buttermilk	500 mL
1 tsp	maple extract or vanilla	5 mL
$1/4$ cup	unsalted butter, melted and cooled slightly	50 mL
	Vegetable oil	
	Maple syrup	

1. In a medium bowl, combine flour, pecans, chocolate chips, sugar, baking powder, baking soda and salt.

2. In a large bowl, whisk together egg yolks, buttermilk, maple extract and melted butter. Add flour mixture, stirring just until moistened.

3. In a separate bowl, using electric mixer, beat egg whites until soft peaks form. Gently fold egg whites into batter just until there are no streaks. Do not overmix.

4. Heat waffle iron to medium–high and lightly brush with vegetable oil. Scoop about $1/2$ cup (125 mL) of the batter onto waffle iron (some waffle irons may take smaller or larger portions). Cook until waffle is crisp and golden brown, about 3 to 5 minutes. Remove from iron. Repeat with remaining batter.

5. Drizzle waffles with maple syrup and serve immediately.

Chocolate Orange French Toast

SERVES 4

This is a fun and absolutely delicious breakfast treat. It's like a breakfast sandwich that is stuffed with a chocolate-cinnamon filling. You can add maple syrup if you want, but you might find the French toast is sweet enough without any additional syrup.

TIP

If you are using a narrow loaf of bread, such as a baguette, just increase the number of French toast sandwiches per serving. Depending on the size of bread used, there will probably be some extra batter and filling. Do not use sourdough bread for this recipe.

$3/4$ cup	semisweet chocolate chips	175 mL
$1/4$ cup	unsalted butter	50 mL
2 tbsp	packed light brown sugar	25 mL
1 tbsp	unsweetened Dutch-process cocoa powder	15 mL
$1/4$ tsp	ground cinnamon	1 mL
8	slices French bread, about $1/2$ inch (1 cm) thick (see Tip, at left)	8
5	eggs	5
$1/2$ cup	orange juice	125 mL
$1/2$ cup	milk	125 mL
2 tbsp	orange liqueur	25 mL
1 tsp	vanilla	5 mL
2 tbsp	butter	25 mL
	Warm maple syrup (optional)	
	Orange slices (optional)	

1. In a food processor fitted with a metal blade, mix together chocolate chips, butter, brown sugar, cocoa powder and cinnamon. Process until blended but still somewhat chunky.

2. Spread mixture on 4 of the bread slices. Top with remaining slices.

3. In a large bowl, whisk eggs. Add orange juice, milk, orange liqueur and vanilla. Whisk well. Carefully dip each sandwich in egg mixture, turning to coat each side well.

4. In a large skillet over medium heat, melt butter. Carefully place dipped sandwiches in skillet and cook until browned and crisp on both sides, about 3 to 5 minutes. If sandwiches start to slide apart, gently press down on tops with spatula.

5. Serve French toast with warm maple syrup and fresh orange slices, if desired.

Raspberry Dutch Baby with Chocolate Chips

When I was growing up, Dutch Babies were always a special breakfast treat in our house. This is my mother's original Dutch Baby recipe, which I have updated with raspberries and chocolate chips. I think that she'll approve.

TIP

No matter how tempted you might be not to use the blender, it really makes a big difference in the final product. The blender whips more volume into the eggs than you can by hand. Also, it is important to follow the directions exactly; the Dutch Baby will not rise properly if you blend everything together at once.

Preheat oven to 425°F (220°C)
9- or 10-inch (23 or 25 cm) deep-dish glass pie plate

1 tbsp	unsalted butter	15 mL
3	eggs	3
3/4 cup	milk	175 mL
3/4 cup	all-purpose flour	175 mL
1/2 cup	fresh or frozen raspberries	125 mL
1/3 cup	semisweet chocolate chips	75 mL
	Confectioner's (icing) sugar, for garnish	

1. Place butter in glass dish and set in preheated oven.

2. In a blender, beat eggs on high speed for 1 minute. With motor running, gradually pour in milk, then slowly add flour. Continue blending for 30 seconds.

3. Remove dish from oven and pour batter over hot, melted butter. Sprinkle with raspberries and chocolate chips.

4. Bake in preheated oven for 20 to 22 minutes or until puffed and golden brown. Dust with confectioner's sugar and serve immediately.

Variation
You can substitute cranberries or cherries for the raspberries.

Breads, Sandwiches and Scones

Chocolate Swirl Bread *38*

Jay's Double Chocolate Cinnamon Bread *40*

Banana Chocolate Breads *43*

Chocolate Challah *44*

Pumpkin Chocolate Chip Loaves *46*

Chocolate Buns *47*

Chocolate Club *48*

Grilled Chocolate *49*

Chocolate Quesadillas *50*

Milk Chocolate Latte Scones *51*

Chocolate-Stuffed Scones *52*

Chocolate Chip Jammer Scones *54*

Chocolate Raisin Scones *56*

Apricot Chip Scones *57*

Chocolate Swirl Bread

This is the best bread I've ever tasted in my life. Try it untoasted, toasted, as French toast, or any way that strikes your fancy. Just try it!

TIP

This bread makes fabulous French toast. Dip slices in an egg-and-milk batter and pan-fry until golden brown.

All of the recipes in this book were tested using large eggs. Using medium or extra-large eggs may adversely affect the outcome of the recipe.

Baking sheet, lined with parchment paper

Dough

1 1/4 cups	warm water	300 mL
1 tbsp	active dry yeast	15 mL
Pinch	granulated sugar	Pinch
1/4 cup	vegetable oil	50 mL
1/4 cup	granulated sugar	50 mL
2	eggs	2
5 1/2 cups	all-purpose flour (approx.), divided	1.375 L
2 tsp	grated orange zest	10 mL
2 tsp	salt	10 mL
1 1/2 cups	semisweet chocolate chips	375 mL
1 cup	coarsely chopped walnuts	250 mL
1/3 cup	packed light brown sugar	75 mL
1 tsp	ground cinnamon	5 mL

Egg Wash

1	egg yolk	1
1 tbsp	water	15 mL

1. *Dough:* In a large bowl, combine water, yeast and pinch of sugar. Let stand for 10 minutes or until foamy.

2. Whisk in oil, 1/4 cup (50 mL) sugar and eggs. Beat in 4 cups (1 L) of the flour, orange zest and salt. Gradually stir in 1/2 cup (125 mL) more of the flour to make a soft workable dough. Turn out onto floured work surface. Knead dough with palms of hands, pushing down and out and folding farthest side back toward you in a continual pattern until you can feel the dough becoming smoother. While kneading, add in just enough of remaining flour, 1 tbsp (15 mL) at a time, to make a firm dough (it shouldn't be sticky or wet but it shouldn't be dry, either). Continue kneading and adding flour for 10 to 15 minutes or until dough is smooth and silky.

3. Place dough in a large oiled bowl, turning to coat lightly. Cover bowl with plastic wrap and a clean kitchen towel. Place bowl in a warm place and let rise for 1 to 1½ hours or until doubled in bulk.

4. Roll dough into a 21- by 14-inch (52 by 35 cm) rectangle with long edge closest to you. Sprinkle with chocolate chips, walnuts, brown sugar and cinnamon, leaving a ¼-inch (0.5 cm) border. Starting with edge closest to you, roll up dough jelly-roll style into a rope. Pinch edge and ends to seal. Then, starting from the center of the rope, gently squeeze the dough as you move your hands toward the ends, stretching the rope slightly as you go until the rope is 30 inches (75 cm) long. Twist the roll into a knot, tucking the end through the center. Carefully transfer to prepared baking sheet. Cover with a kitchen towel and let rise again for 30 minutes or until the dent does not fill in when dough is lightly pressed with a fingertip (do not let double in bulk). Preheat oven to 350°F (180°C).

5. *Egg Wash:* In a small bowl, whisk egg yolk with water. Brush over top of loaf. Bake in preheated oven for about 50 minutes or until golden brown and loaf sounds hollow when tapped. Transfer loaf to a wire rack and let cool.

Variation
Add an additional ½ cup (125 mL) chocolate chips. Once the dough has risen the first time, divide it in half and make two smaller loaves instead of one. Roll up as directed and stretch each rope until it is 22 inches (55 cm) long. Shape and place on separate baking sheets. Let rise as directed. Reduce baking time to 30 to 35 minutes.

Jay's Double Chocolate Cinnamon Bread

MAKES 1 LOAF

My husband has had an ongoing love affair with babka for years. But he always has the same gripe: not enough chocolate. I've taken Jay's suggestion and turned this into an über chocolate creation! Although the recipe may look labor intensive, it really is an easy bread and can be made ahead.

TIP

The richness of this dough makes it difficult to knead by hand. If you don't have a heavy-duty electric mixer, it may take about 20 minutes of kneading to get a smooth and stretchy dough. Be sure to knead it enough so that the structure of the bread holds when rising and baking.

9- by 5-inch (2 L) metal loaf pan, greased

Dough

³⁄₄ cup	warm milk	175 mL
1 tbsp	active dry yeast	15 mL
Pinch	granulated sugar	Pinch
2	egg yolks	2
1	egg	1
¹⁄₂ tsp	almond extract	2 mL
3 cups	all-purpose flour (approx.)	750 mL
¹⁄₃ cup	granulated sugar	75 mL
²⁄₃ cup	unsweetened Dutch-process cocoa powder, sifted	150 mL
1 tsp	salt	5 mL
¹⁄₂ cup	unsalted butter, melted and cooled	125 mL

Filling

1 cup	semisweet chocolate chips	250 mL
¹⁄₃ cup	packed light brown sugar	75 mL
2 tbsp	unsweetened Dutch-process cocoa powder, sifted	25 mL
¹⁄₂ tsp	ground cinnamon	2 mL
2 tbsp	unsalted butter, at room temperature	25 mL

Streusel

¹⁄₃ cup	confectioner's (icing) sugar, sifted	75 mL
¹⁄₃ cup	all-purpose flour	75 mL
2 tbsp	unsalted butter, melted and cooled	25 mL
¹⁄₄ tsp	almond extract	1 mL

Egg Wash

1	egg yolk	1
1 tbsp	water	15 mL

1. *Dough:* In large bowl of a heavy-duty stand mixer, combine warm milk, yeast and pinch of sugar. Let stand for 10 minutes or until foamy.

TIP

You can start this dough at night, letting the dough slowly rise in the refrigerator overnight (just let it come to room temperature before proceeding with Step 4). You can also make the filling and streusel the day before, making sure to refrigerate them separately in airtight containers. Let them soften at room temperature for 30 minutes before using.

2. Using whisk attachment of mixer, whisk in egg yolks, egg and almond extract. Beat in 2 cups (500 mL) flour, $\frac{1}{3}$ cup (75 mL) sugar, cocoa powder and salt. Using dough hook attachment, add butter, kneading until dough is smooth and silky. Gradually add $\frac{1}{2}$ cup (125 mL) more of the flour until a soft workable dough forms. Continue kneading in mixer, adding in just enough flour, 1 tbsp (15 mL) at a time, to make a firm dough (it shouldn't be sticky or wet but it shouldn't be dry, either). Continue kneading and adding flour for 8 minutes or until dough is smooth and silky.

3. Place dough in a large oiled bowl, turning to coat lightly. Cover bowl with plastic wrap and a clean kitchen towel. Let rise in a warm place for 1 to $1\frac{1}{2}$ hours or until doubled in bulk.

4. *Filling:* In a food processor fitted with a metal blade, pulse chocolate chips, brown sugar, cocoa powder and cinnamon until blended. Add butter and pulse until mixture just comes together. Set aside.

5. Turn out dough onto a lightly floured work surface. Roll out to a 17- by 12-inch (43 by 30 cm) rectangle with long edge closest to you. Sprinkle filling over surface, leaving a $\frac{1}{2}$-inch (1 cm) border. Lightly press filling into dough. Starting with edge closest to you, roll up dough jelly-roll style into a rope. Pinch edge and ends together to seal. Then, starting from the center of the rope, gently squeeze the dough as you move your hands toward the ends, stretching the rope slightly as you go until the rope is now 20 inches (50 cm) long. Fold rope in half, bringing ends together with the seams inside. Lightly pressing halves together and holding each end, twist ends of rope once in opposite directions like wringing a towel. Pinch ends tightly. Place in prepared loaf pan. (It won't fill the pan completely, but don't worry, it will as it rises.) Cover pan loosely with plastic wrap and let rise in a warm place for 40 minutes or

continued on next page...

TIP

This cake-like bread will keep for several days if you wrap it well in plastic wrap.

until the dent does not fill in when dough is lightly pressed with a fingertip. Preheat oven to 350°F (180°C).

6. *Streusel:* In a small bowl, mix together confectioner's sugar, flour, butter and almond extract. The mixture should be crumbly, not smooth.

7. *Egg Wash:* In a small bowl, whisk egg yolk with water. Brush over top of loaf and sprinkle with streusel. Bake in prepared oven for 45 to 55 minutes or until top is browned and sounds hollow when tapped and streusel is golden. Let cool in pan on a wire rack for 15 minutes. Transfer to rack and let cool completely.

Banana Chocolate Breads

It's fun to help a recipe evolve. This one started out as a chocolate banana muffin, but then I decided that it would be fabulous as little loaves. If you can't find mini-loaf pans, don't worry. You can bake the batter in an ordinary muffin pan. See how things evolve?

TIPS

You should be able to find mini loaf pans at a well-stocked grocery or home store.

If you can't bake 12 mini loaves at a time, bake the extra batter in a muffin tin or refrigerate the remaining batter and bake once the mini loaf pan is cooled. Be sure to grease the cooled pan before adding the second batch of batter.

These cakes freeze very well. Store them in resealable plastic freezer bags for up to 1 month.

Preheat oven to 350°F (180°C)
1 mini loaf pan or 12-cup muffin tin, greased

7 oz	semisweet chocolate, coarsely chopped, divided	210 g
2 cups	all-purpose flour	500 mL
1 tsp	baking soda	5 mL
1/2 tsp	baking powder	2 mL
1/4 tsp	salt	1 mL
1 cup	mashed ripe bananas	250 mL
3/4 cup	granulated sugar	175 mL
1/2 cup	vegetable oil	125 mL
1/3 cup	sour cream	75 mL
2	eggs	2
1 tsp	vanilla	5 mL
1 cup	walnut pieces	250 mL

1. In a microwave-safe bowl, microwave 3 oz (90 g) chocolate on Medium (50%) for 1 to $1\frac{1}{2}$ minutes, stirring every 30 seconds, or until chocolate is shiny and almost melted. Stir until smooth. Let cool slightly.

2. In a small bowl, mix together flour, baking soda, baking powder and salt.

3. In a large bowl, beat together bananas, sugar, oil, sour cream, eggs and vanilla until smooth. Mix in melted chocolate.

4. Stir flour mixture into banana mixture just until combined. Stir in walnuts and remaining chocolate. Scoop batter into prepared pans.

5. Bake in preheated oven for 20 minutes or until a tester inserted in center comes out clean. Let cakes cool in pan on a wire rack for 5 minutes. Transfer to rack and let cool completely.

Chocolate Challah

One night I was at my friend Erika's house for Shabbat dinner. As she showed me her beautiful, freshly baked challah, she suggested that I create a chocolate one for my new book. Here it is.

TIP

All of the recipes in this book were tested using large eggs. Using medium or extra-large eggs may adversely affect the outcome of the recipe.

2 baking sheets, lined with parchment paper

Dough

1$\frac{1}{4}$ cups	warm water	300 mL
1 tbsp	active dry yeast	15 mL
Pinch	granulated sugar	Pinch
$\frac{1}{4}$ cup	vegetable oil	50 mL
$\frac{3}{4}$ cup	granulated sugar	175 mL
2	eggs	2
4$\frac{1}{2}$ cups	all-purpose flour (approx.), divided	1.125 L
$\frac{1}{2}$ cup	unsweetened Dutch-process cocoa powder, sifted	125 mL
2 tsp	salt	10 mL
1 cup	semisweet chocolate chips	250 mL
1 cup	dried cherries	250 mL

Egg Wash

1	egg yolk	1
1 tbsp	water	15 mL

1. *Dough:* In a large bowl, combine water, yeast and pinch of sugar. Let stand for 10 minutes or until foamy.

2. Whisk in oil, $\frac{3}{4}$ cup (175 mL) sugar and eggs. Add 4 cups (1 L) of the flour, cocoa powder and salt, beating well. Gradually stir in $\frac{1}{2}$ cup (125 mL) more of the flour to make a soft workable dough. Turn dough out onto a lightly floured work surface. Knead dough with palms of hands, pushing down and out and folding farthest side back toward you in a continual pattern until you can feel the dough becoming smoother. While kneading, add in just enough flour, 1 tbsp (15 mL) at a time, to make a firm dough (it shouldn't be sticky or wet but it shouldn't be dry, either). Continue kneading and adding flour for 10 to 15 minutes or until dough is smooth and silky. Knead in chocolate chips and cherries. Shape into a ball.

3. Place dough in a large oiled bowl, turning to coat lightly. Cover bowl with plastic wrap and a clean kitchen towel. Let rise in a warm place for 1 to 1$\frac{1}{2}$ hours or until doubled in bulk.

TIP

Cocoa powder needs to be sifted before use because it can be very lumpy, which makes it difficult to incorporate. Use a fine-meshed sieve to remove any lumps before adding cocoa powder to other dry ingredients.

4. Turn dough out onto a lightly floured work surface. Divide in half and shape each half into a round loaf. Carefully transfer to prepared baking sheets and lightly press down tops to flatten slightly, making a 6-inch (15 cm) circle. Cover with a kitchen towel and let rise again for 20 to 30 minutes or until the dent does not fill in when dough is lightly pressed with a fingertip. Preheat oven to 325°F (160°C).

5. *Egg Wash:* In a small bowl, whisk egg yolk with water. Using a very sharp knife, make two slashes on top of each loaf. Brush tops with egg wash. Bake in preheated oven for 30 to 40 minutes or until firm to the touch and loaves sound hollow when tapped on top. Transfer loaves to a wire rack and let cool.

Variation

You can omit the dried cherries or substitute raisins for them.

Pumpkin Chocolate Chip Loaves

MAKES 2 LOAVES

Pumpkin and spice make this a great quick bread to serve in the fall. It is amazing how well the flavors of pumpkin and chocolate go together.

TIP

These loaves freeze very well for up to 1 month. I like to keep a few on hand for brunch or a last-minute dessert.

Preheat oven to 350°F (180°C)
Two 9- by 5-inch (2 L) metal loaf pans, lined with parchment paper, greased

3 cups	all-purpose flour	750 mL
2 tsp	ground cinnamon	10 mL
1 1/2 tsp	baking powder	7 mL
1 1/2 tsp	baking soda	7 mL
1 tsp	ground allspice	5 mL
1 tsp	ground nutmeg	5 mL
1/2 tsp	salt	2 mL
1 cup	vegetable oil	250 mL
3 cups	granulated sugar	750 mL
4	eggs	4
2 cups	canned pumpkin purée (not pie filling)	500 mL
1/4 cup	water	50 mL
1 1/3 cups	semisweet chocolate chips	325 mL

1. In a medium bowl, combine flour, cinnamon, baking powder, baking soda, allspice, nutmeg and salt.

2. In a large bowl, using electric mixer, beat oil and sugar. Beat in eggs, one at a time, beating well after each addition. Beat in pumpkin and water. Stir in flour mixture just until smooth. Stir in chocolate chips.

3. Spread batter in prepared pans. Bake in preheated oven for 70 minutes or until a tester inserted into center comes out clean. Let cakes cool in pans on rack for 10 minutes. Run a sharp knife around edge of loaves and remove from pan. Place loaves on racks and let cool completely. Remove parchment paper.

Variation

Add 1 cup (250 mL) coarsely chopped walnuts or pecans when you stir in the chocolate chips.

Chocolate Buns

My grandfather used to make these buns for me when I was a little girl. I don't know if this recipe was his creation or something that he ate in his native France. Whatever the case, they are delicious any time of the day. Plus, every time I eat one I feel connected to my heritage.

TIP

You can double or even triple this recipe. It's delicious with a cup of hot coffee or tucked into a lunch box.

$\frac{1}{2}$	freshly baked crusty baguette	$\frac{1}{2}$
2 tbsp	unsalted butter, at room temperature	25 mL
4 oz	bittersweet chocolate, cut into 4 chunks	125 g

1. Cut baguette into four 3-inch (7.5 cm) sections. Slice each section in half lengthwise. Butter both halves of bread.

2. Top one half of bread with one chunk of chocolate, then cover with other half of buttered bread. Repeat with remaining bread and chocolate.

Variation
Substitute milk chocolate for the bittersweet chocolate.

Chocolate Club

These sandwiches could work for either breakfast (try it as French toast) or lunch (potassium and protein). You can also substitute peanut butter for the almond butter or serve the sandwiches open-faced on thick slices of rustic bread for a chocolaty twist on bruschetta. Any way you serve it, this is one delicious sandwich.

TIPS

The banana slices may darken if you make these sandwiches ahead. If this bothers you, make the rest ahead and add the banana slices right before serving.

To toast hazelnuts: Place hazelnuts in a single layer on a foil or parchment-lined baking sheet. Bake in center of preheated 350°F (180°C) oven for 10 to 15 minutes or until lightly browned and skins are blistered. Wrap nuts in a clean dry kitchen towel and let stand for 1 minute. Rub nuts in towel to remove loose skins (it's okay if you can't remove all of them). Let nuts cool completely.

$1/2$ cup	almond or other nut butter	125 mL
2 oz	bittersweet chocolate, chopped	60 g
1 oz	milk chocolate, chopped	30 g
2 tbsp	liquid honey	25 mL
$1/4$ cup	toasted chopped hazelnuts (optional) (see Tips, left)	50 mL
8	slices buttermilk, egg or good-quality white bread	8
1	banana, sliced	1

1. In a microwave-safe bowl, combine almond butter and bittersweet and milk chocolates. Microwave, uncovered, on Medium (50%) for 1 to $1\frac{1}{2}$ minutes, stirring every 30 seconds, or until chocolate is warm and almost melted. Stir until smooth.

2. Stir in honey and hazelnuts, if using. Spread on 4 slices of the bread. Top with banana slices. Cover with remaining 4 slices of bread. Serve immediately.

Variation
Toast bread before spreading with the chocolate mixture.

Apricot Chip Scones (page 57)

Double Chocolate Apricot Muffins (page 79)
and Chocolate Swirl Bread (page 38)

Maple Pecan Muffins with Chocolate Chips (page 77)
and Chocolate Chip Cranberry Muffins (page 70)

Chocolate Mousse Cake (page 88)

Little Chocolate Cakes (page 127)
and Chocolate-Drizzled Almond Cake (page 93)

Almond Chocolate Coconut Torte (page 94)

Grilled Chocolate

Come on, you know this sounds interesting! This take on the grilled cheese sandwich is a great chocolate recipe suggested by my brother, Jon. The lightly buttered white or buttermilk bread is pan-fried, and instead of Cheddar cheese, I've used a chocolate-and-marshmallow filling. This sandwich is Decadent with a capital D.

TIPS

I use soft white sandwich bread for this recipe, but you can use thickly sliced white French bread (not sourdough) instead, if you prefer.

You can easily double this recipe.

4	slices soft white or buttermilk bread	4
3 oz	milk or bittersweet chocolate, chopped, divided	90 g
6	large marshmallows, sliced in half lengthwise (optional)	6
4 tsp	unsalted butter, softened, divided	20 mL

1. Top 2 slices of the bread with half of the chocolate and 6 marshmallow pieces, if using. Cover with remaining bread.

2. In a large nonstick skillet over medium heat, melt 2 tsp (10 mL) butter. Carefully place one of the sandwiches in the hot skillet. Cook, turning once, for 3 to 5 minutes or until lightly golden and chocolate is melted. Repeat with remaining butter and sandwich.

3. Let cool slightly. Cut in half and serve immediately.

Variation
Omit the marshmallows and spread one side of the bread with peanut butter, then top with the chopped chocolate and second slice of bread. Proceed with recipe.

Chocolate Quesadillas

This recipe might sound a bit over-the-top, but trust me — it's not! If you have access to homemade or freshly made flour tortillas, by all means use them. Otherwise, store-bought flour tortillas will work just fine. Quesadillas are usually filled with cheese, but I find that chocolate makes a fine substitute.

TIP

You can double or triple this recipe.

½ cup	chopped pecans	125 mL
1 tbsp	granulated sugar	15 mL
Pinch	salt	Pinch
2	8-inch (20 cm) flour tortillas	2
3 oz	bittersweet or semisweet chocolate, chopped	90 g
¼ cup	sour cream	50 mL
2 tsp	packed light brown sugar	10 mL

1. In a large nonstick skillet over medium–high heat, cook pecans, granulated sugar and salt, stirring with a wooden spoon, for 2 to 4 minutes or until pecans are toasted and sugar is melted and caramelized on nuts. If sugar or nuts start to burn, reduce heat. Transfer to a plate or baking sheet and let cool.

2. In a clean large nonstick skillet over medium–high heat, heat one of the tortillas until warm. Leaving tortilla in skillet, arrange half of the chocolate on one half of tortilla; fold opposite half over chocolate to cover. Cook quesadilla, turning once, for 3 to 4 minutes or until golden brown on both sides and chocolate is melted. Set aside on a plate. Repeat with remaining tortilla and chocolate.

3. In a small bowl, stir sour cream with brown sugar until smooth. Dollop over top of each quesadilla. Sprinkle candied pecans over sour cream mixture. Serve immediately.

Variation

You can use butter, if desired, to crisp the tortillas in the hot skillet.

Milk Chocolate Latte Scones

MAKES 8 SCONES

Coffee! Coffee! Coffee! Need I say more? Rich, bold and aromatic, these scones are one of my favorites.

TIP

Scones are best eaten the day that they're made.

Preheat oven to 400°F (200°C)
Baking sheet, lined with parchment paper or greased

2¼ cups	all-purpose flour	550 mL
7 oz	milk chocolate, chopped	210 g
¼ cup	granulated sugar	50 mL
1 tbsp	baking powder	15 mL
1 tbsp	finely ground espresso or French-roast coffee	15 mL
¼ tsp	salt	1 mL
1¼ cups	whipping (35%) cream	300 mL
Topping		
¾ cup	confectioner's (icing) sugar, sifted	175 mL
4 tsp	freshly brewed coffee, cooled	20 mL

1. In a large bowl, mix together flour, chocolate, sugar, baking powder, ground coffee and salt.

2. Stir cream into flour mixture, mixing just until a soft, shaggy dough forms.

3. On a lightly floured work surface, knead dough lightly just until it holds together. Divide dough into 8 pieces and roll into balls. Transfer balls to prepared baking sheet, about 2 inches (5 cm) apart. Lightly press each ball to flatten slightly into a ¾-inch (2 cm) thick disk.

4. Bake in preheated oven for 20 to 25 minutes or until top and edges are very firm to the touch. Transfer to a wire rack and let cool completely.

5. *Topping:* In a bowl, stir confectioner's sugar with coffee to make a thin icing. Drizzle over cooled scones.

Chocolate-Stuffed Scones

MAKES ABOUT
14 LARGE SCONES

The stuffing for this scone recipe was inspired by Marcy Goldman's chocolate babka in her book *A Treasury of Jewish Holiday Baking*. I thought that my scones could use a chocolate facelift, and this marvelous chocolate filling fits the bill.

TIP

One scant cup (250 mL) means just barely that amount, i.e., just slightly under.

Preheat oven to 425°F (220°C)
Baking sheet, lined with parchment paper or greased

Chocolate Filling

1/2 cup	semisweet chocolate chips	125 mL
3 tbsp	packed light brown sugar	45 mL
2 tbsp	unsalted butter	25 mL
1 tbsp	unsweetened Dutch-process cocoa powder	15 mL
1/2 tsp	ground cinnamon	2 mL

Dough

3 cups	all-purpose flour	750 mL
1/2 cup	granulated sugar	125 mL
2 1/2 tsp	baking powder	12 mL
1/2 tsp	baking soda	2 mL
1/8 tsp	salt	0.5 mL
3/4 cup	unsalted butter, chilled and cut into pieces	175 mL
1 scant cup	buttermilk (see Tip, at left)	250 mL

Topping

1 tbsp	granulated sugar	15 mL
1/4 tsp	ground cinnamon	1 mL
1 tbsp	whipping (35%) cream	15 mL

1. *Chocolate Filling:* In a food processor fitted with a metal blade, combine chocolate chips, brown sugar, butter, cocoa powder and cinnamon. Pulse until mixture is blended. Transfer chocolate mixture to a dish and wipe out food processor.

2. *Dough:* In clean food processor fitted with a metal blade, combine flour, sugar, baking powder, baking soda and salt. Pulse for 5 seconds. Add butter and pulse until mixture resembles coarse meal. Add buttermilk and pulse just until dough starts to form a ball.

3. With lightly floured hands, roll dough into 16 equal balls. Place 8 balls on prepared baking sheet, at least 3 inches (7.5 cm) apart. Flatten slightly with your fingers or the heel of your hand. Spoon a heaping tablespoonful (15 mL) of filling in the center of each scone. Place one of remaining balls on top of each and press down lightly to flatten top.

4. *Topping:* In a small bowl, mix together sugar and cinnamon. Brush tops of scones with cream and sprinkle with cinnamon-sugar topping.

5. Bake in preheated oven for about 20 minutes or until crusty and golden brown. Transfer scones to a rack to cool slightly. Serve warm.

Chocolate Chip Jammer Scones

**MAKES ABOUT
12 SCONES**

These scones have been a part of my catering repertoire for years. I love the flavor of the baked raspberry jam with the chocolate chips. They are especially fun to serve on Valentine's Day or for a special brunch.

TIP

I love parchment paper! It's a grease- and heat-resistant paper used to line baking pans. It keeps your baked goods from sticking and burning and makes cleanup a breeze.

Preheat oven to 425°F (220°C)
Baking sheet, lined with parchment paper or greased

1/4 cup	raspberry jam	50 mL
1/4 cup	semisweet chocolate chips	50 mL
3 cups	all-purpose flour	750 mL
1/4 cup	granulated sugar	50 mL
2 1/2 tsp	baking powder	12 mL
1/2 tsp	baking soda	2 mL
1/2 tsp	salt	2 mL
1 1/2 cups	unsalted butter, chilled and cut into pieces	375 mL
3/4 cup	buttermilk	175 mL

Topping

2 tbsp	whipping (35%) cream	25 mL
2 tbsp	granulated sugar	25 mL
	Confectioner's (icing) sugar, for dusting (optional)	

1. In a small bowl, mix together raspberry jam and chocolate chips. Set aside.

2. In a food processor fitted with a metal blade, combine flour, sugar, baking powder, baking soda and salt. Pulse for 5 seconds. Add butter and pulse using on/off motion until mixture resembles coarse meal. Add buttermilk and pulse just until the dough forms a ball.

TIPS

This recipe can be doubled.

These scones are best served the day they are made.

3. Scooping dough with rounded $\frac{1}{4}$-cup (50 mL) ice cream scoop or measuring cup, place balls on prepared sheets, about 3 inches (7.5 cm) apart. Using your thumb, make a deep indentation on top of each scone. Place a scoop of the reserved raspberry mixture in each indentation.

4. *Topping:* Brush tops of scones with cream and sprinkle with sugar.

5. Bake in preheated oven for about 20 minutes, until crusty and golden brown. Transfer scones to rack to cool. Dust lightly with confectioner's sugar before serving, if desired.

Variation
Substitute strawberry or cherry jam for the raspberry.

Chocolate Raisin Scones

MAKES
12 SCONES

These scones are great for brunch, and the variations you can make on the raisins, such as dried cranberries or cherries, are endless. The scones are very unusual, with a bittersweet chocolate flavor.

TIP

Cocoa powder needs to be sifted before use because it can be very lumpy, which makes it difficult to incorporate. Use a fine-meshed sieve to remove any lumps before adding cocoa powder to other dry ingredients.

Preheat oven to 400°F (200°C)
Baking sheet, lined with parchment paper or greased

2¹/₂ cups	all-purpose flour	625 mL
4 oz	semisweet chocolate, finely chopped	125 g
¹/₂ cup	unsweetened Dutch-process cocoa powder, sifted	125 mL
¹/₂ cup	raisins	125 mL
¹/₃ cup	packed light brown sugar	75 mL
¹/₃ cup	granulated sugar	75 mL
1¹/₂ tbsp	baking powder	22 mL
¹/₄ tsp	salt	1 mL
1¹/₂ cups plus 3 tbsp	whipping (35%) cream	420 mL

Topping

2 tbsp	whipping (35%) cream	25 mL
2 tsp	granulated sugar	10 mL
	Confectioner's (icing) sugar	

1. In a large bowl, mix together flour, chocolate, cocoa powder, raisins, brown and granulated sugars, baking powder and salt. Stir cream into flour mixture, mixing just until a soft, shaggy dough forms.

2. On a lightly floured work surface, shape dough into a 10-inch (25 cm) circle. Cut into 12 pie-shaped wedges. Transfer wedges to prepared baking sheet, keeping circle shape and placing wedges about ¹/₂ inch (1 cm) apart.

3. *Topping:* Brush tops with cream and sprinkle with granulated sugar.

4. Bake in preheated oven for 16 to 18 minutes or until top and edges are very firm to the touch. Transfer to a wire rack and let cool completely. Dust with confectioner's sugar before serving.

Apricot Chip Scones

These scones go together beautifully in the food processor, which effortlessly cuts the butter into the flour, resulting in the most tender and flaky scones imaginable.

TIPS

This recipe can be doubled.

These scones are best served the day they are made.

Preheat oven to 425°F (220°C)
Baking sheets, lined with parchment paper or greased

3 cups	all-purpose flour	750 mL
1/3 cup	granulated sugar	75 mL
2 1/2 tsp	baking powder	12 mL
1/2 tsp	baking soda	2 mL
1/2 tsp	salt	2 mL
1 1/2 cups	unsalted butter, chilled and cut into pieces	375 mL
1 cup	buttermilk	250 mL
2/3 cup	dried apricots, snipped into strips	150 mL
1/2 cup	semisweet chocolate chips	125 mL

Topping

1 tbsp	granulated sugar	15 mL
1/4 tsp	ground cinnamon	1 mL
2 tbsp	whipping (35%) cream	25 mL
	Confectioner's (icing) sugar, for dusting	

1. In a food processor fitted with a metal blade, combine flour, sugar, baking powder, baking soda and salt. Pulse for 5 seconds. Add butter and pulse using on/off motion until mixture resembles coarse meal. Add buttermilk and pulse just until the dough forms a ball. Stir in apricots and chocolate chips.

2. Scooping dough with rounded 1/4-cup (50 mL) ice cream scoop or measuring cup, place balls of dough on prepared baking sheets, about 3 inches (7.5 cm) apart.

3. *Topping:* In a small bowl, mix together sugar and cinnamon. Brush tops of scones with cream and sprinkle with cinnamon–sugar topping.

4. Bake in preheated oven for 18 to 20 minutes or until crusty and golden brown. Transfer scones to a rack to cool. Dust lightly with confectioner's sugar before serving.

Muffins

Chocolate Muffins *60*

Double Chocolate Chip Muffins *61*

Crumbcake Muffins *62*

Donut Muffins *63*

High-Octane Espresso Chip Morning Muffins *64*

Ginger Muffins *66*

Chocolate Chip Eggnog Muffins *67*

Apricot Chocolate Chip Cheesecake Muffins *68*

Chocolate Chip Cranberry Muffins *70*

Raspberry Chocolate Chip Muffins *71*

Strawberry Chocolate Chip Muffins *72*

Chocolate Chip Lemon Muffins *73*

Chocolate Chip Orange Muffins *74*

Chocolate Chip Pumpkin Muffins *75*

Almond Poppy Seed Chocolate Chip Muffins *76*

Maple Pecan Muffins with Chocolate Chips *77*

Sour Cream Coffee Cake Muffins *78*

Double Chocolate Apricot Muffins *79*

Chocolate Muffins

Serve these muffins warm, when they're at their tastiest. They have a bittersweet chocolate flavor and a tickle of orange.

TIP

All of the recipes in this book were tested using large eggs. Using medium or extra-large eggs may adversely affect the outcome of the recipe.

Preheat oven to 375°F (190°C)
12-cup muffin pan, lined with paper liners

1$\frac{1}{2}$ cups	all-purpose flour	375 mL
$\frac{2}{3}$ cup	unsweetened Dutch-process cocoa powder, sifted	150 mL
1 tbsp	baking powder	15 mL
$\frac{1}{4}$ tsp	salt	1 mL
1 cup	packed light brown sugar	250 mL
2	eggs	2
$\frac{1}{2}$ cup	milk	125 mL
$\frac{1}{2}$ cup	brewed coffee, cooled	125 mL
$\frac{1}{3}$ cup	vegetable oil	75 mL
1 tsp	vanilla	5 mL
4 oz	bittersweet chocolate, coarsely chopped	125 g
2 tsp	grated orange zest	10 mL

Topping

2 tbsp	granulated sugar	25 mL

1. In a medium bowl, mix together flour, cocoa powder, baking powder and salt.

2. In a large bowl, mix together brown sugar, eggs, milk, coffee, oil and vanilla. Mix in dry ingredients just until combined. Fold in chopped chocolate and orange zest.

3. Spoon batter into prepared muffin cups. Sprinkle evenly with the 2 tbsp (25 mL) sugar.

4. Bake in preheated oven for 18 to 20 minutes or until a tester inserted into center comes out clean. Let muffins cool in pan on a wire rack for 5 minutes. Transfer to rack and let cool completely.

Variation
Substitute chopped semisweet or milk chocolate for the bittersweet chocolate.

Double Chocolate Chip Muffins

A cross between a brownie and chocolate cake, these muffins are a chocoholic's dream, delivering a double dose of chocolate in every bite.

TIP
Cocoa powder needs to be sifted before use because it can be very lumpy, which makes it difficult to incorporate. Use a fine-meshed sieve to remove any lumps before adding cocoa powder to other dry ingredients.

Preheat oven to 375°F (190°C)
12-cup muffin pan, lined with paper liners

1¾ cups	all-purpose flour	425 mL
½ cup	unsweetened Dutch-process cocoa powder, sifted	125 mL
2 tsp	baking powder	10 mL
¼ tsp	salt	1 mL
1 cup	granulated sugar	250 mL
2	eggs	2
¾ cup	milk	175 mL
½ cup	vegetable oil	125 mL
2 tsp	vanilla	10 mL
1 cup	semisweet chocolate chips	250 mL

Topping

2 tbsp	granulated sugar	25 mL

1. In a medium bowl, combine flour, cocoa powder, baking powder and salt.

2. In a large bowl, whisk together sugar, eggs, milk, oil and vanilla. Stir in flour mixture just until combined. Fold in chocolate chips. Do not overmix.

3. Spoon batter into prepared muffin cups. Sprinkle evenly with the 2 tbsp (25 mL) sugar.

4. Bake in preheated oven for 22 minutes or until puffed and a tester inserted into center comes out clean. Let cool in pan on rack for 5 minutes. Remove from pan and let cool completely on rack.

Crumbcake Muffins

This is a great basic muffin, equally delish with a cup of joe. Try making this recipe with an assortment of other muffins for a weekend brunch.

TIP

When measuring, always remember to spoon your dry ingredients into the cup and level the top by scraping across it with the flat side of a knife or skewer. This will give you an accurate measurement.

Preheat oven to 375°F (190°C)
12-cup muffin pan, lined with paper liners

Topping

1/2 cup	confectioner's (icing) sugar	125 mL
1/2 cup	all-purpose flour	125 mL
1/2 tsp	ground cinnamon	2 mL
1/8 tsp	salt	0.5 mL
1/4 cup	unsalted butter, melted	50 mL

Batter

2 cups	all-purpose flour	500 mL
3/4 cup	semisweet chocolate chips	175 mL
2 tsp	baking powder	10 mL
1/4 tsp	salt	1 mL
3/4 cup	granulated sugar	175 mL
2	eggs	2
3/4 cup	milk	175 mL
1/2 cup	vegetable oil	125 mL
1 tsp	vanilla	5 mL
	Ground cinnamon	

1. *Topping:* In a medium bowl, whisk together confectioner's sugar, flour, cinnamon and salt. Pour in melted butter and whisk until crumbly. Set aside.

2. *Batter:* In a medium bowl, combine flour, chocolate chips, baking powder and salt.

3. In a large bowl, whisk together granulated sugar, eggs, milk, oil and vanilla. Stir in flour mixture just until combined. Do not overmix.

4. Spoon batter into prepared muffin cups. Sprinkle evenly with reserved topping, then ground cinnamon.

5. Bake in preheated oven for 22 to 24 minutes or until puffed, golden and a tester inserted into center comes out clean. Let cool in pan on rack for 5 minutes. Remove from pan and let cool completely on rack.

Donut Muffins

Caution: These buttery treats will disappear fast. You might need to make a double batch. The nutmeg-scented muffins are dipped in melted butter, then rolled in cinnamon sugar.

TIP

To bring cold butter to room temperature in a hurry, use a microwave oven. I usually set it on Medium (50%) for 10 to 20 seconds, making sure not to melt the butter.

Preheat oven to 350°F (180°C)
12-cup muffin pan, lined with paper liners

1 1/2 cups	all-purpose flour	375 mL
1 1/2 tsp	baking powder	7 mL
1/4 tsp	ground nutmeg	1 mL
1/4 tsp	salt	1 mL
1/2 cup	unsalted butter, at room temperature	125 mL
1/2 cup	granulated sugar	125 mL
1	egg	1
1/2 cup	milk	125 mL
1/2 cup	semisweet chocolate chips	125 mL

Topping

1/2 cup	granulated sugar	125 mL
1 tsp	ground cinnamon	5 mL
1/2 cup	unsalted butter, melted	125 mL

1. In a medium bowl, combine flour, baking powder, nutmeg and salt.

2. In a large bowl, using electric mixer, beat butter and sugar until light and fluffy. Beat in egg. Beat in flour mixture alternately with milk, making three additions of flour mixture and two of milk. Do not overmix. Stir in chocolate chips.

3. Spoon batter into prepared muffin cups. Bake in preheated oven for 20 to 22 minutes or until puffed, golden and a tester inserted into center comes out clean. Let cool in pan on rack for 5 minutes. Remove from pan and let cool completely on rack.

4. *Topping:* In a bowl, combine sugar and cinnamon. Place melted butter in another bowl. Dip warm muffins in melted butter, then roll in cinnamon-sugar topping. Serve warm or let cool on rack.

High-Octane Espresso Chip Morning Muffins

When my family and I were in Victoria, British Columbia, on a road trip, we stopped by a fabulous little bakeshop, Cascadia Wholefoods Bakery. My son devoured one of the delicious coffee muffins, immediately giving me the orders to recreate them upon our return. This is my version.

TIP

All of the recipes in this book were tested using large eggs. Using medium or extra-large eggs may adversely affect the outcome of the recipe.

Preheat oven to 350°F (180°C)
12-cup muffin pan, lined with paper liners

2 cups	all-purpose flour	500 mL
2 tsp	baking powder	10 mL
1 tsp	ground cinnamon	5 mL
1/4 tsp	salt	1 mL
1 cup	granulated sugar	250 mL
2	eggs	2
3/4 cup	milk	175 mL
1/2 cup	vegetable oil	125 mL
2 tbsp	finely ground espresso	25 mL
1 1/2 tbsp	instant coffee granules	22 mL
1 tsp	vanilla	5 mL
3/4 cup	semisweet chocolate chips	175 mL

Topping

2 tbsp	granulated sugar	25 mL
1/2 tsp	ground cinnamon	2 mL

1. In a medium bowl, combine flour, baking powder, cinnamon and salt.

2. In a large bowl, whisk together sugar, eggs, milk, oil, finely ground and instant coffees and vanilla. Stir in flour mixture just until combined. Fold in chocolate chips. Do not overmix.

TIP

Use a cookie scoop for both consistency and a professional appearance. Your scones, cookies and muffins will bake more evenly if they are all the same size.

3. *Topping:* In a small bowl, combine sugar and cinnamon. Set aside.

4. Spoon batter into prepared muffin cups. Sprinkle evenly with cinnamon–sugar topping.

5. Bake in preheated oven for 20 to 22 minutes or until puffed, firm to the touch and a tester inserted into center comes out clean. Let cool in pan on rack for 5 minutes. Remove from pan and let cool completely on rack.

Variations

Substitute milk chocolate chips for the semisweet chocolate chips.

Add ½ cup (125 mL) coarsely chopped toasted pecans with the chocolate chips.

Ginger Muffins

Crystallized or candied ginger almost tickles the funny bone, awakening the senses as you eat it. The best part is that it can be found in most supermarkets these days. It has a long shelf life if stored in an airtight jar or container.

TIP

All of the recipes in this book were tested using large eggs. Using medium or extra-large eggs may adversely affect the outcome of the recipe.

Preheat oven to 375°F (190°C)
12-cup muffin pan, lined with paper liners

2 cups	all-purpose flour	500 mL
5 tsp	ground ginger	25 mL
2 tsp	baking powder	10 mL
1 tsp	ground allspice	5 mL
$\frac{1}{4}$ tsp	salt	1 mL
$\frac{1}{4}$ tsp	ground nutmeg	1 mL
1 cup	granulated sugar, divided	250 mL
$\frac{1}{3}$ cup	packed dark brown sugar	75 mL
2	eggs	2
$\frac{2}{3}$ cup	milk	150 mL
$\frac{1}{2}$ cup	vegetable oil	125 mL
$\frac{1}{4}$ cup	fancy molasses	50 mL
$\frac{3}{4}$ cup	semisweet chocolate chips	175 mL
$\frac{1}{4}$ cup	finely chopped crystallized ginger	50 mL

1. In a medium bowl, combine flour, ground ginger, baking powder, allspice, salt and nutmeg.
2. In a large bowl, whisk together $\frac{3}{4}$ cup (175 mL) of the granulated sugar, brown sugar, eggs, milk, oil and molasses. Stir in flour mixture just until combined. Fold in chocolate chips. Do not overmix.
3. Spoon batter into prepared muffin cups. Sprinkle evenly with remaining sugar and crystallized ginger.
4. Bake in preheated oven for 22 minutes or until puffed, golden and a tester inserted into center comes out clean. Let cool in pan on rack for 5 minutes. Remove from pan and let cool completely on rack.

Chocolate Chip Eggnog Muffins

This is a great seasonal muffin. Eggnog is usually available from October through January. The creamy nutmeg flavor always makes me think of winter.

TIP

The taste of freshly grated nutmeg is far superior to that of packaged ground nutmeg. Buy whole nutmeg and grate it with a rasp or nutmeg grater (available in kitchenware shops). Whole nutmeg can be found in the spice section of your supermarket or online.

Preheat oven to 375°F (190°C)
12-cup muffin pan, lined with paper liners

2 cups	all-purpose flour	500 mL
¾ cup	semisweet chocolate chips	175 mL
2 tsp	baking powder	10 mL
1 tsp	ground nutmeg	5 mL
¼ tsp	salt	1 mL
1 cup	granulated sugar, divided	250 mL
2	eggs	2
¾ cup	eggnog (not low-fat)	175 mL
½ cup	vegetable oil	125 mL

1. In a medium bowl, combine flour, chocolate chips, baking powder, nutmeg and salt.

2. In a large bowl, whisk together ¾ cup (175 mL) of the sugar, eggs, eggnog and oil. Stir in flour mixture just until combined. Do not overmix.

3. Spoon batter into prepared muffin cups. Sprinkle evenly with remaining sugar.

4. Bake in preheated oven for 20 to 24 minutes or until puffed, golden and a tester inserted into center comes out clean. Let cool in pan on rack for 5 minutes. Remove from pan and let cool completely on rack.

Apricot Chocolate Chip Cheesecake Muffins

**MAKES
12 MUFFINS**

I was trying to develop a recipe for a deliciously different muffin, which is how this one was born. It has a chocolate chip cream cheese filling, which is an unexpected surprise.

TIPS

Read through the entire recipe before starting. That way, you know both the steps and the ingredients in the recipe before you start.

Make sure your oven is fully preheated before baking. It will likely take between 15 and 20 minutes to preheat, depending on your oven.

Preheat oven to 375°F (190°C)
12-cup muffin pan, lined with paper liners

2 cups	all-purpose flour	500 mL
1/2 cup	finely chopped dried apricots	125 mL
2 tsp	baking powder	10 mL
1/4 tsp	salt	1 mL
3/4 cup	granulated sugar	175 mL
2	eggs	2
3/4 cup	milk	175 mL
1/2 cup	vegetable oil	125 mL
1 tsp	vanilla	5 mL
Filling		
3 oz	cream cheese, at room temperature	90 g
3 tbsp	granulated sugar	45 mL
1/8 tsp	almond extract	0.5 mL
1/3 cup	semisweet chocolate chips	75 mL
Topping		
2 tbsp	granulated sugar	25 mL
1/2 tsp	ground cinnamon	2 mL

1. In a medium bowl, combine flour, apricots, baking powder and salt.

2. In a large bowl, whisk together sugar, eggs, milk, oil and vanilla. Stir in flour mixture, mixing just until combined. Do not overmix.

3. *Filling:* In a medium bowl, using electric mixer, beat together cream cheese, sugar and almond extract. Mix in chocolate chips. Set aside.

TIP

When measuring, always remember to spoon your dry ingredients into the cup and level the top by scraping across it with the flat side of a knife or skewer. This will give you an accurate measurement.

4. *Topping:* In a small bowl, combine sugar and cinnamon. Set aside.

5. Spoon batter into prepared muffin cups, filling halfway. Drop 1 tsp (5 mL) filling onto center of batter in each muffin cup. Top with more batter. Sprinkle evenly with cinnamon-sugar topping.

6. Bake in preheated oven for 22 to 24 minutes or until puffed, golden and a tester inserted into center comes out clean. Let cool in pan on rack for 5 minutes. Remove from pan and let cool completely on rack.

Variations
Substitute ½ cup (125 mL) dried cherries or cranberries for the apricots.

Chocolate Chip Cranberry Muffins

This is a great muffin, especially if you're a cranberry fan. The delightful tartness of the cranberries wedded with the sweetness of the chocolate chips makes for a very yummy treat.

Preheat oven to 375°F (190°C)
12-cup muffin pan, lined with paper liners

2 cups	all-purpose flour	500 mL
2 tsp	baking powder	10 mL
1/4 tsp	salt	1 mL
1 1/2 cups	fresh or frozen cranberries	375 mL
1 1/4 cups	granulated sugar, divided	300 mL
2	eggs	2
3/4 cup	milk	175 mL
1/2 cup	vegetable oil	125 mL
1 tsp	grated orange zest	5 mL
1 tsp	vanilla	5 mL
1/2 cup	semisweet chocolate chips	125 mL

1. In a medium bowl, combine flour, baking powder and salt.

2. In a food processor fitted with a metal blade, coarsely chop cranberries.

3. In a large bowl, whisk together 1 cup (250 mL) of the sugar, eggs, milk, oil, orange zest and vanilla. Stir in flour mixture, just until combined. Fold in chopped cranberries and chocolate chips. Do not overmix.

4. Spoon batter into prepared muffin cups. Sprinkle evenly with remaining sugar.

5. Bake in preheated oven for 20 to 24 minutes or until puffed, golden and a tester inserted into center comes out clean. Let cool in pan on rack for 5 minutes. Remove from pan and let cool completely on rack.

Raspberry Chocolate Chip Muffins

Fresh or frozen raspberries make this easy-to-prepare recipe a favorite in my household. The tart raspberries, sweet chocolate chips and delicate batter are a perfect combination to wake up the taste buds.

TIP

All of the recipes in this book were tested using large eggs. Using medium or extra-large eggs may adversely affect the outcome of the recipe.

Preheat oven to 375°F (190°C)
12-cup muffin pan, lined with paper liners

2 cups	all-purpose flour	500 mL
2 tsp	baking powder	10 mL
1/4 tsp	salt	1 mL
1 1/4 cups	granulated sugar, divided	300 mL
2	eggs	2
3/4 cup	milk	175 mL
1/2 cup	vegetable oil	125 mL
1 tsp	almond extract	5 mL
2 cups	raspberries, fresh or frozen (do not thaw)	500 mL
1/2 cup	semisweet chocolate chips	125 mL

1. In a medium bowl, combine flour, baking powder and salt.

2. In a large bowl, whisk together 1 cup (250 mL) of the sugar, eggs, milk, oil and almond extract. Stir in flour mixture just until combined. Fold in raspberries and chocolate chips. Do not overmix.

3. Spoon batter into prepared muffin cups. Sprinkle evenly with remaining sugar.

4. Bake in preheated oven for 22 to 25 minutes or until puffed, golden and a tester inserted into center comes out clean. Let cool in pan on rack for 5 minutes. Remove from pan and let cool completely on rack.

Strawberry Chocolate Chip Muffins

· ·

This light cornmeal batter is the perfect housing for the strawberry and chocolate chip filling. Don't worry if there is filling left over. Save it and spread it on warm toast for breakfast.

TIP

To give the muffin tops a sparkly appearance, sprinkle lightly with sugar.

Preheat oven to 375°F (190°C)
12-cup muffin pan, lined with paper liners

Filling

1/3 cup	semisweet chocolate chips	75 mL
1/4 cup	strawberry jam	50 mL

Batter

1 3/4 cups	all-purpose flour	425 mL
3/4 cup	cornmeal	175 mL
2 tsp	baking powder	10 mL
1/4 tsp	salt	1 mL
1 cup	sour cream	250 mL
1/2 cup	granulated sugar	125 mL
1/2 cup	unsalted butter, melted and cooled	125 mL
2	eggs	2

1. *Filling:* In a small bowl, combine chocolate chips and strawberry jam. Set aside.

2. *Batter:* In a medium bowl, combine flour, cornmeal, baking powder and salt.

3. In a large bowl, whisk together sour cream, sugar, melted butter and eggs until smooth. Stir in flour mixture just until combined.

4. Spoon batter into prepared muffin cups. Using a spoon, make an indentation in center of each. Fill indentations with a scant teaspoon (5 mL) of the filling.

5. Bake in preheated oven for 22 to 24 minutes or until puffed, golden and a tester inserted into center comes out clean. Let cool in pan on rack for 5 minutes. Remove from pan and let cool completely on rack.

Chocolate Chip Lemon Muffins

**MAKES
12 MUFFINS**

This muffin is delish! Lemon and chocolate are always a smashing combo, and here they result in an out-of-sight muffin. My young taste testers were very impressed with these tender little cakes.

Preheat oven to 375°F (190°C)
12-cup muffin pan, lined with paper liners

2 cups	all-purpose flour	500 mL
1 1/4 cups	granulated sugar, divided	300 mL
2 tsp	baking powder	10 mL
2	eggs	2
3/4 cup	milk	175 mL
1/2 cup	butter, melted	125 mL
2 tsp	grated lemon zest	10 mL
1/4 cup	freshly squeezed lemon juice	50 mL
1/2 cup	semisweet chocolate chips	125 mL

1. In a medium bowl, combine flour, 1 cup (250 mL) of the sugar and baking powder.

2. In a large bowl, whisk together eggs, milk, butter, lemon zest and lemon juice. Stir in flour mixture, mixing just until combined. Fold in chocolate chips. Do not overmix.

3. Scoop batter into prepared muffin cups. Sprinkle remaining sugar evenly over tops.

4. Bake in preheated oven for 20 to 24 minutes or until puffed, light golden and a skewer inserted into center comes out clean. Let cool in pan on rack for 5 minutes. Remove from pan and let cool completely on rack.

Chocolate Chip Orange Muffins

I have always thought that the combination of chocolate and orange is a treat for the senses. The two flavors can truly turn something ordinary into something extraordinary! This muffin proves the point.

TIP

When measuring, always remember to spoon your dry ingredients into the cup and level the top by scraping across it with the flat side of a knife or skewer. This will give you an accurate measurement.

Preheat oven to 375°F (190°C)

12-cup muffin pan, lined with paper liners

2 cups	all-purpose flour	500 mL
2 tsp	baking powder	10 mL
1/4 tsp	salt	1 mL
1 1/4 cups	granulated sugar, divided	300 mL
2	eggs	2
3/4 cup	milk	175 mL
1/2 cup	vegetable oil	125 mL
2 tsp	grated orange zest	10 mL
1 tsp	vanilla	5 mL
1 tsp	orange extract	5 mL
3/4 cup	semisweet chocolate chips	175 mL

1. In a medium bowl, combine flour, baking powder and salt.

2. In a large bowl, whisk together 1 cup (250 mL) of the sugar, eggs, milk, oil, orange zest, vanilla and orange extract. Stir in flour mixture just until combined. Fold in chocolate chips. Do not overmix.

3. Spoon batter into prepared muffin cups. Sprinkle evenly with remaining sugar.

4. Bake in preheated oven for 20 to 24 minutes or until puffed, golden and a tester inserted into center comes out clean. Let cool in pan on rack for 5 minutes. Remove from pan and let cool completely on rack.

Chocolate Chip
Pumpkin Muffins

Pumpkin is high in beta-carotene, making these scrumptious muffins as virtuous as they are delicious. They are a great lunch box stuffer or a quick breakfast on the go.

TIP

For a less sweet muffin, reduce the sugar in the batter to ³/₄ cup (175 mL).

Preheat oven to 375°F (190°C)
12-cup muffin pan, lined with paper liners

2 cups	all-purpose flour	500 mL
³/₄ cup	semisweet chocolate chips	175 mL
2 tsp	baking powder	10 mL
1¹/₂ tsp	ground cinnamon	7 mL
³/₄ tsp	ground allspice	4 mL
³/₄ tsp	ground nutmeg	4 mL
¹/₄ tsp	salt	1 mL
1¹/₄ cups	granulated sugar, divided	300 mL
2	eggs	2
³/₄ cup	canned pumpkin purée (not pie filling)	175 mL
¹/₂ cup	vegetable oil	125 mL
¹/₄ cup	milk	50 mL
1 tsp	vanilla	5 mL

1. In a medium bowl, combine flour, chocolate chips, baking powder, cinnamon, allspice, nutmeg and salt.

2. In a large bowl, whisk together 1 cup (250 mL) of the sugar, eggs, pumpkin, oil, milk and vanilla. Stir in flour mixture just until combined. Do not overmix.

3. Spoon batter into prepared muffin cups. Sprinkle evenly with remaining sugar.

4. Bake in preheated oven for 20 to 24 minutes or until puffed, golden and a tester inserted into center comes out clean. Let cool in pan on rack for 5 minutes. Remove from pan and let cool completely on rack.

Almond Poppy Seed Chocolate Chip Muffins

MAKES 12 MUFFINS

These muffins have a great combination of flavors and the added crunch of almonds, poppy seeds and chocolate chips. For a charming way to serve muffins, line a basket with a beautiful cloth napkin and fill with fresh-baked muffins.

Preheat oven to 375°F (190°C)
12-cup muffin pan, lined with paper liners

2 cups	all-purpose flour	500 mL
3/4 cup	semisweet chocolate chips	175 mL
1 1/2 tbsp	poppy seeds	22 mL
2 tsp	baking powder	10 mL
1/4 tsp	salt	1 mL
1 1/4 cups	granulated sugar, divided	300 mL
2	eggs	2
3/4 cup	milk	175 mL
1/2 cup	vegetable oil	125 mL
2 tsp	almond extract	10 mL
1/4 cup	sliced almonds	50 mL

1. In a medium bowl, combine flour, chocolate chips, poppy seeds, baking powder and salt.

2. In a large bowl, whisk together 1 cup (250 mL) of the sugar, eggs, milk, oil and almond extract. Stir in flour mixture, mixing just until combined. Do not overmix.

3. Spoon batter into prepared muffin cups. Sprinkle remaining sugar and sliced almonds evenly over tops.

4. Bake in preheated oven for 20 to 24 minutes or until puffed, golden and a tester inserted into center comes out clean. Let cool in pan on rack for 5 minutes. Remove from pan and let cool completely on rack.

Maple Pecan Muffins with Chocolate Chips

MAKES 12 MUFFINS

If you love the taste of maple and pecan, you will love these muffins. If you can't find pecans, you can easily substitute walnuts.

Preheat oven to 375°F (190°C)

12-cup muffin pan, lined with paper liners

2 cups	all-purpose flour	500 mL
2 tsp	baking powder	10 mL
1/4 tsp	salt	1 mL
2 tbsp	granulated sugar	25 mL
3/4 cup	chopped pecans, divided	175 mL
1/2 cup	unsalted butter, melted	125 mL
3/4 cup	packed light brown sugar	175 mL
2	eggs	2
3/4 cup	milk	175 mL
1 tsp	vanilla	5 mL
1 tsp	maple extract	5 mL
3/4 cup	semisweet chocolate chips	175 mL

1. In a medium bowl, combine flour, baking powder and salt.

2. In a small bowl, combine granulated sugar and half of the pecans. Set aside.

3. In a large bowl, beat butter and brown sugar. Add eggs, one at a time, beating well after each addition. Stir in milk, vanilla and maple extract. Stir in flour mixture just until combined. Fold in chocolate chips and remaining pecans. Do not overmix.

4. Spoon batter into prepared muffin cups. Sprinkle evenly with reserved pecan mixture.

5. Bake in preheated oven for 20 to 24 minutes or until puffed, golden and a tester inserted into center comes out clean. Let cool in pan on rack for 5 minutes. Remove from pan and let cool completely on rack.

Sour Cream Coffee Cake Muffins

∙ ∙

**MAKES
12 MUFFINS**

This is an ideal recipe when you have a craving for coffee cake but don't have the time to make it. The rich, tender batter is the perfect partner for the tasty chocolate chip walnut topping.

TIP

To bring cold butter to room temperature in a hurry, use a microwave oven. I usually set it on Medium (50%) for 10 to 20 seconds, making sure not to melt the butter.

Preheat oven to 375°F (190°C)
12-cup muffin pan, lined with paper liners

2 cups	all-purpose flour	500 mL
2 tsp	baking powder	10 mL
1/4 tsp	salt	1 mL
1/2 cup	unsalted butter, at room temperature	125 mL
1 cup	granulated sugar	250 mL
1 tsp	vanilla	5 mL
2	eggs	2
1 cup	sour cream	250 mL

Topping

1/2 cup	granulated sugar	125 mL
1/2 cup	coarsely chopped walnuts	125 mL
1/2 cup	semisweet chocolate chips	125 mL
1 tsp	ground cinnamon	5 mL

1. In a medium bowl, combine flour, baking powder and salt.

2. In a large bowl, using electric mixer, beat butter and sugar until light and fluffy. Beat in vanilla. Add eggs, one at a time, beating well after each addition. Add sour cream and beat until smooth. Add flour mixture and beat just until combined.

3. *Topping:* In a small bowl, combine sugar, walnuts, chocolate chips and cinnamon. Spoon batter into prepared muffin cups, filling halfway. Sprinkle evenly with half of the topping. Spoon in remaining batter and sprinkle with remaining topping.

4. Bake in preheated oven for 24 minutes or until puffed, golden and a tester inserted into center comes out clean. Let cool in pan on rack for 5 minutes. Remove from pan and let cool completely on rack.

Double Chocolate Apricot Muffins

· ·

MAKES
12 MUFFINS

I love to whip together muffins for Sunday breakfast. This recipe is one that I make often. You can vary the dried fruit, depending on your mood or what you've got on hand.

TIP

Cocoa powder needs to be sifted before use because it can be very lumpy, which makes it difficult to incorporate. Use a fine-meshed sieve to remove any lumps before adding cocoa powder to other dry ingredients.

Preheat oven to 375°F (190°C)
12-cup muffin pan, lined with paper liners

1³⁄₄ cups	all-purpose flour	425 mL
¹⁄₂ cup	unsweetened Dutch-process cocoa powder, sifted	125 mL
2 tsp	baking powder	10 mL
¹⁄₄ tsp	salt	1 mL
1 cup	granulated sugar	250 mL
2	eggs	2
³⁄₄ cup	milk	175 mL
¹⁄₂ cup	vegetable oil	125 mL
2 tsp	vanilla	10 mL
5 oz	semisweet chocolate, coarsely chopped	150 g
²⁄₃ cup	coarsely chopped dried apricots	150 mL

Topping

2 tbsp	granulated sugar	25 mL

1. In a medium bowl, mix together flour, cocoa powder, baking powder and salt.

2. In a large bowl, mix together sugar, eggs, milk, oil and vanilla. Mix in dry ingredients just until combined. Fold in chocolate and apricots. Scoop batter into prepared muffin cups.

3. *Topping:* Sprinkle with sugar.

4. Bake in preheated oven for 22 minutes or until a tester inserted into center comes out clean. Let muffins cool in pan on a wire rack for 5 minutes. Transfer to rack and let cool completely.

Variation
Substitute dried cherries for the apricots.

Cakes

Cookies and Cream Cake *82*

Lone Star Double Chocolate
Chip Cake *84*

Mud Cake *86*

Chocolate Mousse Cake *88*

Banana Chocolate Cake *90*

Banana Chocolate Chip Cake *91*

Chocolate Midnight Cake *92*

Chocolate-Drizzled Almond
Cake *93*

Almond Chocolate Coconut
Torte *94*

Walnut Chocolate Chip Cake *96*

Tish's Date Flapjack Cake *97*

Chocolate Port Torte *98*

Irish Cream Cake *99*

24 Carrot Cake *100*

Chocolate Potato Cake *102*

Double Chocolate Zucchini
Cake *103*

Chocolate Cherry Bundt Cake *104*

Cranberry Sour Cream
Bundt Cake *106*

Rich Lemon Chocolate Chip
Bundt Cake *108*

Coconut Chocolate Chip
Bundt Cake *110*

Brown Sugar Chocolate
Chunk Pound Cake *112*

Chocolate Chip Cream Cheese
Pound Cake *113*

Sour Cream Coffee Cake with
Chocolate Pecan Streusel *114*

Café Mocha Cake *116*

Mocha Chocolate Chip Cake *117*

Chocolate Espresso Cake *118*

Chocolate Chip Calypso Cake *120*

Chocolate Chip Chai Cake *122*

Eggnog Chocolate Chip
Tea Cake *124*

Chocolate Espresso Lava
Cakes *125*

Chocolate Brownie
Baby Cakes *126*

Little Chocolate Cakes *127*

Chocolate Cherry Rum Cakes *128*

Cookies and Cream Cake

A huge thank-you to Valerie Schucht, who generously shared her family's favorite cake recipe with me. Valerie says that this delicious cake has been in her family for more than 40 years. I hope that Valerie will forgive me for tinkering with the recipe (I couldn't resist adding a "cookies and cream" frosting). This cake is beyond good, with a moist, tender chocolaty crumb and a creamy chocolate cookie frosting.

TIP

All of the recipes in this book were tested using large eggs. Using medium or extra-large eggs may adversely affect the outcome of the recipe.

Preheat oven to 350°F (180°C)

13- by 9-inch (3 L) metal baking pan, bottom and sides greased

Cake

1 cup	packed light brown sugar	250 mL
1 cup	granulated sugar	250 mL
1/2 cup	shortening	125 mL
2	eggs	2
1/2 cup	buttermilk	125 mL
1 tsp	vanilla	5 mL
2 cups	all-purpose flour	500 mL
1/2 cup	unsweetened Dutch-process cocoa powder, sifted	125 mL
2 tsp	baking soda	10 mL
1/2 tsp	salt	2 mL
1 cup	boiling water	250 mL
1 cup	semisweet chocolate chips	250 mL

Frosting

2 cups	confectioner's (icing) sugar	500 mL
1 cup	unsalted butter, at room temperature	250 mL
1/4 cup	whipping (35%) cream	50 mL
1 tsp	vanilla	5 mL
1/8 tsp	salt	0.5 mL
10	chocolate sandwich cookies, crushed	10
7 to 8	chocolate sandwich cookies, broken	7 to 8

1. *Cake:* In a large bowl, using an electric mixer, beat together brown and granulated sugars and shortening. Add eggs, one at a time, beating well after each addition. Add buttermilk and vanilla, mixing well.

2. In a medium bowl, stir together flour, cocoa powder, baking soda and salt. Add to butter mixture, mixing well. Add boiling water, mixing until smooth. Stir in chocolate chips.

3. Spread batter in prepared pan, smoothing top. Bake in preheated oven for 40 to 45 minutes or until a tester inserted in center comes out clean. Let cake cool completely in pan on rack.

4. *Frosting:* In a bowl, using an electric mixer, combine confectioner's sugar, butter, cream, vanilla and salt. Whip on high speed until smooth and fluffy. Mix in crushed sandwich cookies until almost smooth, with little bits of chocolate cookies.

5. Spread top of cake with frosting. Garnish cake with broken chocolate sandwich cookies.

Variation
Frost cake with Cream Cheese Icing (see recipe, page 100).

Lone Star Double Chocolate Chip Cake

SERVES 12

Several years ago, large chocolate sheet cakes called Texas Sheet Cakes (I guess for their big size) were all the rage. I thought that they needed something new, so here is a twist. This rich, dark chocolate cake is studded with chocolate chips and a creamy chocolate coffee icing. One of the great things about this cake (without the icing) is that it contains no dairy or eggs, perfect for vegans or people with allergies.

TIP

A great ratio for strong brewed coffee is 2 tbsp (25 mL) finely ground French-roast coffee or espresso for every ¾ cup (175 mL) water.

Preheat oven to 350°F (180°C)

13- by 9-inch (3 L) metal baking pan, greased

2⅓ cups	all-purpose flour	575 mL
¾ cup	unsweetened Dutch-process cocoa powder	175 mL
1 tsp	baking soda	5 mL
¼ tsp	salt	1 mL
¾ cup	vegetable oil	175 mL
2 cups	granulated sugar	500 mL
1¼ cups	strong brewed coffee, cooled to room temperature (see Tip, at left)	300 mL
1 tsp	vanilla	5 mL
½ tsp	almond extract	2 mL
1½ tbsp	balsamic vinegar	22 mL
1 cup	semisweet chocolate chips	250 mL

Icing

2½ cups	confectioner's (icing) sugar	625 mL
1½ cups	unsweetened Dutch-process cocoa powder	375 mL
1 cup	unsalted butter or margarine, at room temperature	250 mL
2 tbsp	strong brewed coffee, at room temperature (see Tip, at left)	25 mL
2 tsp	vanilla	10 mL
2 tbsp	milk	25 mL
1 tbsp	dark rum	15 mL

1. In a medium bowl, sift together flour, cocoa powder, baking soda and salt.

2. In a large bowl, using electric mixer, beat oil and sugar. Beat in coffee, vanilla and almond extract. Add flour mixture, beating until smooth. Beat in balsamic vinegar just until mixed.

TIP

To bring cold butter to room temperature in a hurry, use a microwave oven. I usually set it on Medium (50%) for 10 to 20 seconds, making sure not to melt the butter.

3. Quickly pour batter into prepared pan and sprinkle with chocolate chips. Bake in preheated oven for 50 minutes or until a tester inserted into center of cake comes out clean. Let cake cool completely in pan on rack.

4. *Icing:* Meanwhile, in a food processor fitted with a metal blade, combine confectioner's sugar, cocoa powder, butter, coffee and vanilla. Process until smooth. Add milk and rum. Process until smooth, scraping down side of bowl as necessary. Spread desired amount of icing over cooled cake. Any extra icing can be covered and refrigerated for another use. Bring to room temperature before using.

Variation

To make this cake dairy-free, substitute dairy-free chocolate chips, soy beverage for the milk and margarine for the butter.

Mud Cake

SERVES 24

This recipe percolates into an ooey-gooey fudgy ooze of flavors that melds into sweet delectable mud. It's a bit messy, so wear a bib. If you're looking for something rich, chocolaty and creamy (and who isn't?), then this is your cake. The base of this cake is adapted from a recipe generously shared with me by Cindy Pauldine.

TIP

Cocoa powder needs to be sifted before use because it can be very lumpy, which makes it difficult to incorporate. Use a fine-meshed sieve to remove any lumps before adding cocoa powder to other dry ingredients.

Preheat oven to 350°F (180°C)
13- by 9-inch (3 L) metal baking pan, greased

Cake

2 cups	all-purpose flour	500 mL
2/3 cup	unsweetened Dutch-process cocoa powder, sifted	150 mL
2 tsp	baking soda	10 mL
1 3/4 cups	granulated sugar	425 mL
1/2 cup	shortening	125 mL
2	eggs	2
2 tsp	vanilla	10 mL
1/2 tsp	almond extract	2 mL
1/4 cup	bourbon, dark rum or whiskey	50 mL
1/4 cup	milk	50 mL
2 tsp	instant coffee granules	10 mL
1 cup	boiling water	250 mL

Filling

7 oz	marshmallow cream	210 g

Topping

10 oz	semisweet chocolate, chopped	300 g
1 cup	whipping (35%) cream	250 mL
1 tbsp	bourbon, dark rum or whiskey	15 mL

1. *Cake:* In a medium bowl, mix together flour, cocoa powder and baking soda.

2. In a large bowl, beat together sugar and shortening. Add eggs, one at a time, beating well after each addition. Beat until fluffy. Add vanilla, almond extract and bourbon, mixing well.

3. In a measuring cup, mix together milk and instant coffee. Stir to dissolve. Add to shortening mixture, mixing well. Stir dry ingredients into shortening mixture alternately with boiling water, making three additions of dry and two of water. Beat until almost smooth. Batter will still have a few small lumps in it.

4. Spread batter in prepared pan, smoothing top. Bake in preheated oven for 40 minutes or until a tester inserted in center comes out clean. Let cool in pan on a rack for 5 minutes.

5. *Filling:* Spread marshmallow cream over top of warm cake. This might take a few minutes to spread, but the marshmallow cream will begin to soften from the cake's warmth. Let cake cool completely.

6. *Topping:* In a microwave-safe bowl, combine chocolate and cream. Microwave, uncovered, on Medium (50%) for 1 to 2 minutes, stirring every 30 seconds, or until cream is hot and chocolate is starting to melt. Stir well until chocolate is melted and mixture is thick and smooth. If chocolate is not completely melted, return to microwave for another 10 to 20 seconds or until chocolate is soft and melted. Add bourbon, stirring well. Spread over marshmallow layer. Refrigerate until chocolate is firm, at least 2 hours or for up to 2 days.

Variation
Substitute milk chocolate for the semisweet chocolate in the topping.

Chocolate Mousse Cake

Although this seems like a very labor-intensive cake, it really isn't. In fact, it can be made a day ahead, making it a perfect do-ahead dessert. Plus, as an added bonus, it freezes beautifully.

TIP

Read through the entire recipe before starting. That way, you know both the steps and the ingredients in the recipe before you start.

10-inch (25 cm) springform pan, greased

36	cream-filled chocolate sandwich cookies	36
1/4 cup	unsalted butter, melted	50 mL
Filling		
2 3/4 cups	semisweet chocolate chips	675 mL
4 cups	whipping (35%) cream, chilled and divided	1 L
1 tbsp	kirsch or other liqueur (see Variation, opposite)	15 mL
Topping		
1 cup	whipping (35%) cream, chilled	250 mL
3 tbsp	confectioner's (icing) sugar	45 mL
1/2 tsp	vanilla	2 mL

1. In a food processor fitted with a metal blade, pulse chocolate sandwich cookies until finely ground. (You should have about 3 cups/750 mL.) Add melted butter and process just until combined. Firmly press cookie mixture onto bottom and up side of prepared pan. Freeze for 20 minutes to firm up crust.

2. *Filling:* Meanwhile, in a large microwave-safe bowl, combine chocolate chips and 1 cup (250 mL) of the cream. Microwave on High for 2 1/2 minutes, stirring every 30 seconds, until chocolate is shiny and almost melted. Stir until smooth. In clean food processor bowl, process chocolate mixture and Kirsch until smooth.

TIP

You can garnish cake with a sprinkling of chocolate chips or sprinkle it with pieces of broken sandwich cookies.

3. In a large bowl, whip remaining cream until stiff peaks form. Add cooled chocolate mixture and whip until incorporated. Spread filling over prepared crust and refrigerate until firm, about 6 hours, or overnight.

4. *Topping:* Whip cream with confectioner's sugar and vanilla until stiff peaks form. Spread over chocolate mousse layer and refrigerate for 1 hour or until firm, or freeze for 20 minutes. Carefully run a knife around edge of pan before removing side. Do not remove bottom of pan. Slice and serve cake directly from bottom of pan.

Variation

Substitute another liqueur for the kirsch (cherry brandy), such as Irish cream, crème de cacao or crème de menthe.

Banana Chocolate Cake

I am so easily influenced when it comes to challenges. My friend Erika Novick gave me some ripe bananas and said, "Make something with these." This recipe embodies the richness of a coffee cake with the flavor of banana bread. Of course, I added chocolate to the batter — no big surprise there. This cake was adapted from a recipe by Beth Hensperger.

TIP

This cake freezes very well. To prepare a cake for the freezer, wrap it well in two layers of plastic wrap. Then cover with one layer of foil. This will keep the cake from getting freezer burn for up to 1 month. I also like to set the cake on a 10-inch (25 cm) round piece of cardboard for stability in the freezer. You can buy precut 10-inch (25 cm) cardboard cake circles at restaurant supply or cake decorating stores (or sometimes even craft stores).

Preheat oven to 350°F (180°C)
10-inch (3 L) Bundt pan, greased

3 cups	all-purpose flour, divided	750 mL
5 oz	semisweet chocolate, coarsely chopped	150 g
2 tsp	baking powder	10 mL
1/2 tsp	baking soda	2 mL
1/2 tsp	salt	2 mL
1 1/2 cups	granulated sugar	375 mL
3/4 cup	unsalted butter, at room temperature	175 mL
1 tsp	vanilla	5 mL
2	eggs	2
1 1/2 cups	mashed ripe bananas (about 3 large)	375 mL
1 cup	sour cream	250 mL
1 cup	walnut halves, coarsely chopped	250 mL

1. In a food processor fitted with a metal blade, pulse 1 cup (250 mL) flour and chocolate until flour looks somewhat brown and there are little bits of chocolate throughout. Transfer mixture to a bowl, adding remaining flour, baking powder, baking soda and salt.

2. In a large bowl, using electric mixer, beat together sugar, butter and vanilla until light and fluffy. Add eggs, one at a time, beating well after each addition. Beat in bananas and sour cream. Add flour mixture, beating just until combined. Stir in walnut pieces.

3. Spread batter in prepared pan, smoothing top. Bake in preheated oven for 60 to 70 minutes or until a tester inserted into center comes out clean. Let cake cool in pan on a rack for 15 minutes. Invert onto rack and let cool completely before cutting and serving.

Banana Chocolate Chip Cake

This is not only the ultimate banana bread but also the perfect vehicle for overripe bananas. It is based on a recipe that my mom used to make when my brother and I were growing up. I thought that chocolate chips were needed in an otherwise perfect cake. This cake freezes beautifully, so eat one now and freeze one to enjoy later.

TIPS

You can easily freeze overripe bananas, skin and all. Just be sure to thaw them before mashing.

For a more intense walnut flavor, toast the nuts before adding to the batter. Simply spread the nuts on a rimmed baking sheet and bake in a preheated 350°F (180°C) oven until lightly browned and fragrant, about 8 to 10 minutes. Let cool before mixing into batter.

Preheat oven to 350°F (180°C)
Two 9-by 5-inch (2 L) metal loaf pans, lined with parchment paper, greased

2¹/₂ cups	all-purpose flour	625 mL
2 tsp	baking soda	10 mL
¹/₄ tsp	salt	1 mL
1 cup	canola oil	250 mL
2 cups	granulated sugar	500 mL
4	eggs	4
2 cups	mashed ripe bananas (about 4 large)	500 mL
1 tsp	vanilla	5 mL
1¹/₃ cups	semisweet chocolate chips	325 mL
³/₄ cup	toasted walnuts (optional) (see Tip, at left)	175 mL

1. In a medium bowl, combine flour, baking soda and salt.

2. In a large bowl, using electric mixer, beat oil and sugar. Add eggs, one at a time, beating well after each addition. Add bananas and vanilla, beating well. Add flour mixture, beating just until smooth. Stir in chocolate chips and walnuts, if using.

3. Spread batter in prepared pans. Bake in preheated oven for 60 to 65 minutes or until a tester inserted into center of cakes comes out clean. Let cakes cool in pans on racks for 15 minutes. Invert cakes to remove from pans and peel off parchment paper. Return cakes to racks to cool completely.

Chocolate Midnight Cake

This flourless cake is a delectable blend of dark chocolate and espresso. Serve slices with a scoop of premium vanilla ice cream.

TIP

To remove cake from springform pan, run a knife around edge of pan to loosen. Remove side of pan. Invert cake onto platter and remove parchment.

Preheat oven to 350°F (180°C)

10-inch (25 cm) springform pan, lined with parchment paper, greased

1 1/2 cups	semisweet chocolate chips	375 mL
1 cup	unsalted butter	250 mL
1 tbsp	rum	15 mL
1 tsp	vanilla	5 mL
6	eggs	6
1 cup	granulated sugar	250 mL
1 cup	unsweetened Dutch-process cocoa powder, sifted	250 mL
2 tbsp	finely ground espresso	25 mL
1/4 tsp	salt	1 mL

1. In a microwave-safe bowl, combine chocolate chips and butter. Microwave on High for 2 minutes, stirring every 30 seconds, until chocolate is shiny and almost melted. Stir until smooth. Whisk in rum and vanilla. Set aside.

2. In a large bowl, whisk eggs. Whisk in sugar, cocoa powder, chocolate mixture, ground espresso and salt just until smooth.

3. Pour mixture into prepared pan and bake in preheated oven, about 55 minutes or until a tester inserted into center comes out clean. Let cool in pan on a rack. Remove from pan (see Tip, at left) and serve.

Variation
Omit ground espresso.

Chocolate-Drizzled Almond Cake

This almond cake has a dense, spongy texture. Freshly whipped cream and strawberries are the perfect accompaniment.

TIP

To bring cold butter to room temperature in a hurry, use a microwave oven. I usually set it on Medium (50%) for 10 to 20 seconds, making sure not to melt the butter.

Preheat oven to 350°F (180°C)

8-inch (20 cm) round cake pan, lined with parchment paper, greased

1 cup	granulated sugar	250 mL
1/2 cup	unsalted butter, at room temperature	125 mL
7 oz	almond paste	210 g
1 1/2 tsp	almond extract	7 mL
5	eggs	5
1 cup	all-purpose flour	250 mL
1/2 tsp	baking powder	2 mL
1/4 tsp	salt	1 mL
1/2 cup	semisweet chocolate chips	125 mL
1 1/2 tsp	shortening	7 mL
	Fresh strawberries (optional)	
	Whipped cream (optional)	

1. In a food processor fitted with a metal blade, combine sugar, butter, almond paste and almond extract. Process until smooth. Add eggs, one at a time, processing well after each addition.

2. In a small bowl, sift together flour, baking powder and salt. Add to almond mixture and process just until blended. Pour into prepared pan, smoothing top. Bake in preheated oven for 55 to 60 minutes or until a tester inserted into center comes out clean. Let cake cool in pan on a rack. Run a knife around the side to loosen and invert cake onto a serving plate. Remove parchment.

3. In a microwave-safe bowl, combine chocolate chips and shortening. Microwave on High for 2 minutes, stirring every 30 seconds, until chocolate is shiny and almost melted. Stir until smooth. Using a fork, randomly drizzle the melted chocolate over top of cake. Refrigerate cake until chocolate hardens.

4. Serve cake with fresh strawberries and whipped cream, if desired.

Almond Chocolate Coconut Torte

This thin, fudgy cake is better than good. Its coconut and almond interior is enrobed in a creamy chocolate glaze. This is a great dessert to serve for company.

TIP

To make almond meal: Finely grind about 2/3 cup (150 mL) unsalted whole blanched or unblanched almonds (raw or toasted) in a food processor with a metal blade until finely ground. Do not overprocess or you will wind up with almond butter.

Preheat oven to 325°F (160°C)

9-inch (23 cm) springform pan, bottom and sides greased, then bottom lined with parchment paper

Cake

7 oz	semisweet chocolate, chopped	210 g
1 cup	unsalted butter	250 mL
2/3 cup	packed light brown sugar	150 mL
4	eggs	4
1/2 cup	almond meal or finely ground almonds (see Tip, at left)	125 mL
1/4 cup	all-purpose flour	50 mL
1/3 cup	sweetened flaked coconut	75 mL
1/4 tsp	salt	1 mL
1 tsp	vanilla	5 mL
1/2 tsp	almond extract	2 mL

Chocolate Glaze

5 oz	semisweet chocolate, chopped	150 g
1/2 cup	whipping (35%) cream	125 mL

1. *Cake:* In a large microwave-safe bowl, combine chocolate and butter. Microwave, uncovered, on Medium (50%) for 1 to 2 minutes, stirring every 30 seconds, or until chocolate and butter are soft and almost melted. Stir until melted and smooth. Stir in brown sugar until smooth. Let cool slightly. Add eggs, one at a time, whisking well after each addition. Stir in vanilla and almond extract.

2. In a small bowl, mix together almond meal, flour, coconut and salt. Add to chocolate mixture, stirring until smooth.

TIPS

Serve cake on plates that have been drizzled with Raspberry Sauce (see Variation, page 325).

The glazed cake keeps well for several days in the refrigerator.

3. Spread batter in prepared pan, smoothing top. Bake in preheated oven for 25 minutes. Top of cake will be puffed (do not overbake). Let cool completely in pan on a rack.

4. *Chocolate Glaze:* In a microwave-safe bowl, combine chocolate and cream. Microwave, uncovered, on Medium (50%) for 1 minute, stirring every 30 seconds, or until cream is hot and chocolate is starting to melt. Stir well until chocolate is melted and mixture is thick and smooth. If chocolate is not completely melted, return to microwave for another 10 to 20 seconds or until chocolate is soft and melted. Stir well. If glaze is very thin, let stand for a few minutes to thicken slightly.

5. Invert cake onto a platter and remove parchment paper. Pour glaze over top and evenly spread with a spatula, letting glaze drip down the sides. Refrigerate until glaze is firm. Cut into wedges and serve.

Variation
Top batter with ½ cup (125 mL) chopped chocolate or chocolate chips before baking.

Walnut Chocolate Chip Cake

Although this cake is rich, it's slightly sweet with a subtle maple flavor from the walnuts and brown sugar. I love it with a cup of tea.

TIP

All of the recipes in this book were tested using large eggs. Using medium or extra-large eggs may adversely affect the outcome of the recipe.

Preheat oven to 350°F (180°C)
10-inch (4 L) tube pan, greased and floured

4 cups	all-purpose flour	1 L
2 tsp	baking soda	10 mL
1/2 tsp	salt	2 mL
1 cup	unsalted butter, at room temperature	250 mL
1 cup	packed light brown sugar	250 mL
1 cup	granulated sugar	250 mL
4	eggs	4
2 cups	sour cream	500 mL
2 tsp	vanilla	10 mL
1 cup	walnut pieces	250 mL
1 cup	semisweet chocolate chips	250 mL
	Confectioner's (icing) sugar (optional)	

1. In a large bowl, combine flour, baking soda and salt.

2. In a large bowl, using electric mixer, beat butter and brown and granulated sugars until light and fluffy. Beat in eggs, one at a time, beating well after each addition. Beat in sour cream and vanilla. Add flour mixture, beating just until smooth. Stir in nuts and chocolate chips.

3. Spread batter in prepared pan. Bake in preheated oven for 70 minutes or until golden and a tester inserted into center comes out clean. Remove from pan and let cool completely on rack. Dust cooled cake with confectioner's sugar, if desired.

Variation
Substitute pecans for the walnuts.

Tish's Date Flapjack Cake

The original recipe for this delicious dessert came from my good friend Tish Thornton, hence the name. I played with the recipe a bit to give it that chocolate edge. This cake is almost like a very thick cookie, with a chocolate date filling.

TIP

Store chocolate in a cool, dry place for up to one year. Chocolate will sometimes develop a white "bloom," or coating, when it gets too warm, causing the cocoa butter to separate. The chocolate is still fine to use in recipes or for melting.

Preheat oven to 350°F (180°C)
8-inch (20 cm) round metal baking pan, greased

2 cups	dates, coarsely chopped (about 10 oz/300 g)	500 mL
²/₃ cup	red wine, such as Cabernet or Merlot	150 mL
3 oz	bittersweet or semisweet chocolate, chopped	90 g
2 cups	old-fashioned rolled oats (not quick-cooking oats)	500 mL
1 cup	all-purpose flour	250 mL
³/₄ cup	unsalted butter, melted	175 mL
³/₄ cup	packed light brown sugar	175 mL
¹/₂ tsp	ground cinnamon	2 mL
	Confectioner's (icing) sugar for dusting	

1. In a small saucepan, combine chopped dates and wine. Cook over low heat for 5 minutes or until dates are very soft and mixture is thick. Stir date mixture with a wooden spoon until it forms a thick purée. Stir in chopped chocolate until smooth and chocolate is melted.

2. In a large bowl, stir together rolled oats, flour, butter, brown sugar and cinnamon. Press half of the oat mixture into prepared pan. Top with date mixture. Press remaining oat mixture over dates.

3. Bake flapjack in preheated oven for 30 minutes or until golden brown. Let cool completely in pan on a rack, gently scoring the top into 8 wedges while warm. When cool, wrap cake with plastic wrap and let stand overnight. This gives the flavors a chance to meld (plus the cake is too crumbly when warm or freshly made). Before serving, dust with confectioner's sugar. Cut completely into wedges and serve.

Chocolate Port Torte

Do you like grown-up desserts that can be assembled in a jiffy and, above all else, taste fantastic? Then this one's for you! One of my husband's favorites, it has a truffle-like texture with the deep flavors of dark chocolate and port wine.

TIPS

Don't be daunted by the water bath. It is actually a very simple technique to ensure a smooth-textured cake.

Dust with unsweetened cocoa powder or confectioner's sugar.

Preheat oven to 350°F (180°C)
10-inch (25 cm) round cake pan, lined with parchment paper, greased
Roasting pan large enough to hold cake pan for water bath

2$\frac{1}{2}$ cups	semisweet chocolate chips	625 mL
2 cups	unsalted butter	500 mL
3 oz	unsweetened chocolate, chopped	90 g
2 cups	granulated sugar	500 mL
1 cup	port wine	250 mL
$\frac{1}{8}$ tsp	salt	0.5 mL
8	eggs	8

1. In a large microwave–safe bowl, combine chocolate chips, butter and unsweetened chocolate. Microwave on High for 2 minutes, stirring every 30 seconds, until chocolate is shiny and almost melted. Stir until smooth. Whisk in sugar, port wine and salt.

2. In a large bowl, whisk eggs until blended. Add melted chocolate mixture, whisking until smooth. Pour chocolate mixture into prepared cake pan.

3. Place pan in a roasting pan in preheated oven. Pour in enough warm water to come 1 inch (2.5 cm) up side of cake pan. Bake for 70 to 75 minutes or until top of cake has risen, feels firm and crisp to the touch and a knife inserted into center comes out almost clean (it will look a little moist). Do not overbake.

4. Transfer pan with water bath to a cooling rack. Let stand for 20 minutes. Remove cake from water bath and let cool completely on rack. Refrigerate until firm. To serve, invert cake onto a serving platter. Remove parchment paper.

Irish Cream Cake

Here's a very versatile chocolate pound cake with the deep flavor of Irish cream. The cake has a slightly dry yet silky texture, making it a perfect partner for ice cream, fresh berry sauce, whipped cream or for layering into a trifle. The possibilities are endless.

TIP

This cakes freezes very well. To prepare a cake for the freezer, wrap it well in two layers of plastic wrap. Then cover with one layer of foil. This will keep the cake from getting freezer burn for up to 1 month. I also like to set the cake on a 10-inch (25 cm) round piece of cardboard for stability in the freezer. You can buy precut 10-inch (25 cm) cardboard cake circles at restaurant supply or cake decorating stores (or sometimes even craft stores).

Preheat oven to 350°F (180°C)
9- by 5-inch (1.5 L) metal loaf pan, greased

1 1/2 cups	cake flour	375 mL
1/2 cup	unsweetened Dutch-process cocoa powder	125 mL
1/4 tsp	salt	1 mL
1 cup	unsalted butter, at room temperature	250 mL
1 cup	granulated sugar	250 mL
4	eggs	4
2 tsp	vanilla	10 mL
1/2 cup	Irish cream liqueur	125 mL
	Confectioner's (icing) sugar for dusting	

1. In a small bowl, sift together flour, cocoa powder and salt.

2. In a large bowl, using electric mixer, beat together butter and sugar until light and fluffy. Add eggs, one at a time, beating well after each addition. Add vanilla, mixing well. Stir in dry ingredients alternately with liqueur, making three additions of dry and two of liqueur, just until combined.

3. Spread batter in prepared pan, smoothing top. Bake in preheated oven for 50 to 60 minutes or until a tester inserted into center comes out clean. Let cake cool in pan on a rack for 15 minutes. Transfer cake to rack and let cool completely before slicing.

4. Dust cake with confectioner's (icing) sugar before serving.

Variations

You could very successfully substitute rum or another liqueur for the Irish cream. You could also stir 1/2 cup (125 mL) chocolate chips into the batter before baking or drizzle the cooled cake with a chocolate glaze.

24 Carrot Cake

SERVES 16

Your jeweler couldn't recreate this if he tried! It's one of a kind. One bite of this chocolate carrot cake and you will see what I mean. As much as you may be tempted to skip the frosting, don't. The cream cheese icing completes the entire carrot cake experience — it's truly the icing on the cake! Enjoy.

TIPS

To soften cream cheese, let stand at room temperature for 20 minutes or remove from wrapper and microwave on High for 20 seconds.

This cake will keep wrapped in plastic wrap and refrigerated for up to 2 days.

Preheat oven to 350°F (180°C)
13- by 9-inch (3 L) metal baking pan, greased

Cake

2¼ cups	all-purpose flour	550 mL
1 cup	sweetened flaked coconut	250 mL
¾ cup	unsweetened Dutch-process cocoa powder, sifted	175 mL
1½ tsp	baking soda	7 mL
1 tsp	baking powder	5 mL
1 tsp	ground cinnamon	5 mL
½ tsp	salt	2 mL
2 cups	granulated sugar	500 mL
1½ cups	vegetable oil	375 mL
3	eggs	3
1 tsp	vanilla	5 mL
1 cup	crushed pineapple, undrained	250 mL
2 cups	grated carrots (about 3 large carrots)	500 mL
½ cup	semisweet chocolate chips	125 mL

Cream Cheese Icing

1	package (8 oz/250 g) cream cheese, softened (see Tips, left)	1
½ cup	unsalted butter, at room temperature	125 mL
2½ cups	confectioner's (icing) sugar	625 mL
½ tsp	vanilla	2 mL

1. *Cake:* In a medium bowl, mix together flour, coconut, cocoa powder, baking soda, baking powder, cinnamon and salt.

2. In a large bowl, beat together sugar, oil, eggs and vanilla. Beat in pineapple with juice and carrots. Add flour mixture, beating just until smooth. Stir in chocolate chips.

I like to ice the cake right
in the pan after it's cooled
and serve it that way. But
you can also turn it out
onto a serving plate and
ice it once it's cool.

3. Spread batter in prepared pan, smoothing top. Bake in preheated oven for 50 to 60 minutes or until a tester inserted into center comes out clean. Let cool in pan or transfer to a rack to let cool completely (see Tip, at left).

4. *Cream Cheese Icing:* While cake is cooling, in a bowl and using electric mixer, beat together cream cheese and butter until smooth and fluffy. Add confectioner's sugar and vanilla, beating until smooth. Spread over cool cake and refrigerate until ready to serve.

Variation
Decorate the cream cheese icing with shaved chocolate (use a vegetable peeler and a chunk of semisweet chocolate).

Chocolate Potato Cake

This is a surprisingly simple cake, with a light chocolate spice flavor. No one will guess the secret ingredient! It's divine with a drizzle of dark chocolate sauce or raspberry sauce or served à la mode. You be the judge. This recipe is courtesy of Susan Morelli.

TIPS

Using a paper doily as a template on top of the cake, dust with confectioner's sugar for a decorative look. Serve with a drizzle of dark chocolate or fudge sauce for an extra special treat.

I don't use leftover potatoes because they are usually seasoned and they become hardened in the refrigerator. I like to cook up a potato in a small saucepan just before beginning the recipe.

Preheat oven to 350°F (180°C)
9-inch (23 cm) round cake pan, bottom lined with parchment paper, greased

1 cup	all-purpose flour	250 mL
1/3 cup	unsweetened Dutch-process cocoa powder, sifted	75 mL
1/2 tsp	baking powder	2 mL
1/2 tsp	ground cinnamon	2 mL
1/4 tsp	baking soda	1 mL
1/4 tsp	salt	1 mL
Pinch	ground nutmeg	Pinch
1 cup	granulated sugar	250 mL
1/2 cup	vegetable oil	125 mL
2	eggs	2
1/2 cup	mashed potatoes, at room temperature (about 1 small potato) (see Tips, left)	125 mL
1/2 cup	buttermilk	125 mL
	Confectioner's (icing) sugar for dusting	

1. In a small bowl, stir together flour, cocoa powder, baking powder, cinnamon, baking soda, salt and nutmeg.

2. In a large bowl, whisk together sugar, oil and eggs. Whisk in potato. Using a spoon or rubber spatula, stir in dry ingredients alternately with buttermilk, making three additions of dry and two of buttermilk, just until combined.

3. Spread batter in prepared pan, smoothing top. Bake in preheated oven for 30 to 35 minutes or until top springs back when touched lightly. Let cool in pan on a rack for 10 minutes. Invert cake onto a rack, remove parchment paper and let cool completely. Transfer to a serving platter and dust with confectioner's sugar.

Double Chocolate Zucchini Cake

MAKES 2 CAKES

This cake has been a favorite over the years. Unless you mention it, no one would guess that there is zucchini in it. The shredded zucchini provides incredible moisture, while the cocoa and chocolate chips provide the fudge flavor.

TIP

This cake freezes very well for up to 2 months, so if you find yourself with a bumper crop of zucchini, be sure to make this cake.

Preheat oven to 350°F (180°C)

Two 9- by 5-inch (2 L) metal loaf pans, lined with parchment paper, greased

2 cups	all-purpose flour	500 mL
1/2 cup	unsweetened Dutch-process cocoa powder, sifted	125 mL
1 tsp	baking soda	5 mL
1 tsp	baking powder	5 mL
1 tsp	ground cinnamon	5 mL
1/2 tsp	ground nutmeg	2 mL
1/2 tsp	ground allspice	2 mL
1/4 tsp	salt	1 mL
1 cup	vegetable oil	250 mL
2 cups	granulated sugar	500 mL
4	eggs	4
1 tsp	vanilla	5 mL
3 cups	lightly packed shredded zucchini (about 3 zucchini)	750 mL
1 cup	semisweet chocolate chips	250 mL

1. In a medium bowl, combine flour, cocoa powder, baking soda, baking powder, cinnamon, nutmeg, allspice and salt.

2. In a large bowl, using electric mixer, beat oil and sugar. Add eggs, one at a time, beating well after each addition. Beat in vanilla. Add flour mixture, beating just until smooth. Stir in zucchini and chocolate chips.

3. Spread batter in prepared pans. Bake in preheated oven for 1 hour or until a tester inserted into center comes out clean. Let cakes cool in pans on racks for 15 minutes. Invert cakes to remove from pans and peel off parchment paper. Return cakes to racks to cool completely.

Chocolate Cherry Bundt Cake

SERVES 16

Here's a great cake that marries my favorite combo of chocolate and cherries. When you're called upon to bring dessert to a gathering, this is a real crowd pleaser. It looks beautiful (as do most Bundt cakes), freezes well and is very delicious.

TIP

This cake freezes very well. To prepare a cake for the freezer, wrap it well in two layers of plastic wrap. Then cover with one layer of foil. This will keep the cake from getting freezer burn for up to 1 month. I also like to set the cake on a 10-inch (25 cm) round piece of cardboard for stability in the freezer. You can buy precut 10-inch (25 cm) cardboard cake circles at restaurant supply or cake decorating stores (or sometimes even craft stores).

Preheat oven to 350°F (180°C)
10-inch (3 L) Bundt pan, greased

½ cup	unsalted butter	125 mL
8 oz	unsweetened chocolate, chopped	250 g
2 cups	all-purpose flour	500 mL
2 tsp	baking soda	10 mL
½ tsp	salt	2 mL
2 cups	granulated sugar	500 mL
½ cup	vegetable oil	125 mL
4	eggs	4
2 tsp	vanilla	10 mL
1 tsp	almond extract	5 mL
1	can (21 oz/595 g) cherry pie filling	1
½ cup	semisweet chocolate chips	125 mL
	Confectioner's (icing) sugar for dusting	

1. In a large microwave-safe bowl, combine butter and unsweetened chocolate. Microwave, uncovered, on Medium (50%) for 1 to 2 minutes, stirring every 30 seconds, or until chocolate is shiny and almost melted. Stir until smooth.

2. In a small bowl, mix together flour, baking soda and salt. Add to chocolate mixture, stirring until smooth.

3. Beat in sugar and oil until smooth. Add eggs, one at a time, beating well after each addition. Stir in vanilla and almond extract. Add cherry pie filling, stirring well. Stir in chocolate chips.

4. Spread batter in prepared pan, smoothing top. Bake in preheated oven for 50 to 60 minutes or until a tester inserted into center comes out clean. Let cake cool in pan on a rack for 10 minutes. Invert cake onto rack and let cool completely.

5. Lightly dust with confectioner's sugar before serving.

Variations

Top this cake with Chocolate Glaze (see recipe, page 336) or Killer Mocha Frosting (see recipe, page 339) or serve with a warm chocolate sauce on the side.

You can also make this cake in two 8- or 9-inch (20 to 23 cm) round pans and layer the two together with some frosting in the middle.

Cranberry Sour Cream Bundt Cake

My daughter suggested I mention that this is a very grown-up cake. As I was developing this recipe, I decided to send the cake with her to her sixth grade class. The teachers demolished the cake in mere minutes, while the kids waited patiently for chocolate chip cookies. Go figure.

TIP

To bring cold butter to room temperature in a hurry, use a microwave oven. I usually set it on Medium (50%) for 10 to 20 seconds, making sure not to melt the butter.

Preheat oven to 325°F (160°C)
10-inch (3 L) Bundt pan, greased and floured

3 cups	all-purpose flour	750 mL
1/2 tsp	baking powder	2 mL
1/4 tsp	baking soda	1 mL
1/4 tsp	salt	1 mL
1 cup	unsalted butter, at room temperature	250 mL
2 cups	granulated sugar	500 mL
1 cup	sour cream	250 mL
6	eggs	6
2 tbsp	orange liqueur	25 mL
1 tbsp	grated orange zest	15 mL
1 tsp	vanilla	5 mL
1 1/3 cups	fresh or frozen cranberries	325 mL
3/4 cup	semisweet chocolate chips	175 mL

Icing

1 cup	confectioner's (icing) sugar, sifted	250 mL
1 1/2 tbsp	freshly squeezed orange juice (approx.)	22 mL
	Confectioner's sugar, for dusting (optional)	

1. In a medium bowl, combine flour, baking powder, baking soda and salt.

2. In a large bowl, using electric mixer, beat butter and sugar until light and fluffy. Beat in sour cream. Add eggs, one at a time, beating well after each addition. Add orange liqueur, orange zest and vanilla. Add flour mixture, beating just until smooth. Fold in cranberries and chocolate chips.

TIP
Although this cake is delicious the day it is made, the flavors and textures are even better the next day.

3. Spread batter in prepared pan. Bake in preheated oven for 75 to 80 minutes or until a tester inserted into center of cake comes out clean. Let cake cool in pan on a rack for 15 minutes. Carefully invert cake onto a large plate. Let cool completely.

4. *Icing:* Meanwhile, whisk together confectioner's sugar and orange juice until smooth, adding up to 1 tsp (5 mL) more juice if necessary for desired consistency. Set aside until cake is cool. Whisk again before drizzling or pouring over top of cake. When icing hardens, transfer cake to a serving platter. Lightly dust with confectioner's sugar, if desired.

Variation
Substitute dried cranberries for the fresh or frozen cranberries.

Rich Lemon Chocolate Chip Bundt Cake

Sometimes strange bedfellows make the best relationships. Take chocolate and lemon, for example. This is a dynamite combination, one that often catches people by surprise — and a pleasant one at that. You can make this cake ahead of time as it is good for several days.

TIPS

This cake needs to be made in a stand mixer; otherwise, the cream cheese separates from the batter during baking.

Do not freeze this cake or it will become very rubbery.

Preheat oven to 350°F (180°C)
Electric stand mixer
10-inch (3 L) Bundt pan, greased and floured

3 cups	all-purpose flour	750 mL
1/2 tsp	baking soda	2 mL
1/4 tsp	salt	1 mL
1 cup	unsalted butter, at room temperature	250 mL
2 cups	granulated sugar	500 mL
1	package (8 oz/250 g) cream cheese, softened	1
3	eggs	3
1 tsp	lemon extract	5 mL
1 tbsp	grated lemon zest	15 mL
2 tbsp	freshly squeezed lemon juice	25 mL
1 cup	buttermilk	250 mL
1 cup	semisweet chocolate chips	250 mL

Icing

1 cup	confectioner's (icing) sugar, sifted	250 mL
1 1/2 tbsp	freshly squeezed lemon juice (approx.)	22 mL

1. In a medium bowl, combine flour, baking soda and salt.

2. In a large bowl, using electric mixer, beat butter and sugar until light and fluffy. Add cream cheese, beating until smooth. Add eggs, one at a time, beating well after each addition. Add lemon extract, lemon zest and lemon juice, beating well. Mix in flour mixture alternately with buttermilk, making three additions of flour mixture and two of buttermilk, just until smooth. Stir in chocolate chips.

TIP

When measuring, always remember to spoon your dry ingredients into the cup and level the top by scraping across it with the flat side of a knife or skewer. This will give you an accurate measurement.

3. Spread batter in prepared pan, smoothing top. Bake in preheated oven for about 70 minutes or until a tester inserted into center of cake comes out clean and cake starts to pull away from sides of pan. Let cake cool in pan on a rack for 15 minutes. Carefully invert cake onto a large plate. Let cool completely.

4. *Icing:* Meanwhile, whisk together confectioner's sugar and lemon juice until smooth, adding up to 1 tsp (5 mL) more juice if necessary for desired consistency. Set aside until cake is cool. Whisk again before drizzling or pouring over top of cake. When icing hardens, transfer cake to a serving platter.

Variation

For an Orange Chocolate Chip Bundt Cake, substitute orange extract, zest and juice for the lemon extract, zest and juice. In the frosting, substitute orange juice for the lemon juice.

Coconut Chocolate Chip Bundt Cake

This name is fun to repeat over and over. It is equally fun to enjoy the combination of chocolate and coconut time and time again. To "gild the lily," I've combined them in one cake.

TIP

If you are out of buttermilk, you can make your own sour milk: Pour 1 tbsp (15 mL) lemon juice or white vinegar into a measuring cup. Add enough milk to make 1 cup (250 mL). Let stand for about 5 minutes before using.

Preheat oven to 325°F (160°C)
10-inch (3 L) Bundt pan, greased and floured

3 cups	all-purpose flour	750 mL
1/2 tsp	baking soda	2 mL
1/4 tsp	salt	1 mL
1 cup	unsalted butter, at room temperature	250 mL
2 cups	granulated sugar	500 mL
1	package (8 oz/250 g) cream cheese, softened	1
3	eggs	3
1 tsp	vanilla	5 mL
1/2 cup	unsweetened coconut milk	125 mL
3/4 cup	buttermilk	175 mL
1 cup	lightly packed sweetened flaked coconut	250 mL
3/4 cup	semisweet chocolate chips	175 mL

Icing

1 cup	confectioner's (icing) sugar, sifted	250 mL
1 1/2 tbsp	milk	22 mL
1/2 tsp	rum	2 mL
1/2 cup	sweetened flaked coconut, toasted (see Tip, opposite)	125 mL

1. In a medium bowl, combine flour, baking soda and salt.

2. In a large bowl, using electric mixer, beat butter and sugar until light and fluffy. Beat in cream cheese until smooth. Add eggs, one at a time, beating well after each addition. Add vanilla, beating well. Combine coconut milk and buttermilk. Mix in flour mixture alternately with coconut milk–buttermilk mixture, making three additions of flour mixture and two of milk mixture, just until smooth. Stir in chocolate chips.

TIP

A great way to toast coconut is in a nonstick skillet. Heat coconut in skillet over medium-high heat, stirring constantly. Cook, stirring, just until coconut starts to turn light golden brown, about 3 minutes. Be careful not to burn. Transfer to a plate and let cool.

3. Spread batter in prepared pan, smoothing top. Bake in preheated oven for 65 to 80 minutes or until a tester inserted into center of cake comes out clean and cake starts to pull away from sides of pan. Let cake cool in pan on a rack for 15 minutes. Carefully invert cake onto a large plate. Let cool completely.

4. *Icing:* Meanwhile, whisk together confectioner's sugar, milk and rum until smooth. Set aside until cake is cool. Whisk again before drizzling or spooning over top of cake. Sprinkle with toasted coconut.

Variation

Substitute dried coconut shavings for the sweetened flaked coconut.

Brown Sugar Chocolate Chunk Pound Cake

Hands down, this is one awesome cake. Everyone loves it, and I am always being asked for the recipe. It's a cross between a chocolate chip cookie and a pound cake that combines the best of both. It's delish with a cup of hot tea or coffee for dessert or for breakfast the next morning.

TIP

Make sure to line the bottom of the pan with parchment paper or the chocolate chunks will stick to the bottom of the pan.

Preheat oven to 350°F (180°C)

9-inch (2.5 L) square metal baking pan, bottom and sides greased, then bottom lined with parchment paper

2 cups	all-purpose flour	500 mL
1/4 tsp	salt	1 mL
1 3/4 cups	packed light brown sugar	425 mL
1 cup	unsalted butter, at room temperature	250 mL
5	eggs	5
2 tsp	vanilla	10 mL
12 oz	milk chocolate, coarsely chopped	375 g
1/2 cup	walnut pieces, toasted	125 mL
	Confectioner's (icing) sugar for dusting (optional)	

1. In a small bowl, mix together flour and salt.

2. In a large bowl, using electric mixer, beat together brown sugar and butter until fluffy. Add eggs, one at a time, beating well after each addition. Beat in vanilla. Add flour mixture, beating just until smooth. Stir in chocolate and walnuts.

3. Spread batter in prepared pan, smoothing top. Bake in preheated oven for 50 to 60 minutes or until a tester inserted in center comes out clean. Let cool in pan on a rack for 15 minutes. Carefully loosen edges of cake and invert onto rack. Remove parchment paper. Invert cake right side up and let cool completely on rack.

4. Dust cake with confectioner's sugar, if using, before serving.

Chocolate Chip Cream Cheese Pound Cake

This is the best pound cake you will ever taste. It is very quick to make and disappears just as quickly. Exercise patience while waiting for it to bake. It will keep, wrapped, for several days.

TIP

Because this recipe makes two cakes, go ahead and freeze one so that you have something on hand for unexpected company.

Preheat oven to 325°F (160°C)
Two 9- by 5-inch (2 L) metal loaf pans, lined with parchment paper, greased

3 cups	all-purpose flour	750 mL
1/4 tsp	salt	1 mL
1 1/2 cups	unsalted butter, at room temperature	375 mL
1	package (8 oz/250 g) cream cheese, softened	1
3 cups	granulated sugar	750 mL
6	eggs	6
1 1/2 tsp	vanilla	7 mL
1 1/2 cups	semisweet chocolate chips	375 mL

1. In a medium bowl, combine flour and salt.

2. In a large bowl, using electric mixer, beat butter, cream cheese and sugar until light and fluffy. Add eggs, one at a time, beating well after each addition. Add flour mixture and vanilla, beating just until smooth. Stir in chocolate chips.

3. Spread batter in prepared pans. Bake in preheated oven for 1 1/2 hours to 1 hour and 40 minutes or until golden and a tester inserted into center comes out clean. Let cakes cool in pans for 15 minutes. Carefully invert cakes onto racks (the cakes can break apart easily). Let cool completely on racks. Peel off parchment.

Variation
Substitute 2 tsp (10 mL) almond extract for the vanilla.

Sour Cream Coffee Cake with Chocolate Pecan Streusel

I created this decadent coffee cake for an article I wrote for *Bon Appétit* magazine. It's an old-fashioned coffee cake, updated with orange, pecans and chocolate chips. It is perfect for picnics, brunches and potlucks.

TIP

To bring cold butter to room temperature in a hurry, use a microwave oven. I usually set it on Medium (50%) for 10 to 20 seconds, making sure not to melt the butter.

Preheat oven to 350°F (180°C)

13- by 9-inch (3 L) metal baking pan, lined with parchment paper, greased

Streusel

1 1/2 cups	packed light brown sugar	375 mL
1 tbsp	ground cinnamon	15 mL
1/3 cup	unsalted butter, chilled and cut into pieces	75 mL
1 1/2 cups	coarsely chopped pecans	375 mL
1 cup	semisweet chocolate chips	250 mL

Cake

3 cups	all-purpose flour	750 mL
1 1/2 tsp	baking soda	7 mL
1 1/2 tsp	baking powder	7 mL
3/4 cup	butter, at room temperature	175 mL
1 1/3 cups	granulated sugar	325 mL
3	eggs	3
1 1/2 tsp	grated orange zest	7 mL
1 1/2 tsp	vanilla	7 mL
1 1/2 cups	sour cream	375 mL
1/4 cup	freshly squeezed orange juice	50 mL
	Confectioner's (icing) sugar (optional)	

1. *Streusel:* In a medium bowl, whisk together brown sugar and cinnamon. Add butter and rub in with fingertips until mixture holds together in small, moist clumps. Mix in pecans and chocolate chips. Set aside.

2. *Cake:* In a medium bowl, stir together flour, baking soda and baking powder.

Line your baking sheets
with parchment paper for
blissful baking. It will keep
your baked goods from
sticking, making cleanup
a snap.

3. In a large bowl, using electric mixer, beat butter and sugar until light and fluffy. Beat in eggs, one at a time, beating well after each addition. Beat in orange zest and vanilla. Stir in flour mixture alternately with sour cream, making three additions of flour mixture and two of sour cream. Stir in orange juice.

4. Spread half of the batter in prepared pan. Sprinkle with half of the streusel. Drop remaining batter over top by heaping tablespoons (15 mL), carefully spreading to make an even layer. Sprinkle with remaining streusel.

5. Bake in preheated oven for 30 minutes. Lay a sheet of foil loosely over pan to keep topping from browning too quickly. Bake for 35 minutes longer or until a tester inserted into center of cake comes out clean. Remove foil.

6. Let cake cool in pan on rack for 20 minutes. Invert cake to remove from pan and peel off parchment paper. Serve warm or at room temperature. Lightly dust cake with confectioner's sugar, if desired.

Variation
Substitute walnuts for the pecans.

Café Mocha Cake

· ·

SERVES 12

This cake, inspired by my brother, Jon, is one of the moistest cakes ever. It has a nice light cappuccino flavor. If you want to dress up the cake further, stir up Chocolate Glaze (see recipe, page 336) and spoon it over the top.

TIP

This cake freezes very well. To prepare a cake for the freezer, wrap it well in two layers of plastic wrap. Then cover with one layer of foil. This will keep the cake from getting freezer burn for up to 1 month. I also like to set the cake on a 10-inch (25 cm) round piece of cardboard for stability in the freezer. You can buy precut 10-inch (25 cm) cardboard cake circles at restaurant supply or cake decorating stores (or sometimes even craft stores).

Preheat oven to 350°F (180°C)
10-inch (3 L) Bundt pan, greased

3 cups	all-purpose flour	750 mL
½ tsp	baking soda	2 mL
¼ tsp	salt	1 mL
2 cups	granulated sugar	500 mL
1 cup	unsalted butter, at room temperature	250 mL
3	eggs	3
1 cup	sour cream	250 mL
2 tsp	vanilla	10 mL
1 cup	buttermilk	250 mL
3 tbsp	instant coffee granules	45 mL
6 oz	semisweet chocolate, chopped	175 g

1. In a medium bowl, mix together flour, baking soda and salt.

2. In a large bowl, using electric mixer, beat sugar and butter until light and fluffy. Add eggs, one at a time, beating well after each addition. Add sour cream and vanilla, beating well.

3. In a microwave-safe bowl, mix together buttermilk and instant coffee. Microwave on High for 20 seconds, stirring well to dissolve coffee.

4. Add dry ingredients to butter mixture alternately with buttermilk mixture, making three additions of dry and two of buttermilk, stirring just until smooth. Stir in chocolate.

5. Spread batter in prepared pan, smoothing top. Bake in preheated oven for 60 to 70 minutes or until a tester inserted into center comes out clean and cake starts to pull away from sides of pan. Let cake cool in pan on a rack for 15 minutes. Carefully invert cake onto rack and let cool completely.

Mocha Chocolate Chip Cake

SERVES 10

For years, people have begged me to share this loaf cake recipe. This has been a closely guarded secret — until now. It is pure nirvana for coffee lovers.

TIP

A great ratio for strong brewed coffee is 2 tbsp (25 mL) finely ground French-roast coffee or espresso for every $3/4$ cup (175 mL) water.

Preheat oven to 350°F (180°C)
9- by 5-inch (2 L) metal loaf pan, lined with parchment paper, greased

$1/2$ cup	hot strong brewed coffee (see Tip, at left)	125 mL
$1/4$ cup	finely ground espresso or French-roast coffee	50 mL
2 tbsp	instant coffee granules	25 mL
2 cups	all-purpose flour	500 mL
2 tsp	baking powder	10 mL
2 tsp	ground cinnamon	10 mL
$1/4$ tsp	salt	1 mL
1 cup	vegetable oil	250 mL
$1^3/4$ cups	granulated sugar	425 mL
3	eggs	3
2 tsp	vanilla	10 mL
$1/2$ cup	semisweet chocolate chips	125 mL

1. In a small bowl, combine brewed coffee and finely ground and instant coffee, stirring well. Set aside to cool.

2. In a medium bowl, combine flour, baking powder, cinnamon and salt.

3. In a large bowl, using electric mixer, beat oil, sugar and eggs until smooth. Add cooled coffee mixture and vanilla, beating well. Add flour mixture and beat on medium–high speed for 10 seconds, just until blended.

4. Pour batter into prepared pan. Sprinkle chocolate chips over top, lightly pressing some of the chips into batter. Bake in preheated oven for 65 to 70 minutes or until a tester inserted into center of cake comes out clean.

5. Let cake cool in pan on rack for 15 minutes. Invert cake to remove from pan and peel off parchment paper. Return cake to rack to cool completely.

Chocolate Espresso Cake

SERVES 12

You can have your cake and coffee and eat them, too — in one bite! This cake is a favorite with my friends, family and anyone else who eats a piece.

TIP

A great ratio for strong brewed coffee is 2 tbsp (25 mL) finely ground French-roast coffee or espresso for every ¾ cup (175 mL) water.

Preheat oven to 350°F (180°C)

10-inch (4 L) tube pan, bottom lined with parchment paper, sides greased

Cake

2 cups	all-purpose flour	500 mL
1 cup	unsweetened Dutch-process cocoa powder, sifted	250 mL
1 tbsp	finely ground espresso or French-roast coffee	15 mL
1½ tsp	baking soda	7 mL
1 tsp	ground cinnamon	5 mL
½ tsp	salt	2 mL
¼ tsp	baking powder	1 mL
2⅓ cups	granulated sugar	575 mL
¾ cup	vegetable oil	175 mL
3	eggs	3
2 tsp	vanilla	5 mL
¼ cup	milk	50 mL
2 tbsp	instant coffee granules	25 mL
1 cup	strong brewed coffee, cooled to room temperature (see Tip, at left)	250 mL
6 oz	milk chocolate, finely chopped	175 g

Chocolate Glaze

5 oz	semisweet chocolate, chopped	150 g
½ cup	whipping (35%) cream	125 mL

1. In a medium bowl, combine flour, cocoa powder, ground coffee, baking soda, cinnamon, salt and baking powder, mixing well.

2. In a large bowl, using electric mixer, beat together sugar and oil. Add eggs, one at a time, beating well after each addition. Add vanilla, beating well.

3. In a microwave-safe bowl, mix together milk and instant coffee. Microwave, uncovered, on High for 20 seconds, until just slightly warm. Mix until coffee is dissolved. Add to egg mixture, mixing well.

4. Stir in dry ingredients alternately with brewed coffee, making three additions of dry and two of coffee, mixing just until smooth.

5. Spread batter in prepared pan, smoothing top. Sprinkle chopped chocolate over batter. Lightly press chocolate into batter, but not too much or else it will all sink to bottom of pan. Bake in preheated oven for 50 to 60 minutes or until a tester inserted in center comes out clean and cake starts to pull away from sides of pan. Let cake cool in pan on a rack for 15 minutes.

6. *Chocolate Glaze:* In a microwave-safe bowl, combine chocolate and cream. Microwave, uncovered, on Medium (50%) for 1 minute, stirring every 30 seconds, or until cream is hot and chocolate is starting to melt. Stir well until chocolate is melted and mixture is thick and smooth. If chocolate is not completely melted, return to microwave for another 10 to 20 seconds or until chocolate is soft and melted. Stir well. If glaze is very thin, let stand for a few minutes to thicken slightly.

7. Carefully invert cake onto a large plate and remove parchment paper. When cake is cool, pour glaze over top. Refrigerate until glaze is firm.

Variations

This cake can be baked in a Bundt pan, but omit the chopped chocolate. (The chocolate will sink to the bottom and make pan removal almost impossible.) If baking it into a Bundt cake, serve it with a dark chocolate sauce to make up for the missing chopped chocolate in the cake.

This cake looks great garnished with a sprinkle of chocolate-covered espresso beans or grated or finely chopped chocolate.

Chocolate Chip Calypso Cake

SERVES 12

Chocolate and ginger are a magical combination, transforming an otherwise plain cake into something extraordinary. This cake is divine with a cup of hot tea, preferably Earl Grey.

TIP

When measuring, always remember to spoon your dry ingredients into the cup and level the top by scraping across it with the flat side of a knife or skewer. This will give you an accurate measurement.

Preheat oven to 350°F (180°C)

13- by 9-inch (3 L) metal baking pan, lined with parchment paper, greased

2¹/₂ cups	all-purpose flour	625 mL
1 tbsp	ground ginger	15 mL
2 tsp	baking soda	10 mL
1 tsp	ground cinnamon	5 mL
¹/₂ tsp	baking powder	2 mL
¹/₂ tsp	ground allspice	2 mL
¹/₄ tsp	ground nutmeg	1 mL
¹/₄ tsp	salt	1 mL
³/₄ cup	unsalted butter, melted and cooled	175 mL
³/₄ cup	granulated sugar	175 mL
³/₄ cup	light fancy molasses	175 mL
2	eggs	2
1 cup	hot brewed tea, preferably Earl Grey (see Tip, opposite)	250 mL
¹/₃ cup	chopped crystallized ginger	75 mL
³/₄ cup	semisweet chocolate chips	175 mL
	Confectioner's (icing) sugar (optional)	

1. In a medium bowl, combine flour, ground ginger, baking soda, cinnamon, baking powder, allspice, nutmeg and salt.

2. In a large bowl, using electric mixer, beat butter and sugar until light and fluffy. Beat in molasses. Add eggs, one at a time, beating well after each addition. Stir in flour mixture alternately with hot tea, making three additions of flour mixture and two of tea, beating just until smooth. Stir in crystallized ginger.

TIP

To make hot brewed Earl Grey tea, combine 1¼ cups (300 mL) boiling water with 2 Earl Grey tea bags in a glass measuring cup. Let stand for 5 minutes before using.

3. Spread batter in prepared pan. Sprinkle top evenly with chocolate chips. Bake in preheated oven for 30 minutes or until a tester inserted into center comes out clean. Let cake cool completely in pan on rack.

4. Carefully invert cake onto a large plate and remove parchment paper. Serve lightly dusted with confectioner's sugar, if desired.

Variation
Substitute boiling water for the tea.

Chocolate Chip Chai Cake

This is a delightful cake filled with the creamy, slightly spicy flavors of chai tea. It's great on its own, but I also thought a caramel frosting would be good, so I developed a brown sugar icing inspired by a recipe by Lee Bailey.

TIPS

To substitute loose chai tea, grind it in a coffee or spice grinder until you have little bits (it doesn't have to be finely powdered). For 2 tea bags, substitute 2 tsp (10 mL) ground loose tea.

If you are out of buttermilk, you can make your own sour milk: Pour 1 tbsp (15 mL) lemon juice or white vinegar into a measuring cup. Add enough milk to make 1 cup (250 mL). Let stand for about 5 minutes before using.

Preheat oven to 350°F (180°C)
13-by 9-inch (3 L) metal baking pan, greased

2 cups	all-purpose flour	500 mL
1 tsp	baking powder	5 mL
1/2 tsp	baking soda	2 mL
1/2 tsp	ground cardamom	2 mL
1/4 tsp	ground allspice	1 mL
1/4 tsp	salt	1 mL
2	chai spice tea bags (see Tip, at left)	2
1/2 cup	unsalted butter, at room temperature	125 mL
1 3/4 cups	granulated sugar	425 mL
4	egg whites	4
1 tsp	vanilla	5 mL
1 1/3 cups	buttermilk	325 mL
3/4 cup	semisweet chocolate chips	175 mL

Icing (optional)

1 cup	packed light or medium brown sugar	250 mL
1/2 cup	whipping (35%) cream	125 mL
1/4 cup	butter	50 mL
2 cups	confectioner's (icing) sugar, sifted	500 mL
1 tsp	vanilla	5 mL

1. In a medium bowl, combine flour, baking powder, baking soda, cardamom, allspice, salt and contents of tea bags.

2. In a large bowl, using electric mixer, beat butter and sugar until light and fluffy. Add egg whites, one at a time, beating well after each addition. Stir in vanilla.

TIP

Leftover cake freezes very well for about 1 month (that is, if you happen to have any left).

3. Beat flour mixture into butter mixture alternately with buttermilk, making three additions of flour mixture and two of buttermilk. Beat just until smooth. Stir in chocolate chips.

4. Spread batter in prepared pan. Bake in preheated oven for 35 to 40 minutes or until cake is golden brown and pulling away from sides of pan and a tester inserted into center comes out clean. Let cake cool in pan on a rack while preparing icing.

5. *Icing:* In a large saucepan over medium heat, bring brown sugar, cream and butter to a rolling boil. Remove pan from heat and transfer mixture to a mixing bowl. Whisk in confectioner's sugar and vanilla until blended. Using an electric mixer, beat icing until thick and just warm to the touch. Spread over cake. Let cool completely.

Eggnog Chocolate Chip Tea Cake

This cake has all of the flavors of Christmas. You can usually find eggnog in the grocery store from October through January.

TIP

To bring cold butter to room temperature in a hurry, use a microwave oven. I usually set it on Medium (50%) for 10 to 20 seconds, making sure not to melt the butter.

Preheat oven to 350°F (180°C)

9- by 5-inch (2 L) metal loaf pan, lined with parchment paper, greased

3 cups	all-purpose flour	750 mL
1 tbsp	baking powder	15 mL
1 1/2 tsp	ground nutmeg	7 mL
1/2 cup	unsalted butter, at room temperature	125 mL
3/4 cup	granulated sugar	175 mL
2	eggs	2
1 3/4 cups	eggnog	425 mL
1/4 cup	dark rum	50 mL
1/2 cup	semisweet chocolate chips	125 mL

1. In a medium bowl, combine flour, baking powder and nutmeg.

2. In a large bowl, using electric mixer, beat butter and sugar until light and fluffy. Add eggs, one at a time, beating well after each addition. Add eggnog and rum, beating well. Add flour mixture, beating just until combined. Fold in chocolate chips.

3. Spread batter in prepared pan. Bake in preheated oven for 70 minutes or until cake is golden and a tester inserted into center comes out clean.

4. Let cake cool in pan on rack for 15 minutes. Invert cake to remove from pan and peel off parchment paper. Return cake to rack to cool completely.

Variation

You can garnish this cake with a light dusting of confectioner's sugar or you can drizzle it with an eggnog glaze. To make a glaze, simply whisk together 2 cups (500 mL) confectioner's (icing) sugar, sifted, 3 tbsp (45 mL) eggnog and 1 tsp (5 mL) rum. Drizzle over cake.

Chocolate Espresso Lava Cakes

I developed this recipe for *Bon Appétit* magazine. It was such a huge hit that it was prepared on the *Today Show*. These cakes are really chocolate brownie soufflés that are baked in coffee mugs. They are truly delicious, embodying everything that a chocolate dessert should be. You can make them ahead of time, then pop them in the oven as your guests sit down for the main course.

TIP

All of the recipes in this book were tested using large eggs. Using medium or extra-large eggs may adversely affect the outcome of the recipe.

Six 1-cup (250 mL) ovenproof ceramic coffee mugs, greased

1 cup	all-purpose flour	250 mL
³/₄ cup	unsweetened Dutch-process cocoa powder	175 mL
5 tsp	instant espresso powder	25 mL
1¹/₂ tsp	baking powder	7 mL
1 cup	butter, melted	250 mL
1 cup	granulated sugar	250 mL
1 cup	packed light brown sugar	250 mL
4	eggs	4
1¹/₂ tsp	vanilla	7 mL
¹/₄ tsp	almond extract	1 mL
³/₄ cup	semisweet chocolate chips	175 mL

Topping

1 cup	whipping (35%) cream, chilled	250 mL
3 tbsp	confectioner's (icing) sugar	45 mL
1 tsp	instant espresso powder	5 mL

1. In a medium bowl, sift together flour, cocoa powder, espresso powder and baking powder.

2. In a large bowl, whisk together melted butter and granulated and brown sugars until well blended. Whisk in eggs, one at a time, then vanilla and almond extract. Whisk in flour mixture. Divide batter among prepared coffee mugs (about ²/₃ cup/150 mL in each). Top each with 2 tbsp (25 mL) of the chocolate chips. Gently press chips into batter. Cover and refrigerate mugs for at least 1 hour or for up to 1 day.

3. *Topping:* In a medium bowl, combine cream, confectioner's sugar and espresso powder. Whisk until stiff peaks form. Chill for 1 hour.

4. Preheat oven to 350°F (180°C). Let mugs with batter stand at room temperature for 5 minutes. Bake, uncovered, until cakes are puffed and crusty and tester inserted into center comes out with thick batter attached, about 30 minutes. Let cool in mugs on a rack for 5 minutes. Top hot cakes with espresso whipped cream and serve.

Chocolate Brownie Baby Cakes

MAKES
24 MINI CAKES

You can never own too many pans, although my husband seems to disagree. If you don't have a mini Bundt pan (with 12 molds per pan), substitute a mini muffin pan (with 24 molds per pan). The baking time will be shorter with the muffin pan though, so alter the baking time accordingly.

TIP

This recipe for homemade nonstick coating is a keeper! In fact, I now grease all of my baking pans with this mixture. In a mixer, blender or food processor, blend together 1/2 cup (125 mL) vegetable oil, 1/2 cup (125 mL) solid white vegetable shortening and 1/2 cup (125 mL) all-purpose flour until smooth. Store mixture in a glass jar in the refrigerator. Bring to room temperature or warm slightly in the microwave before using. Simply "paint" the mixture in the pan with a pastry brush and chill the pan for 5 minutes in the freezer before using. If I'm greasing a regular baking pan without lots of nooks and crannies, I don't bother chilling the pan in the freezer.

Preheat oven to 350°F (180°C)
2 mini Bundt pans (with 12 molds per pan), greased

1 cup	butter	250 mL
4 oz	unsweetened chocolate, chopped	125 g
2 cups	packed light brown sugar	500 mL
4	eggs	4
2 tsp	vanilla	10 mL
1/2 tsp	almond extract	2 mL
1 cup	all-purpose flour	250 mL
1 tsp	ground cinnamon	5 mL

1. In a microwave-safe bowl, combine butter and chocolate. Microwave, uncovered, on Medium (50%) for 1 to 1 1/2 minutes, stirring every 30 seconds, or until chocolate is soft and almost melted. Stir until completely smooth. Set aside and let cool slightly.

2. In a large bowl, whisk together brown sugar, eggs, vanilla and almond extract, beating until well mixed and slightly frothy. Stir in melted chocolate mixture. Add flour and cinnamon, mixing just until combined.

3. Scoop batter into prepared pans. Bake in preheated oven for 23 minutes or just until springy or spongy to the touch. Your finger will leave a slight indentation in the top when touched. Let cool in pans on a rack for 3 to 5 minutes. Transfer to racks and let cool completely.

Little Chocolate Cakes

Serve these elegant little cakes warm so that the center is soft and gooey. I like to make them for special occasions, dressed up with a little raspberry sauce or a scoop of raspberry sorbet.

TIP

These cakes lend themselves nicely to several different garnishes. You can lightly dust with confectioner's (icing) sugar or serve with a scoop of vanilla ice cream.

Preheat oven to 350°F (180°C)
Six $^3/_4$ cup (175 mL) ramekins, greased
Baking sheet

$^3/_4$ cup	semisweet chocolate chips	175 mL
2 oz	unsweetened chocolate, chopped	60 g
$^2/_3$ cup	unsalted butter, at room temperature	150 mL
1 tsp	brandy	5 mL
$^1/_8$ tsp	salt	0.5 mL
2	eggs	2
4	egg yolks	4
$^1/_2$ cup	granulated sugar	125 mL
2 tbsp	all-purpose flour	25 mL
1 tbsp	unsweetened Dutch-process cocoa powder	15 mL

1. In a medium microwave–safe bowl, combine chocolate chips, unsweetened chocolate and butter. Microwave on High for 2 minutes, stirring every 30 seconds, until chocolate is shiny and almost melted. Stir until smooth. Whisk in brandy and salt. Set aside to cool slightly.

2. In a large bowl, using electric mixer, beat eggs and egg yolks with sugar for 2 to 3 minutes or until thickened, pale and the consistency of soft whipped cream. Fold in half of the chocolate mixture until blended. Fold in remaining chocolate mixture.

3. In a small bowl, combine flour and cocoa powder. Sift over top of batter and gently fold in until incorporated.

4. Divide batter among prepared ramekins and place on baking sheet. Bake in preheated oven for 15 minutes or until tops of cakes are puffed and just starting to crack. Remove from pan and let cool on rack for 3 minutes. Gently run a sharp paring knife around edge of cakes and invert onto serving plates. Serve immediately.

Variation
Lightly sprinkle cakes with ground cinnamon before serving.

Chocolate Cherry Rum Cakes

I have always loved chocolate and cherries together, but then again, who doesn't? One day a thought occurred to me: What would happen if I added these two ingredients to a rum cake batter? The answer lies in this fantastic cake.

TIP

To bring cold butter to room temperature in a hurry, use a microwave oven. I usually set it on Medium (50%) for 10 to 20 seconds, making sure not to melt the butter.

Preheat oven to 375°F (190°C)
Four 6- by 3-inch (375 mL) loaf pans, lined with parchment paper, greased

2¹/₂ cups	all-purpose flour	625 mL
2¹/₂ tsp	baking powder	12 mL
¹/₄ tsp	salt	1 mL
²/₃ cup	unsalted butter, at room temperature	150 mL
1³/₄ cups	granulated sugar	425 mL
2	eggs	2
1 tsp	vanilla	5 mL
³/₄ cup	milk	175 mL
¹/₂ cup	light rum	125 mL
²/₃ cup	semisweet chocolate chips	150 mL
²/₃ cup	dried sour cherries	150 mL

Glaze

³/₄ cup	granulated sugar	175 mL
¹/₂ cup	unsalted butter	125 mL
¹/₄ cup	light rum	50 mL
¹/₄ cup	water	50 mL

1. In a medium bowl, combine flour, baking powder and salt.

2. In a large bowl, using electric mixer, beat butter and sugar. Add eggs, one at a time, beating well after each addition. Beat in vanilla. Add flour mixture to butter mixture alternately with milk, making three additions of flour mixture and two of milk. Add rum, beating just until smooth. Stir in chocolate chips and cherries.

TIP

When measuring, always remember to spoon your dry ingredients into the cup and level the top by scraping across it with the flat side of a knife or skewer. This will give you an accurate measurement.

3. Divide batter among prepared pans. Bake in preheated oven for 36 to 38 minutes or until a tester inserted into center of cakes comes out clean. Remove cakes from oven and, using a skewer or toothpick, poke holes randomly over tops.

4. *Glaze:* Meanwhile, in a medium saucepan over medium heat, combine sugar, butter, rum and water. Let simmer for 3 to 4 minutes, until sugar is dissolved. Remove from heat. Spoon glaze over tops of hot cakes. Use most of glaze, even if it takes several applications.

5. Let cakes cool in pans on racks for 30 minutes. Remove cakes from pans, invert onto racks and remove parchment paper. Drizzle with remaining glaze. Let cool completely on racks.

Variation
Substitute dried cranberries for the cherries.

Cupcakes

Chocolate Mousse–Filled Cupcakes *132*

Coconut Cupcakes *134*

Chocolate Cupcakes with Mocha Frosting *136*

Chocolate Peanut Butter Cupcakes *137*

Chocolate Surprise Cupcakes *138*

Chocolate Cinnamon Cupcakes *139*

White Chocolate Macadamia Cupcakes *140*

Chocolate Chili Cupcakes *142*

Chocolate Mint Cupcakes *144*

Espresso Dark Brownie Cupcakes *145*

Chocolate Cheesecake Cupcakes *146*

Chocolate Mousse-Filled Cupcakes

These cupcakes are a grown-up version of the store-bought treats beloved by children. Devil's food cupcakes are filled with a luscious chocolate mousse center and topped with a coating of chocolate ganache.

TIP

A great ratio for strong brewed coffee is 2 tbsp (25 mL) finely ground French-roast coffee or espresso for every ¾ cup (175 mL) water.

Preheat oven to 350°F (180°C)
Two 12-cup muffin pans, greased or lined with paper liners
Baking sheet

1½ cups	all-purpose flour	375 mL
¾ cup	unsweetened Dutch-process cocoa powder	175 mL
1 tsp	baking soda	5 mL
1 tsp	baking powder	5 mL
¼ tsp	salt	1 mL
2	eggs	2
1¾ cups	granulated sugar	425 mL
½ cup	vegetable oil	125 mL
1 tsp	vanilla	5 mL
1¼ cups	strong brewed coffee, cooled to room temperature (see Tip, at left)	300 mL

Filling

⅓ cup	semisweet chocolate chips	75 mL
1 tbsp	strong brewed coffee	15 mL
¾ cup	whipping (35%) cream	175 mL
1 tbsp	confectioner's (icing) sugar	15 mL

Glaze

⅔ cup	whipping (35%) cream	150 mL
1 cup	semisweet chocolate chips	250 mL

1. In a medium bowl, sift together flour, cocoa powder, baking soda, baking powder and salt.

2. In a large bowl, using electric mixer, beat eggs, sugar, oil and vanilla until creamy. Add flour mixture, beating just until combined. Beat in coffee until smooth. Do not overbeat.

3. Fill 18 prepared muffin cups with batter. Bake in preheated oven for 22 to 24 minutes, until cupcakes are just firm to the touch and a tester inserted into center of cupcake comes out clean. Let cool in pans on racks for 10 minutes. Remove from pans and let cool completely on racks. If baked with paper liners, remove liners.

4. *Filling:* In a microwave-safe dish, combine chocolate chips and coffee. Microwave on High for $2\frac{1}{2}$ minutes, stirring every 30 seconds, until chocolate is shiny and almost melted. Stir until smooth. Remove from microwave and stir until chocolate is melted and smooth. Let cool slightly.

5. In a large bowl, using electric mixer, whip cream and confectioner's sugar until almost stiff peaks. Add melted chocolate mixture, beating just until incorporated. Finish mixing by hand with a rubber spatula.

6. Using a sharp paring knife, gently cut a $\frac{3}{4}$-inch (2 cm) cone from the bottom of each cupcake and trim point off cone. Using a small spoon, fill each hole with chocolate cream filling and replace reserved cones. Place on prepared baking sheet and refrigerate while preparing glaze.

7. *Glaze:* In a microwave-safe bowl, microwave cream on High until it starts to simmer, about 40 seconds. Add chocolate chips and whisk until melted and shiny. Stir until smooth. Set aside to cool for 10 minutes. Dip tops of each filled cupcake in chocolate glaze. Place dipped cupcakes on prepared baking sheet and refrigerate until ready to serve.

Coconut Cupcakes

**MAKES
12 CUPCAKES**

These cupcakes have been my brother Jon's favorite for years. The scrumptious chocolate chip cake, creamy icing and toasted coconut make them a winner.

TIP

A great way to toast coconut is in a nonstick skillet. Heat coconut in skillet over medium-high heat, stirring constantly. Cook, stirring, just until coconut starts to turn light golden brown, about 3 minutes. Be careful not to burn. Transfer to a plate and let cool.

Preheat oven to 350°F (180°C)
12-cup muffin pan, lined with paper liners

1 cup	all-purpose flour	250 mL
1/2 tsp	baking powder	2 mL
1/4 tsp	baking soda	1 mL
1/8 tsp	salt	0.5 mL
1/4 cup	unsalted butter, at room temperature	50 mL
3/4 cup	granulated sugar	175 mL
1/2 tsp	vanilla	2 mL
2	egg whites	2
2/3 cup	buttermilk	150 mL
1/2 cup	semisweet chocolate chips	125 mL

Icing

6 oz	cream cheese, softened	175 g
1/2 cup	unsalted butter	125 mL
1 tsp	vanilla	5 mL
1/4 tsp	almond extract	1 mL
2 3/4 cups	confectioner's (icing) sugar, sifted	675 mL
1/2 cup	whipping (35%) cream	125 mL
3/4 cup	sweetened flaked coconut, lightly toasted (see Tip, at left)	175 mL

1. In a small bowl, combine flour, baking powder, baking soda and salt.

2. In a large bowl, using electric mixer, beat butter and sugar until light and fluffy. Beat in vanilla. Add egg whites, one at a time, beating well after each addition. Alternately beat in flour mixture and buttermilk on low speed, making three additions of flour mixture and two of buttermilk, just until combined. Stir in chocolate chips.

These cupcakes are best eaten fresh the day they are made.

3. Divide batter among prepared muffin cups, filling each halfway. Bake in preheated oven for about 25 minutes or until a tester inserted into center comes out clean. Let cool in pan on a rack for 5 minutes. Remove from pan and let cool completely on rack.

4. *Icing:* Meanwhile, beat cream cheese, butter, vanilla and almond extract until fluffy. Gradually beat in confectioner's sugar until light and fluffy. Add cream, beating until incorporated. With mixer on high speed, beat icing until it is whipped, fluffy and forms soft peaks.

5. Spread icing on cooled cupcakes. Generously sprinkle toasted coconut over icing.

Chocolate Cupcakes
with Mocha Frosting

When you have children, cupcakes become a staple in the house. But cupcakes aren't just for kids. They've become so popular these days that they are even being served at weddings in lieu of big cakes. Here's a cupcake that adults will love.

TIPS

A great ratio for strong brewed coffee is 2 tbsp (25 mL) finely ground French-roast coffee or espresso for every ¾ cup (175 mL) water.

This recipe can be doubled. The cupcakes will keep, covered, for 2 days either in the refrigerator or at room temperature.

Preheat oven to 350°F (180°C)
12-cup muffin pan, lined with paper liners

1¼ cups	all-purpose flour	300 mL
½ cup	unsweetened Dutch-process cocoa powder, sifted	125 mL
1 tsp	baking soda	5 mL
1 cup	granulated sugar	250 mL
1 cup	strong brewed coffee, cooled to room temperature (see Tip, at left)	250 mL
¼ cup	vegetable oil	50 mL
1 tsp	vanilla	5 mL
1 tbsp	balsamic vinegar	15 mL
⅓ cup	semisweet chocolate chips	75 mL
½	batch Killer Mocha Frosting (see recipe, page 339)	½
⅓ cup	mini semisweet chocolate chips	75 mL

1. In a small bowl, mix together flour, cocoa powder and baking soda.

2. In a large bowl, mix together sugar, coffee, oil and vanilla. Add dry ingredients, mixing just until smooth. Stir in balsamic vinegar.

3. Scoop batter into prepared muffin cups. Sprinkle regular chocolate chips over top (they will sink slightly).

4. Bake in preheated oven for 18 to 20 minutes or until a tester inserted into center comes out clean. Let cool in pan on a rack for 10 minutes. Transfer to rack and let cool completely.

5. Frost cupcakes with Killer Mocha Frosting. Sprinkle tops with mini chocolate chips.

Chocolate Peanut Butter Cupcakes

MAKES
12 CUPCAKES

Chocolate and peanut butter are blended together in this recipe to create a fabulously delicious, habit-forming cupcake. I bet you can't eat just one!

TIP

Regular peanut butter, rather than natural-style peanut butter, works best in this recipe.

Frosting suggestions:
Peanut Butter Fudge Frosting (see recipe, page 338) or Chocolate Fudge Frosting (see recipe, page 337).

Preheat oven to 350°F (180°C)
12-cup muffin pan, lined with paper liners

³⁄₄ cup	all-purpose flour	175 mL
¼ cup	unsweetened Dutch-process cocoa powder, sifted	50 mL
1½ tsp	baking powder	7 mL
Pinch	salt	Pinch
½ cup	granulated sugar	125 mL
½ cup	packed light or medium brown sugar	125 mL
¼ cup	unsalted butter, at room temperature	50 mL
½ cup	crunchy peanut butter	125 mL
1	egg	1
½ tsp	vanilla	2 mL
⅔ cup	milk	150 mL
½ cup	semisweet chocolate chips	125 mL
	Frosting (see Frosting suggestions, left)	

1. In a small bowl, mix together flour, cocoa powder, baking powder and salt.

2. In a large bowl, using electric mixer, beat together granulated and brown sugars and butter until well combined. Add peanut butter, beating until smooth. Beat in egg and vanilla until mixture is smooth. Alternately beat in flour mixture and milk, making three additions of flour mixture and two of milk, beating until smooth. Stir in chocolate chips.

3. Scoop batter into prepared muffin cups. Bake in preheated oven for 20 to 25 minutes or until tops of cupcakes spring back when lightly touched. Let cool in pan on rack for 10 minutes. Remove from pan and let cool completely on rack. Top cooled cupcakes with frosting.

Variation

Omit the chocolate chips.

Chocolate Surprise Cupcakes

My mom called me the other day to tell me about a recipe she saw in *Donna Hay Magazine* for a great-looking cupcake with marshmallow filling. I didn't have a copy of the magazine, so I was inspired to come up with my own concoction. This cupcake has been voted a "10" by friends and family. Thanks, Mom and Donna!

TIP

For vegetarians, you can now find vegetarian marshmallows in some specialty health food stores.

Frosting suggestions:

Chocolate Fudge Frosting (see recipe, page 337) or Chocolate Glaze (see recipe, page 336).

Preheat oven to 350°F (180°C)
12-cup muffin pan, lined with paper liners

1 cup	all-purpose flour	250 mL
1/2 tsp	baking powder	2 mL
1/4 tsp	baking soda	1 mL
1/4 tsp	salt	1 mL
1 cup	granulated sugar	250 mL
1/4 cup	vegetable oil	50 mL
2	egg whites	2
1 tsp	vanilla	5 mL
2 oz	unsweetened chocolate, melted and cooled slightly	60 g
2/3 cup	buttermilk	150 mL
2 tbsp	chocolate cream liqueur	25 mL
12	large marshmallows (see Tip, at left)	12
	Frosting (see Frosting suggestions, left)	

1. In a small bowl, mix together flour, baking powder, baking soda and salt.

2. In a large bowl, using electric mixer, beat together sugar and oil until well combined. Add egg whites, one at a time, beating well after each addition. Beat in vanilla and melted chocolate. Alternately beat in flour mixture and buttermilk, making three additions of flour mixture and two of buttermilk, beating until smooth. Beat in chocolate liqueur.

3. Scoop batter into prepared muffin cups. Bake in preheated oven for 20 to 25 minutes or until tops of cupcakes spring back when lightly touched. Let cool in pan on rack for 5 minutes. Remove cupcakes from pan.

4. While cupcakes are still hot, using a spoon, scoop a hole in the top of each cupcake, scooping down to the center. Push a marshmallow into each hole. Don't worry if the marshmallows stick up a bit from the top of the cupcakes. The warmth of the cupcakes will soften the marshmallows and they will smoosh down. (Discard scooped out cupcake or save to nibble on.) Let cool completely on rack. Top cooled cupcakes with frosting.

Chocolate Cinnamon Cupcakes

MAKES
12 CUPCAKES

Mexican chocolate —
a blend of chocolate,
almond and cinnamon
flavors — is usually
served hot, blended with
milk. I took the delicious
flavors of Mexican
chocolate and added
them to this delectable
cupcake. Viva el chocolate!

TIPS

A great ratio for strong
brewed coffee is 2 tbsp
(25 mL) finely ground
French-roast coffee or
espresso for every 3/4 cup
(175 mL) water.

Although it might seem
weird to add the balsamic
vinegar to the batter, it
reacts with the baking soda
to make the cupcakes rise
(since there are no eggs
in the batter). The vinegar
evaporates while baking,
so there is no vinegary
taste.

Preheat oven to 350°F (180°C)
12-cup muffin pan, lined with paper liners

1 1/2 cups	all-purpose flour	375 mL
1/2 cup	unsweetened Dutch-process cocoa powder, sifted	125 mL
1/2 tsp	ground cinnamon	2 mL
1/2 tsp	baking soda	2 mL
Pinch	salt	Pinch
1 1/4 cups	granulated sugar	300 mL
3/4 cup	strong brewed coffee, cooled to room temperature (see Tip, at left)	175 mL
1/2 cup	vegetable oil	125 mL
1 tsp	vanilla	5 mL
1/2 tsp	almond extract	2 mL
2 tbsp	balsamic vinegar	25 mL
1/2 cup	semisweet chocolate chips	125 mL
	Chocolate Fudge Frosting (see recipe, page 337)	

1. In a small bowl, mix together flour, cocoa powder, cinnamon, baking soda and salt.

2. In a large bowl, whisk together sugar, coffee, oil, vanilla and almond extract. Add flour mixture, beating until smooth. Mix in balsamic vinegar. Stir in chocolate chips.

3. Scoop batter into prepared muffin cups. Bake in preheated oven for 25 minutes or until tops of cupcakes spring back when lightly touched. Let cool in pan on rack for 10 minutes. Remove from pan and let cool completely on rack. Top cooled cupcakes with frosting.

White Chocolate Macadamia Cupcakes

**MAKES
12 CUPCAKES**

White chocolate and macadamia nuts — just think of the possibilities. Whenever I pair these ingredients together, I imagine them as the dynamic duo: always pleasing, always satisfying.

TIP

I like to toast the macadamia nuts in a dry nonstick skillet over medium heat, stirring constantly, for about 5 minutes.

Preheat oven to 350°F (180°C)
12-cup muffin pan, lined with paper liners

1 1/2 cups	all-purpose flour	375 mL
3/4 cup	macadamia nuts, coarsely chopped, toasted and cooled (see Tip, at left)	175 mL
1 1/2 tsp	baking powder	7 mL
1/4 tsp	salt	1 mL
1 cup	granulated sugar	250 mL
1/2 cup	vegetable oil	125 mL
2	eggs	2
1/3 cup	milk	75 mL
1/2 cup	white chocolate chips	125 mL
	Cream Cheese Icing (see recipe, opposite)	
1/4 cup	toasted macadamia nuts for garnish	50 mL

1. In a small bowl, mix together flour, macadamia nuts, baking powder and salt.

2. In a large bowl, whisk together sugar, oil and eggs until smooth. Alternately beat in flour mixture and milk, making three additions of flour mixture and two of milk, beating just until smooth. Stir in white chocolate chips.

3. Scoop batter into prepared muffin cups. Bake in preheated oven for 22 to 26 minutes or until golden brown and tops of cupcakes spring back when lightly touched. Let cool in pan on rack for 10 minutes. Remove from pan and let cool completely on rack. Top cooled cupcakes with Cream Cheese Icing and garnish with macadamia nuts.

Variation
Substitute semisweet chocolate chips for the white chocolate chips and almonds for the macadamia nuts.

**MAKES ABOUT
2 CUPS (500 mL),
enough to frost 16
or more cupcakes**

Cream Cheese Icing

4 oz	cream cheese, at room temperature	125 g
1/2 cup	unsalted butter, at room temperature	125 mL
Pinch	salt	Pinch
2 1/4 cups	confectioner's (icing) sugar, sifted	550 mL

Cream cheese icing tastes great on just about everything. It's a quick mix that can make something go from tasting good to tasting extraordinary.

TIPS

Because cream cheese is perishable, be sure to keep your frosted cupcakes refrigerated until you're ready to eat them.

This frosting will keep in an airtight container in the refrigerator for up to 3 days. Before using, let stand at room temperature for 15 minutes to soften enough to spread.

1. In a large bowl, using an electric mixer on medium-high speed, beat together cream cheese, butter and salt until creamy. With mixer on low speed, beat in confectioner's sugar, 1/2 cup (125 mL) at a time so that the sugar doesn't fly all over the place. Increase speed to medium-high and beat until light and fluffy.

2. Spread frosting over cooled cupcakes and refrigerate until ready to serve or for up to 1 day.

Variation
Add a drop of food coloring to the frosting as you are making it for a touch of beautiful color.

Espresso Dark Brownie Cupcakes

MAKES
24 CUPCAKES

This is an absolutely delicious, fudgy chocolate cupcake. It's a brownie and a cupcake all rolled up into one. When I need a chocolate fix, this cupcake fills the bill.

TIP

All of the recipes in this book were tested using large eggs. Using medium or extra-large eggs may adversely affect the outcome of the recipe.

Preheat oven to 350°F (180°C)
Two 12-cup muffin pans, lined with paper liners

1 cup	unsalted butter, cut into pieces	250 mL
4 oz	unsweetened chocolate, chopped	125 g
1 cup	all-purpose flour	250 mL
¼ cup	unsweetened Dutch-process cocoa powder, sifted	50 mL
2 tbsp	finely ground espresso	25 mL
¼ tsp	salt	1 mL
1¾ cups	packed light or medium brown sugar	425 mL
½ cup	granulated sugar	125 mL
4	eggs	4
	Chocolate Fudge Frosting (see recipe, page 337)	

1. In a microwave-safe bowl, combine butter and chocolate. Microwave, uncovered, on High for 60 seconds, stirring every 30 seconds, or until butter is melted and chocolate is soft. Stir until smooth. Set aside and let cool slightly.

2. In a small bowl, mix together flour, cocoa powder, espresso and salt.

3. In a large bowl, using electric mixer, beat together brown and granulated sugars and reserved chocolate mixture until well combined. Add eggs, one at a time, beating well after each addition. Add flour mixture, mixing just until blended.

4. Scoop batter into prepared muffin cups. Bake in preheated oven for 25 to 30 minutes or until a few moist crumbs cling to tester when inserted in center of cupcakes. Let cool in pans on rack for 10 minutes. Remove from pans and let cool completely on rack. Top cooled cupcakes with frosting.

Variation
Mix $\frac{1}{3}$ to $\frac{1}{2}$ cup (75 to 125 mL) chopped white chocolate into the batter.

Chocolate Chili Cupcakes

MAKES
12 CUPCAKES

I'm sure you're wondering how chocolate and chili go together, but let me assure you that it is a match made in heaven. You don't taste the chili; you feel only a slight amount of heat from it. So what you wind up with is a deep chocolate flavor with a little kick and a slight jump in your heart rate.

TIP

These are best served the day that they're made.

Frosting suggestions:
Chocolate Fudge Frosting (see recipe, page 337) or Chocolate Glaze (see recipe, page 336).

Preheat oven to 350°F (180°C)
12-cup muffin pan, lined with paper liners

1¼ cups	all-purpose flour	300 mL
½ cup	unsweetened Dutch-process cocoa powder, sifted	125 mL
1 tbsp	ancho chili powder or 1 tsp (5 mL) chipotle chili powder	15 mL
2 tsp	finely ground espresso or French-roast coffee	10 mL
¾ tsp	baking soda	4 mL
¼ tsp	salt	1 mL
1 cup	granulated sugar	250 mL
⅓ cup	vegetable oil	75 mL
1	egg	1
1 tsp	vanilla	5 mL
¾ cup	buttermilk	175 mL
1 tbsp	instant coffee granules	15 mL
½ cup	semisweet chocolate chips	125 mL
	Frosting (see Frosting suggestions, left)	

1. In a small bowl, mix together flour, cocoa powder, chili powder, ground coffee, baking soda and salt.

2. In a large bowl, whisk together sugar, oil, egg and vanilla until smooth. In a separate bowl, stir together buttermilk and instant coffee.

3. Alternately whisk flour mixture and buttermilk mixture into oil mixture, making three additions of flour mixture and two of buttermilk mixture, beating until smooth. Mix in chocolate chips.

4. Scoop batter into prepared muffin cups. Bake for 22 to 27 minutes or until tops of cupcakes spring back when lightly touched. Let cool in pan on rack for 10 minutes. Remove from pan and let cool completely on rack. Top cooled cupcakes with frosting.

24 Carrot Cake (page 100)

Café Mocha Cake (page 116)

Chocolate Potato Cake (page 102)

Chocolate Mousse–Filled Cupcakes (page 132)

Chocolate Surprise Cupcakes (page 138) with
Chocolate Fudge Frosting (page 337)

Triple Chocolate Chip Cookies (page 179),
Vancouver Bars (page 234),
Chocolate Coconut Clouds (page 197)
and Ginger Chocolate Shortbread (page 209)

White Chocolate Key Lime Pie (page 156)

Chocolate Mint Cupcakes

**MAKES
12 CUPCAKES**

Let me just say that these little cakes are fudgy and delicious! My son, Noah, tells me that the flavor reminds him of his favorite mint chocolate chip ice cream. If these cupcakes cave in somewhat on top as they cool, the frosting will hide it.

TIP

These cupcakes are best frosted and served the day that they're made.

Frosting suggestions:
Chocolate Fudge Frosting (see recipe, page 337) or Chocolate Glaze (see recipe, page 336).

Preheat oven to 350°F (180°C)
12-cup muffin pan, lined with paper liners

³⁄₄ cup	all-purpose flour	175 mL
¹⁄₃ cup	unsweetened Dutch-process cocoa powder, sifted	75 mL
¹⁄₂ tsp	baking soda	2 mL
¹⁄₂ tsp	baking powder	2 mL
Pinch	salt	Pinch
³⁄₄ cup	granulated sugar	175 mL
¹⁄₃ cup	vegetable oil	75 mL
1	egg	1
¹⁄₄ tsp	peppermint extract	1 mL
¹⁄₂ cup	milk	125 mL
¹⁄₂ cup	semisweet chocolate chips	125 mL
	Frosting (see Frosting suggestions, left)	

1. In a small bowl, mix together flour, cocoa powder, baking soda, baking powder and salt.

2. In a large bowl, whisk together sugar, oil and egg until smooth. Add peppermint extract, mixing well. Alternately whisk in flour mixture and milk, making three additions of flour mixture and two of milk, beating until smooth. Stir in chocolate chips.

3. Scoop batter into prepared muffin cups. Bake in preheated oven for 20 to 25 minutes or until tops of cupcakes spring back when lightly touched. Let cool in pan on rack for 10 minutes. Remove from pan and let cool completely on rack. Top cooled cupcakes with frosting.

Variation
Substitute chocolate mint chips or a chopped chocolate mint candy bar for the semisweet chocolate chips.

Chocolate Cheesecake Cupcakes

**MAKES
12 CUPCAKES**

Cheesecake does not get any easier than this. Instead of a traditional crust, simply place a whole chocolate sandwich cookie in the bottom of the baking cup, then top it with a blend of cream cheese and melted chocolate. This is definitely a to-die-for dessert.

TIP

Do not use paper liners for cheesecakes. Use only foil liners because the paper liners get soggy and the cheesecake will stick to them. The foil liners release the cheesecake cupcakes effortlessly.

Preheat oven to 350°F (180°C)
12-cup muffin pan, lined with foil liners (see Tip, at left)

12	chocolate sandwich cookies	12
3 oz	bittersweet or semisweet chocolate, chopped	90 g
1 oz	unsweetened chocolate, chopped	30 g
12 oz	cream cheese, at room temperature	375 g
1/2 cup	granulated sugar	125 mL
1/4 cup	sour cream	50 mL
2 tbsp	chocolate cream liqueur	25 mL
2	eggs	2

Topping

3/4 cup	sour cream	175 mL
3 tbsp	granulated sugar	45 mL
1 tbsp	chocolate cream liqueur	15 mL
	Unsweetened Dutch-process cocoa powder, sifted	

1. Place one chocolate sandwich cookie in bottom of each foil-lined cup and set aside.

2. In a microwave-safe bowl, combine bittersweet and unsweetened chocolate. Microwave, uncovered, on High for 45 to 50 seconds, stirring after 30 seconds, or until chocolate is soft and almost melted. Stir until smooth. Set aside and let cool slightly.

TIPS

Make sure not to overprocess the cheesecake filling.

These cupcakes freeze well. Wrap them individually in plastic wrap and store them in resealable plastic freezer bags for up to 3 weeks.

3. In a food processor fitted with a metal blade, pulse cream cheese until smooth. Add sugar, pulsing until smooth. Add melted chocolate and process until smooth. Add sour cream and liqueur, blending well. Add eggs, pulsing just until smooth (you don't want to overprocess the mixture; you just want it to be smooth).

4. Scoop batter into cookie-lined cups. Bake in preheated oven for 18 to 22 minutes or until centers of cupcakes are firm. Let cool in pan on rack for 5 minutes.

5. *Topping:* In a small bowl, stir together sour cream, sugar and liqueur. Gently spoon and swirl (with back of spoon) sour cream mixture over cupcakes, covering tops. Return to oven and bake for 4 minutes. Let cupcakes cool in pan on rack to room temperature. Cover and refrigerate for 2 hours or overnight to chill completely. Just before serving, lightly dust tops of cupcakes with cocoa powder.

Variations

Omit sour cream topping. Just before serving, whip together ¾ cup (175 mL) whipping (35%) cream, 2 tbsp (25 mL) confectioner's sugar and ½ tsp (1 mL) vanilla. Spread or dollop whipped cream mixture over tops of cupcakes. Sprinkle grated chocolate over whipped cream and serve.

You can use crème de cacao in place of chocolate cream liqueur.

Pies, Tarts and Pastries

Banana Fanna Pie *150*

Old-Fashioned Chocolate Orange Pie *152*

Sweet Potato Pie with White Chocolate Chunks *154*

White Chocolate Key Lime Pie *156*

Chocolate Chip Coconut Pie *157*

Chocolate Chip Pecan Pie *158*

Brownie Pie *159*

Chocolate Chip Brownie Tart *160*

Almond and Coconut Chocolate Chip Tart *161*

Chocolate Truffle Tart *162*

Chocolate Chip Cheese Tart *164*

Chocolate Chip Mocha Tarts *165*

Cookie Tarts *166*

Chocolate Fruit Tarts *168*

Chocolate Macaroon Tarts *169*

Quick Cinnamon Chocolate Pastries *170*

Baklava with Chocolate, Walnuts and Honey Syrup *172*

Banana Fanna Pie

SERVES 8

My friend Erika Novick and I used to make banana cream pies together all the time. I've added chocolate chips to our original recipe — taking it from fabulous to oh so fabulous.

TIPS

Read through the entire recipe before starting. That way, you know both the steps and ingredients in the recipe before you start.

Make sure your oven is fully preheated before baking. It will likely take between 15 and 20 minutes to preheat, depending on your oven.

Preheat oven to 400°F (200°C)

1	unbaked 9-inch (23 cm) pie shell (frozen or homemade)	1
3/4 cup	semisweet chocolate chips, divided	175 mL
1 cup plus 2 tbsp	whipping (35%) cream, divided	275 mL
3	egg yolks	3
3/4 cup	granulated sugar	175 mL
1/4 cup	all-purpose flour	50 mL
1/3 cup	cornstarch	75 mL
1/8 tsp	salt	0.5 mL
3 cups	half-and-half (10%) cream, divided	750 mL
2 tbsp	unsalted butter	25 mL
1 tbsp	confectioner's (icing) sugar, sifted	15 mL
1/4 tsp	vanilla	1 mL
2	medium bananas, sliced	2

1. If frozen, let pie shell thaw for 10 minutes. Place on a baking sheet. Lightly prick bottom and sides of shell with a fork (be careful not to make large holes). Bake in preheated oven until crust is lightly browned, 13 to 15 minutes. Let cool completely on rack.

2. In a microwave-safe bowl, combine 1/2 cup (125 mL) of the chocolate chips and 2 tbsp (25 mL) of the whipping cream. Microwave on High for 1 to 2 minutes, stirring every 30 seconds, until chocolate is shiny and almost melted. Stir until smooth. Spread chocolate mixture over bottom of cooled crust. Refrigerate until chocolate is firm.

3. Meanwhile, in a small bowl, whisk together egg yolks, granulated sugar, flour, cornstarch and salt. Whisk in 1/2 cup (125 mL) of the half-and-half until smooth.

When measuring, always
remember to spoon your
dry ingredients into the
cup and level the top by
scraping across it with
the flat side of a knife or
skewer. This will give you
an accurate measurement.

4. In a large saucepan, bring remaining half-and-half to boil over medium-high heat. Remove saucepan from heat and gradually whisk in egg yolk mixture. Reduce heat to medium and return pan to stovetop. Cook, whisking constantly, until thick and smooth, 3 to 4 minutes. Whisk in butter. Pour custard into a bowl and place a sheet of plastic wrap directly on surface to prevent a skin from forming. Let cool completely.

5. In a medium bowl, using electric mixer or whisk, whip remaining whipping cream, confectioner's sugar and vanilla until stiff peaks form.

6. Layer banana slices over chocolate in crust. Spoon cooled custard over bananas. Top pie with whipped cream and sprinkle with remaining chocolate chips. Chill for several hours or until firm before serving.

Variation
Whisk ¾ cup (175 mL) semisweet chocolate chips into hot custard mixture for a double chocolate banana pie.

Old-Fashioned Chocolate Orange Pie

SERVES 8

Don't let the name fool you. This dessert is a favorite with all ages. The chocolate-orange flavor lends an air of sophistication to an old-fashioned pie.

TIP

You will find it easiest to cook this pudding in a heavy-bottomed nonstick saucepan.

1/4 cup	granulated sugar	50 mL
2 tbsp	all-purpose flour	25 mL
2 tbsp	cornstarch	25 mL
1/8 tsp	salt	0.5 mL
1 1/2 cups	milk, divided	375 mL
2	egg yolks	2
1 tsp	grated orange zest	5 mL
1/2 cup	orange juice	125 mL
1 cup	semisweet chocolate chips	250 mL
1 tbsp	unsalted butter	15 mL
1/2 tsp	vanilla	2 mL
1	9-inch (23 cm) pie shell, baked and cooled	1
1 cup	whipping (35%) cream	250 mL
1 tbsp	confectioner's (icing) sugar	15 mL
1/2 tsp	vanilla	2 mL
	Semisweet chocolate chips, for garnish (optional)	

1. In a small bowl, whisk together sugar, flour, cornstarch and salt. Whisk in 1/2 cup (125 mL) of the milk and egg yolks. Set aside.

2. In a large saucepan over medium–high heat, bring remaining milk, orange zest and juice to a simmer, whisking often (don't worry if it starts to curdle). Remove saucepan from heat and whisk in egg yolk mixture. Reduce heat to medium, return saucepan to burner and cook, whisking constantly, until thickened. Remove from heat and whisk in chocolate chips, butter and vanilla until smooth. Let cool slightly. Pour into cooled pie crust.

Store chocolate in a cool, dry place for up to one year. Chocolate will sometimes develop a white "bloom," or coating, when it gets too warm, causing the cocoa butter to separate. The chocolate is still fine to use in recipes or for melting.

3. In a medium bowl, with electric mixer or whisk, whip together cream, confectioner's sugar and vanilla until almost stiff peaks. Swirl top of pie with whipped cream and sprinkle with additional chocolate chips, if desired. Chill for several hours before serving.

Variation
For a pure chocolate variation, substitute ½ cup (125 mL) milk for the orange juice and omit the orange zest.

Sweet Potato Pie with White Chocolate Chunks

This is an unusual yet perfect combination. It's a fun change from pumpkin pie and a surprise to the taste buds. It can be made quickly, thanks to the use of a store-bought pie shell and canned sweet potatoes.

TIP
All of the recipes in this book were tested using large eggs. Using medium or extra-large eggs may adversely affect the outcome of the recipe.

Preheat oven to 350°F (180°C)

1¹⁄₂ cups	well-drained canned sweet potatoes	375 mL
3	eggs	3
1 cup	packed dark brown sugar	250 mL
1 cup	evaporated milk	250 mL
1 tsp	ground cinnamon	5 mL
1 tsp	vanilla	5 mL
1	unbaked 9-inch (23 cm) frozen deep-dish pie shell	1
2 oz	white chocolate, chopped	60 g
Pinch	ground cinnamon	Pinch

Topping

1 cup	whipping (35%) cream	250 mL
3 tbsp	confectioner's (icing) sugar, sifted	45 mL
1 tbsp	bourbon or dark rum	15 mL
	White chocolate curls (see Tips, opposite)	

1. In a food processor fitted with a metal blade, purée sweet potatoes. Add eggs, pulsing well. Add brown sugar, evaporated milk, the 1 tsp (5 mL) cinnamon and vanilla, pulsing until smooth. Pour into pie shell. Sprinkle with chopped white chocolate. Using back of spoon, lightly press white chocolate into filling. Sprinkle with pinch of cinnamon.

TIPS

To melt white chocolate, place chocolate in a microwave-safe bowl. Microwave, uncovered, on Medium (50%) for 40 to 60 seconds or just until melted. Let cool slightly.

To make chocolate curls, use a vegetable peeler to peel curls directly off white chocolate bar.

2. Bake pie in preheated oven for 45 minutes or until filling is set in center and pie is slightly puffed (do not overbake). Let pie cool on a rack. Refrigerate pie for 2 to 3 hours or until cold.

3. *Topping:* In a medium bowl, using electric mixer or whisk, whip cream, confectioner's sugar and bourbon until stiff peaks form. Swirl whipped cream over top of pie. Sprinkle white chocolate curls over whipped cream. Serve pie at once or refrigerate for up to 1 day.

Variations

Omit the bourbon from the whipped cream and substitute 1 tsp (5 mL) vanilla.

For a more intense flavor, you can increase the chopped white chocolate to 4 oz (125 g).

White Chocolate Key Lime Pie

SERVES 8

Close your eyes and imagine yourself on a beach in the tropics. Now sink your teeth into a dreamy, luscious pie filled with the flavor of fresh lime juice and creamy white chocolate. Well, you won't have to travel farther than your kitchen, because this recipe will transport you directly to that beach. You don't necessarily have to use Key limes here — any lime will work.

TIPS

To melt white chocolate, place chocolate in a microwave-safe bowl. Microwave, uncovered, on Medium (50%) for 40 to 60 seconds or just until melted. Let cool slightly.

To make chocolate curls, use a vegetable peeler to peel curls directly off white chocolate bar.

1	package (8 oz/250 g) cream cheese, softened slightly	1
1	can (14 oz/398 mL) sweetened condensed milk (about 1 $\frac{1}{3}$ cups/325 mL)	1
3 oz	white chocolate, melted (see Tips, left)	90 g
1 tsp	packed grated lime zest	5 mL
$\frac{3}{4}$ cup	freshly squeezed lime juice	175 mL
1	8-inch (20 cm) store-bought graham cracker pie shell	1
1 cup	whipping (35%) cream	250 mL
2 tbsp	confectioner's (icing) sugar	25 mL
	White chocolate curls (see Tips, at left)	

1. In a food processor fitted with a metal blade, combine cream cheese and sweetened condensed milk. Pulse until puréed and smooth. Add melted white chocolate, pulsing until smooth. Add lime juice and pulse again until smooth and creamy. Stir in lime zest.

2. Spread lime mixture in pie shell, smoothing top. Refrigerate pie for 3 to 4 hours or until firm.

3. In a medium bowl, using an electric mixer, whip cream and confectioner's sugar until stiff peaks form. Swirl whipped cream over top of pie. Sprinkle white chocolate curls over whipped cream. Serve pie at once or refrigerate for up to 1 day.

Chocolate Chip Coconut Pie

This dessert — a chewy, ooey-gooey chocolate chip cookie baked in a flaky pastry crust — acts like a party in your mouth.

TIP

Serve a slice of pie with a scoop of vanilla ice cream.

Preheat oven to 350°F (180°C)

1 cup	granulated sugar	250 mL
1 cup	semisweet chocolate chips	250 mL
1/2 cup	all-purpose flour	125 mL
1/2 cup	sweetened flaked coconut	125 mL
1/8 tsp	salt	0.5 mL
1/2 cup	unsalted butter, melted and cooled slightly	125 mL
2	eggs	2
1 tsp	vanilla	5 mL
1	unbaked 9-inch (23 cm) deep-dish pie shell (frozen or homemade)	1
	Confectioner's (icing) sugar, for garnish	

1. In a large bowl, combine sugar, chocolate chips, flour, coconut and salt. Add melted butter, eggs and vanilla, stirring well.

2. Pour mixture into pie shell. Bake in preheated oven for 45 minutes or until a knife inserted into center comes out almost clean. Let cool completely on rack.

3. Lightly dust the top of the cooled pie with confectioner's sugar.

Variation
Substitute walnuts for the coconut.

Chocolate Chip Pecan Pie

SERVES 8

For Thanksgiving, I was busy baking chocolate chip pecan pies but could not get them to set. Our friend Rick, who is from New Orleans, suggested that I follow the recipe he uses for pecan pie: the one on the back of the corn syrup bottle. This is my version of Rick's favorite recipe.

TIP

To toast pecans: Preheat oven to 350°F (180°C). Spread pecans on baking sheet, lined with parchment paper, and bake for 8 to 10 minutes or until lightly browned.

Preheat oven to 350°F (180°C)

3	eggs	3
³⁄₄ cup	firmly packed dark brown sugar	175 mL
1 cup	light corn syrup	250 mL
2 tbsp	unsalted butter, melted and cooled slightly	25 mL
1 tsp	vanilla	5 mL
¹⁄₈ tsp	salt	0.5 mL
¹⁄₃ cup	semisweet chocolate chips	75 mL
1¹⁄₃ cups	pecans, toasted (see Tip, at left)	325 mL
1	unbaked 9-inch (23 cm) deep-dish pie shell (frozen or homemade)	1

1. In a large bowl, whisk eggs. Add brown sugar, corn syrup, melted butter, vanilla and salt, whisking well. Stir in chocolate chips.

2. Place pecans in bottom of pie shell. Pour filling over top. Bake in preheated oven for 50 to 55 minutes or until a knife inserted into center of pie comes out clean. Let cool completely on rack.

Variation
Substitute walnuts for the pecans.

Brownie Pie

This pie is a year-round favorite of my kids. It's easy enough for children to make (with the guidance of an adult), and not only does it make a fabulous dessert but it's also a fun alternative to standard birthday cakes.

TIP

Instead of refrigerating the tart until firm, you can serve it warm. Unrefrigerated, this tart is soft, chewy and slightly gooey in the center.

Preheat oven to 350°F (180°C)
10-inch (25 cm) deep-dish pie plate, greased

³/₄ cup	all-purpose flour	175 mL
³/₄ cup	unsweetened Dutch-process cocoa powder, sifted	175 mL
1¹/₄ tsp	baking powder	6 mL
1 cup	salted butter, melted	250 mL
1 cup	granulated sugar	250 mL
³/₄ cup	packed light brown sugar	175 mL
2	eggs	2
2 tsp	vanilla	10 mL
1 cup	coarsely chopped chocolate-covered mints	250 mL
¹/₄ cup	semisweet chocolate chips	50 mL

1. In a small bowl, mix together flour, cocoa powder and baking powder.

2. In a large bowl, beat together melted butter and granulated and brown sugars. Add eggs, one at a time, beating well after each addition. Add vanilla, beating well. Add flour mixture, beating just until smooth.

3. Spread batter in prepared pan, smoothing top. Sprinkle chocolate mints and chocolate chips over top. Lightly press chocolates into batter, but not too much.

4. Bake in preheated oven for 35 to 40 minutes or until pie is somewhat firm but not hard to the touch. Let cool on a rack. Refrigerate until firm or for up to 1 day. Serve pie with a scoop of vanilla ice cream.

Variation
Substitute chopped chocolate sandwich cookies or another favorite candy for the chocolate–covered mints.

Chocolate Chip Brownie Tart

This delicious tart will keep, refrigerated, for several days. For such a humble dessert, it has a sophisticated look to it. Serve it with a scoop of your favorite premium ice cream.

TIP

All of the recipes in this book were tested using large eggs. Using medium or extra-large eggs may adversely affect the outcome of the recipe.

Preheat oven to 325°F (160°C)
10-inch (25 cm) glass tart dish or quiche dish, greased

1/3 cup	all-purpose flour	75 mL
1/8 tsp	salt	0.5 mL
4 oz	unsweetened chocolate, chopped	125 g
1/2 cup	unsalted butter	125 mL
1 1/4 cups	packed light brown sugar	300 mL
2	eggs	2
1 tsp	vanilla	5 mL
1/2 cup	semisweet chocolate chips	125 mL

1. In a small bowl, mix together flour and salt. Set aside.

2. In a large microwave-safe bowl, combine unsweetened chocolate and butter. Microwave on High for 2 to 2½ minutes, stirring every 30 seconds, until butter is melted and chocolate is shiny and almost melted. Stir until smooth. Let cool to lukewarm. Whisk in sugar, eggs and vanilla. Stir in flour mixture just until combined.

3. Spread in prepared dish. Sprinkle with chocolate chips. Bake in preheated oven for 30 to 35 minutes or until a toothpick inserted into center comes out clean. Let cool in dish on rack. Cover and refrigerate for several hours or until firm, or overnight.

Almond and Coconut Chocolate Chip Tart

SERVES 12

This elegant and delicious tart is an adaptation of a recipe that I developed for *Bon Appétit* magazine. It is also a fabulous dessert for a dinner party, as you can make the entire dessert ahead of time.

TIPS

To toast almonds: Preheat oven to 350°F (180°C). Spread nuts on a baking sheet lined with foil or parchment. Bake for 5 to 7 minutes or until light brown and fragrant.

Garnish the tart with a light dusting of confectioner's (icing) sugar, if desired.

Preheat oven to 350°F (180°C)
11-inch (28 cm) metal tart pan with removable bottom, greased

Crust

1 1/2 cups	all-purpose flour	375 mL
1/4 cup	granulated sugar	50 mL
1/2 cup	unsalted butter, chilled and cut into pieces	125 mL
2 tbsp	whipping (35%) cream (approx.)	25 mL
1 1/2 tsp	vanilla	7 mL

Filling

3/4 cup	light corn syrup	175 mL
1/4 cup	packed light brown sugar	50 mL
1/4 cup	butter, melted and cooled	50 mL
3	eggs	3
1 tsp	vanilla	5 mL
2 cups	whole almonds, toasted and coarsely chopped (see Tip, at left)	500 mL
1 cup	semisweet chocolate chips	250 mL
1/2 cup	sweetened flaked coconut	125 mL

1. *Crust:* In a food processor fitted with a metal blade, combine flour and sugar. Pulse to combine. Add butter and pulse just until mixture resembles coarse meal. Add cream and vanilla, pulsing just until moist clumps form. If dough is dry, add an additional tbsp (15 mL) cream. Pulse again, just until dough starts to form a ball. Press into prepared pan.

2. *Filling:* In a large bowl, whisk together corn syrup, brown sugar and melted butter. Whisk in eggs and vanilla. Mix in almonds, chocolate chips and coconut. Pour filling over prepared crust.

3. Bake in preheated oven for 50 minutes or until tart is firmly set in center and top is golden brown. Let tart cool in pan on rack. Push up bottom of pan to release. Serve tart warm or at room temperature.

Chocolate Truffle Tart

Back in my bakery days, this chocolate tart was a huge seller. The tart filling is adapted from an old recipe that I found in *Food & Wine* magazine. This bittersweet chocolate tart is sure to please.

TIPS

To check if dough needs more liquid when making a tart dough, break off a piece of dough and squeeze it into a ball. If it's too crumbly, it probably needs a touch more liquid. If it forms into a silky ball, then it's perfect. You do not want the dough too moist.

You can heat cream, milk and chocolate in a microwave-safe bowl instead of on the stove.

Preheat oven to 375°F (190°C)

10-inch (25 cm) metal tart pan with removable bottom, greased

Crust

2 cups	all-purpose flour	500 mL
1/4 cup	granulated sugar	50 mL
3/4 cup	cold salted butter, cut into pieces	175 mL
4 to 5 tbsp	whipping (35%) cream (approx.)	60 to 75 mL
1 tsp	vanilla	5 mL

Filling

1 1/2 cups	whipping (35%) cream	375 mL
2/3 cup	milk (not nonfat or low-fat)	150 mL
14 oz	bittersweet or semisweet chocolate, chopped	420 g
1/4 cup	granulated sugar	50 mL
2	eggs, lightly beaten	2
2 tbsp	dark rum	25 mL
	Unsweetened Dutch-process cocoa powder, sifted, for dusting	

1. *Crust:* In a food processor fitted with a metal blade, pulse flour and sugar until well combined. Add butter, pulsing until mixture is crumbly and resembles coarse meal. Add 4 tbsp (50 mL) cream and vanilla, pulsing until mixture just comes together and starts to form a ball. If dough is still dry, add additional cream, 1 tsp (5 mL) at a time, as needed to make a smooth dough (dough should not be wet — see Tip, at left). Press dough (do not roll) into prepared tart tin. Place in freezer and chill for 20 minutes. Using a fork, gently prick bottom of crust.

TIP

You might wind up with some extra filling after you fill your tart crust (tart pans can be slightly different sizes). Pour this extra filling into a ramekin or two (or an ovenproof espresso or small coffee mug) and bake alongside the tart for the same amount of time.

2. Bake crust in preheated oven for 25 minutes or until lightly golden brown and firm to the touch. Let crust cool on a rack. Leave oven on.

3. *Filling:* In a saucepan over medium heat, combine cream and milk and bring to a simmer. Remove saucepan from heat and add chocolate and sugar, stirring well until melted. Strain chocolate cream into a bowl and let cool slightly. (It can be slightly warm, but if it's too warm, it will cook the eggs.) Whisk in eggs and rum until blended.

4. Pour chocolate mixture into crust. Bake in preheated oven for 15 to 20 minutes or until filling is almost firm but still slightly jiggly in center. Let tart cool completely before removing outer rim of pan. Dust with cocoa powder before serving.

Variation
Substitute milk chocolate for the bittersweet chocolate.

Chocolate Chip Cheese Tart

This is similar to a cheesecake but better. It goes together quickly and looks impressive. The chocolate drizzle on top gives it a striking appearance.

TIP

If you cannot find superfine sugar in your local grocery store, you can make your own: Process granulated sugar in a food processor until very finely ground.

9-inch (23 cm) tart pan with removable bottom, sprayed with nonstick spray

10	whole graham crackers	10
$1/3$ cup	unsalted butter, melted	75 mL
$1/3$ cup	sweetened flaked coconut	75 mL
12 oz	cream cheese, softened	375 g
$1/2$ cup	superfine sugar (see Tip, at left)	125 mL
$1^3/4$ cups	whipping (35%) cream	425 mL
$2^1/2$ tbsp	coconut rum	32 mL
$1/2$ cup	semisweet chocolate chips	125 mL
$1^1/2$ tsp	shortening	7 mL
$1/3$ cup	miniature semisweet chocolate chips	75 mL

1. In a food processor fitted with a metal blade, pulse graham crackers until fine crumbs form. Transfer crumbs to a medium bowl. Stir in melted butter and coconut. Press into bottom and up side of prepared tart pan. Freeze until firm.

2. In a large bowl, using electric mixer, combine cream cheese and sugar. Whip until creamy, scraping down side of bowl as necessary. Add cream and rum, whipping until mixture looks like whipped cream and soft peaks form.

3. Spread whipped cream mixture over frozen crust, using back of spoon to swirl decoratively.

4. In a microwave-safe bowl, combine $1/2$ cup (125 mL) chocolate chips and shortening. Microwave on High for 1 to 2 minutes, stirring every 30 seconds, until chocolate is shiny and almost melted. Stir until smooth.

5. Drizzle melted chocolate over top of cheese mixture. Sprinkle with miniature chocolate chips. Refrigerate for several hours or until firm, or for up to 8 hours. (If left any longer, the crust will get soggy.)

Variation
Substitute light rum for the coconut rum.

Chocolate Chip Mocha Tarts

I usually have a roll or two of homemade chocolate chip cookie dough in my freezer. I have found it makes great tart crust for recipes like this. It is a fun recipe to make with kids as they find the tarts not only delicious but "fancy" too.

TIP

You can freeze the cooled filled tarts. Just be sure to store them in a resealable freezer bag.

Preheat oven to 350°F (180°C)
Mini muffin pans, greased

1 lb	log chocolate chip cookie dough (see Slice-and-Bake Chocolate Chip Almond Cookies, page 186, with or without the almonds) or store-bought cookie dough	500 g
1 pint	coffee ice cream	500 mL
	Miniature semisweet chocolate chips	
	Whipped (35%) cream or fudge sauce (optional)	

1. Remove cookie dough from freezer or refrigerator (if frozen, let stand at room temperature until slightly softened). Cut dough into $\frac{1}{4}$-inch (0.5 cm) thick slices and press into prepared muffin cups. Bake tarts in preheated oven for 10 minutes or until puffed and golden brown. Let cool in tins on rack for 5 minutes. Remove from tins and let cool completely on rack.

2. Place a scoop of ice cream on top of each cookie tart. Sprinkle with miniature chocolate chips. Garnish with whipped cream, if desired. Serve immediately.

Variation
Use a standard-size 12-cup muffin pan to make 8 to 10 larger tarts. Increase baking time to 12 to 14 minutes.

Cookie Tarts

Although this seems like a complicated recipe, it is really easy to make. The recipe can be shortened even further by using store-bought sugar cookie dough for the tart shells and store-bought chocolate pudding or pudding mix for the filling.

TIP

Cocoa powder needs to be sifted before use because it can be very lumpy, which makes it difficult to incorporate. Use a fine-meshed sieve to remove any lumps before adding cocoa powder to other dry ingredients.

Preheat oven to 350°F (180°C)
Mini muffin pan (with 24 cups), greased

Crust

1⅓ cups	all-purpose flour	325 mL
⅓ cup	unsweetened Dutch-process cocoa powder, sifted	75 mL
3 tbsp	granulated sugar	45 mL
¼ tsp	salt	1 mL
⅔ cup	cold unsalted butter, cut into pieces	150 mL
3 tbsp	whipping (35%) cream	45 mL

Filling

½ cup	chocolate milk, divided	125 mL
2 tsp	granulated sugar	10 mL
1 tbsp	cornstarch	15 mL
Pinch	salt	Pinch
1 oz	milk chocolate, chopped	30 g

Topping

⅓ cup	whipping (35%) cream	75 mL
2 tsp	confectioner's (icing) sugar	10 mL
	Finely chopped milk chocolate	

1. *Crust:* In a food processor fitted with a metal blade, pulse flour, cocoa powder, sugar and salt until combined. Add butter and pulse until mixture is crumbly and resembles coarse meal. Add cream and pulse just until mixture starts to come together and form a ball.

2. Scoop dough into balls and place in prepared muffin cups, pressing into bottoms and up sides of cups. Place pan in freezer to chill dough while preparing filling.

TIP

The tart shells can be
made a day ahead. Store
in an airtight container
for 2 days. The filled tarts
will keep for up to 2 days
in the refrigerator, but
the tart shells will soften
slightly. If you're making
this ahead of time, add
the whipped cream topping
right before serving.

3. *Filling:* In a small saucepan over medium heat, heat
   $\frac{1}{3}$ cup (75 mL) chocolate milk and sugar until just
   warm to the touch.

4. In a small bowl, whisk together remaining chocolate
   milk, cornstarch and salt. Whisk into hot chocolate
   milk and cook, whisking continuously, for about
   1 minute or until thick. Remove from heat and whisk
   in milk chocolate until smooth. Pour pudding into
   a bowl. Press a piece of plastic wrap onto the surface.
   Let cool for 20 minutes at room temperature.
   Refrigerate until ready to use.

5. Bake chilled tart shells in preheated oven for 15 to
   20 minutes or until shells start to pull away from sides
   of pan. Let cool in pan on a rack for 15 minutes. Transfer
   to rack and let cool completely.

6. Spoon chocolate pudding into cooled tart shells.

7. *Topping:* In a small bowl, using electric mixer, whip
   cream and confectioner's sugar until stiff peaks form.
   Spoon dollops of whipped cream over chocolate
   pudding. Sprinkle chopped chocolate over whipped
   cream.

Variation
Garnish tops with semisweet or white chocolate chips
instead of the chopped chocolate.

Chocolate Fruit Tarts

MAKES 6 TARTS

Here's a quick and easy dessert that looks like you spent the day in the kitchen but really takes less than an hour to make. Simply top cookie dough, which has been baked into tart shells, with a chocolate ganache and top with fresh fruit. The fruit can be varied depending on the season, making this a spectacular dessert any time of the year.

TIP

Line your baking sheets with parchment paper for blissful baking. It will keep your baked goods from sticking, making cleanup a snap.

Preheat oven to 350°F (180°C)
Baking sheet, lined with parchment paper

Crust

1 1/2 cups	all-purpose flour	375 mL
1/2 cup	packed light brown sugar	125 mL
1 tsp	baking powder	5 mL
1/2 cup	salted butter	125 mL
1	egg yolk	1
2 tsp	vanilla	10 mL

Filling

5 oz	semisweet chocolate, chopped	150 g
1/2 cup	whipping (35%) cream	125 mL

Topping

Fresh or dried fruit of choice, such as sliced bananas, fresh strawberries or raspberries, or a combination of fresh fruit (see Tip, opposite)

1. *Crust:* In a food processor fitted with a metal blade, pulse flour, brown sugar and baking powder until mixed. Add butter, egg yolk and vanilla, pulsing until dough is smooth and begins to form a ball.

2. Scoop dough with 1/4-cup (50 mL) measure and place on prepared baking sheet. Flatten dough into 4-inch (10 cm) circles, crimping edges so they are slightly raised. Bake in preheated oven for 18 to 20 minutes or until golden brown and just firm to the touch.

If using bananas as
your fruit of choice, melt
$^1\!/_3$ cup (75 mL) apricot
jelly or jam in microwave
until warm and soft. Using
a pastry brush, paint a
thin coating of melted jelly
over fruit. This will help
prevent the bananas from
turning brown.

3. *Filling:* In a microwave-safe bowl, combine chocolate
   and cream. Microwave, uncovered, on Medium (50%)
   for 1 minute, stirring every 30 seconds, or until cream
   is hot and chocolate is starting to melt. Stir well until
   chocolate is melted and mixture is thick and smooth.
   If chocolate is not completely melted, return to
   microwave for another 10 to 20 seconds or until
   chocolate is soft and melted. Stir well. Spread filling
   over individual crusts, leaving a small border without
   chocolate filling.

4. *Topping:* Decoratively arrange fruit over melted
   chocolate. Place crusts on a clean parchment paper–lined
   baking sheet. Refrigerate for 30 minutes or until
   chocolate is firm, or for up to 8 hours. For best results,
   serve the same day.

Variation

If you are in a big hurry, you can substitute
store-bought chocolate chip cookie dough for the
homemade crust.

Chocolate Macaroon Tarts

MAKES 24 TARTS

These miniature tarts are dainty but have a powerful chocolate punch. They taste like chocolate macaroons and look like elegant flowers. They are beautiful as part of a dessert tray. These are best eaten the day they're made.

TIPS

These tarts look very pretty lightly dusted with confectioner's (icing) sugar.

If you're not serving them right away, refrigerate until almost ready to serve.

Preheat oven to 350°F (180°C)
Mini muffin pan (with 24 cups), greased

Crust

1$\frac{1}{2}$ cups	packed sweetened flaked coconut (about 6 oz/175 g)	375 mL
2 tbsp	granulated sugar	25 mL
2 tbsp	all-purpose flour	25 mL
2	egg whites	2
$\frac{1}{2}$ tsp	almond extract	2 mL

Filling

$\frac{1}{3}$ cup	whipping (35%) cream	75 mL
4 oz	bittersweet or semisweet chocolate, chopped	125 g

1. *Crust:* In a small bowl, mix together coconut, sugar and flour. Add egg whites and almond extract, mixing well.

2. Scoop tablespoonfuls (15 mL) of dough and, with moistened fingers, press into bottom and up sides of muffin cups. Bake in preheated oven for 15 to 20 minutes or until golden brown. Let tart shells cool for 5 minutes in pan on a rack.

3. Carefully remove each tart shell from pan.

4. *Filling:* In a microwave-safe bowl, combine cream and chocolate. Microwave, uncovered, on Medium (50%) for 1 to 1$\frac{1}{2}$ minutes, stirring every 30 seconds, or until cream is hot and chocolate is soft and almost melted. Stir chocolate mixture until smooth.

5. Spoon chocolate mixture into cooled tart shells and refrigerate for 1 hour or until chocolate is firm, or for up to 1 day.

Quick Cinnamon Chocolate Pastries

MAKES ABOUT 36 PASTRIES

I have always loved the chocolate chip pastries that you find in delicatessens, but unfortunately they are very time-consuming to make. I wanted to develop a recipe that packs the similar chocolate chip cinnamon goodness of those deli treats without the labor. I came up with this dessert, which is quick, easy and delicious.

TIPS

These pastries look great sprinkled with confectioner's (icing) sugar. They are wonderful served with coffee or as an accompaniment to homemade ice cream.

Store in an airtight container for up to 2 days.

Preheat oven to 425°F (220°C)
Baking sheets, lined with parchment paper

1	package (17.3 oz/490 g) frozen puff pastry sheets (about 9½ inches/24 cm square) or 1 package (13 oz/397 g) block puff pastry	1
½ cup	granulated sugar	125 mL
½ tsp	ground cinnamon	2 mL
⅔ cup	miniature semisweet chocolate chips	150 mL

1. Thaw puff pastry at room temperature for 30 minutes or according to package directions.

2. In a small bowl, combine sugar and cinnamon.

3. If pastry is a block, cut in half. On a floured surface, roll out each half to 9½-inch (24 cm) square sheets. Working with one sheet at a time, sprinkle half of the cinnamon sugar over top, then half of the miniature chocolate chips, leaving ½ inch (1 cm) bare at one edge. Brush bare edge with water. Starting at edge opposite, tightly roll up pastry jelly-roll style, gently pressing to help chocolate chips adhere and pinching edge to seal. Repeat with remaining sheet of pastry. Slice into ½-inch (1 cm) thick slices, carefully placing rounds cut side up on prepared baking sheets, about 1 inch (2.5 cm) apart. (Don't worry if some sugar or chocolate chips fall out. Just sprinkle them on top or tuck them back into pastry slice.)

4. Bake in preheated oven for 19 to 22 minutes or until medium brown and crisp. The pastries will look somewhat caramelized on top. Let cool completely on pan on rack.

Baklava with Chocolate, Walnuts and Honey Syrup

MAKES
30 PIECES

I've taken a traditional-style baklava and given it a chocolate babka–like twist. This recipe gets two forks way up.

TIP

If you can't find orange blossom water, you can simply omit it or substitute orange blossom honey or 2 tsp (10 mL) grated orange zest.

Preheat oven to 350°F (180°C)

13- by 9-inch (3 L) metal baking pan, bottom and sides greased, then bottom lined with parchment paper

1/2 cup	liquid honey	125 mL
1/2 cup	granulated sugar	125 mL
1/2 tsp	orange blossom water (see Tip, at left)	2 mL
1 cup	unsalted butter	250 mL
3 cups	walnut halves or pieces	750 mL
2 cups	semisweet chocolate chips	500 mL
1/3 cup	packed light brown sugar	75 mL
1 tsp	ground cinnamon	5 mL
1	package (1 lb/500 g) phyllo dough, thawed	1

1. In a saucepan over medium-high heat, combine 3/4 cup (175 mL) water, honey and sugar and bring to a simmer. Reduce heat to medium and simmer for 10 minutes or until reduced and syrupy. Stir in orange blossom water. Set aside and let cool.

2. In a small saucepan, melt butter over low heat. Skim off foam and discard. Remove saucepan from heat and set aside.

3. In a food processor fitted with a metal blade, pulse walnuts, chocolate chips, brown sugar and cinnamon, in batches if necessary, until finely ground.

4. Stack phyllo sheets on a lightly damp kitchen towel and cover loosely with plastic wrap. Place one sheet of phyllo in bottom of prepared pan and lightly brush with melted butter. Repeat with one-third of the remaining phyllo sheets, brushing each sheet with melted butter after placing in pan. Spread half of the nut mixture evenly over top. Brush next phyllo sheet on both sides with melted butter, placing on top of nuts. Add another one-third of phyllo sheets, brushing each with melted butter. Top with remaining nut mixture. Butter next phyllo sheet on both sides, placing on top of nuts. Top with remaining phyllo sheets, brushing each with melted butter. Drizzle any remaining melted butter over top.

5 Using a sharp knife, cut through pastry, making four cuts lengthwise to make five strips, then five cuts crosswise to make six strips, making 30 rectangles total. Bake in preheated oven for 40 to 45 minutes or until crisp and lightly golden. Remove baklava from oven and immediately pour cooled syrup over top. Let stand on a rack for several hours until cool and softened.

Cookies, Bars and Squares

Chocolate Butter Cookies 176

The Quintessential Chocolate Chip Cookie 177

Double Chocolate Chunkies 178

Triple Chocolate Chip Cookies 179

Raspberry Chocolate Chip Cookies 180

Pumpkin Chocolate Chip Cookies 181

Double Chocolate Mint Chunkers 182

Chocolate Chip Butterscotch Cookies 183

Julie's Chocolate Chip Espresso Cookies 184

Chocolate Cappuccino Chip Cookies 185

Slice-and-Bake Chocolate Chip Almond Cookies 186

Cowgirl Cookies 187

White Chocolate Chunk Fudge Cookies 188

Chocolate Almond Drops 190

Chocolate Almond Chews 191

Hazelnut Chocolate Cookies 192

Cinnamon Chocolate Crisps 193

Ginger Chocolate Molasses Cookies 194

Chocolate Salt and Pepper Cookies 196

Chocolate Coconut Clouds 197

Chocolate-Dipped Coconut Macaroons 198

Chocolate Mint Sandwich Cookies 199

Ice Cream Cookie Cups 200

Chocolate Cappuccino Creams 202

Double Chocolate Dips 204

Chocolate Chip Madeleines 205

Chocolate Tea Cakes 206

Chocolate Chip Meringues 207

Brown Sugar Shortbread 208

Ginger Chocolate Shortbread 209

Chocolate Cherry Biscotti 210

Chocolate Chip Orange Biscotti 211

Snickerdoodle Chip Biscotti 212

White Chocolate Almond Chunk Biscotti 213

Vegan Chocolate Espresso Brownies 214

Double Fudge Espresso Brownies 216

Rum Raisin Spoon Brownies 217

Banana Blondies with Chocolate Chips and Walnuts 218

Butterscotch Pecan Chocolate Chip Blondies 219

Chocolate Brittle Bars 220

Oat Bars 221

Chocolate Chip Cherry Bars 222

Raspberry Chocolate Chip Bars 223

Chocolate Chip Spice Bars with Maple Glaze 224

White Chocolate Sesame Shortbread Bars 226

Chocolate Almond Bars 227

Almond Caramel Bars 228

Chocolate Almond Graham Bars 229

Chocolate Caramel Bars 230

Six-Layer Bars 232

Vancouver Bars 233

Chocolate Butter Cookies

These are buttery, crumbly, melt-in-your-mouth cookies with a tender, lightly sweet bittersweet chocolate flavor. They are a perfect complement to a cup of tea. I like to include them on a cookie platter.

TIPS

Make sure the cookies are completely cooled before removing them from the baking sheet, as they are very fragile.

If you're not going to eat all of these cookies within a day or two of baking them, freeze the extras in resealable plastic freezer bags for up to 2 weeks.

Preheat oven to 350°F (180°C)
Baking sheets, lined with parchment paper

1 cup	all-purpose flour	250 mL
1/2 cup	cornstarch	125 mL
1/2 cup	unsweetened Dutch-process cocoa powder	125 mL
1/8 tsp	salt	0.5 mL
1 cup	unsalted butter, at room temperature	250 mL
1 cup	confectioner's (icing) sugar	250 mL
1/2 cup	semisweet chocolate chips	125 mL
	Confectioner's (icing) sugar, sifted, for dusting	

1. In a small bowl, sift together flour, cornstarch, cocoa powder and salt.

2. In another bowl, using electric mixer, beat butter and 1 cup (250 mL) confectioner's sugar until light and fluffy. Add flour mixture, mixing until smooth. Stir in chocolate chips.

3. Scoop batter by tablespoons (15 mL) and, using your hands, roll into balls. Place on prepared baking sheets, 2 to 3 inches (5 to 7.5 cm) apart. Using the heel of your hand, lightly flatten tops. Bake in preheated oven for 10 to 12 minutes or until firm around edges and a faint indentation is left when touched on top.

4. Generously sprinkle hot cookies with confectioner's sugar. Let cookies cool completely on baking sheets on racks.

Variation
Add up to 5 oz (150 g) chopped bittersweet or semisweet chocolate to the batter. Or you can sandwich the baked and cooled cookies together with melted semisweet chocolate in the middle.

The Quintessential Chocolate Chip Cookie

I have made thousands of chocolate chip cookies in my life. They often take on a life of their own, coming out differently depending on ingredients used, time of year, altitude, oven temperature variations and, of course, my presence of mind. This recipe has never let me down — thus the boastful name. Your taste buds will appreciate the 100% pure ingredients and love that went into these melt-in-your-mouth cookies.

TIP

For a more intense walnut flavor, toast the nuts before adding to the batter. Simply spread the nuts on a rimmed baking sheet and bake in a preheated 350°F (180°C) oven until lightly browned and fragrant, about 8 to 10 minutes. Let cool before mixing into batter.

Preheat oven to 350°F (180°C)
Baking sheets, lined with parchment paper

3 cups	all-purpose flour	750 mL
1 tsp	baking powder	5 mL
$1/4$ tsp	salt	1 mL
1 cup	unsalted butter, at room temperature	250 mL
$2^{1}/_3$ cups	packed light brown sugar	575 mL
2 tsp	vanilla	10 mL
2	eggs	2
2 cups	semisweet chocolate chips	500 mL
$1^{1}/_2$ cups	walnut pieces, toasted	375 mL

1. In a medium bowl, combine flour, baking powder and salt.

2. In a large bowl, using electric mixer, beat butter and sugar until light and fluffy. Add vanilla, mixing well. Add eggs, one at a time, beating well after each addition. Add flour mixture and beat just until combined. Fold in chocolate chips and walnuts.

3. Drop by $1/4$-cup (50 mL) measure on prepared baking sheets, about 2 inches (5 cm) apart. Bake in preheated oven for 15 to 20 minutes or until puffed and pale golden. Cookies will still be soft to the touch in center and look somewhat undercooked. Let cool completely on pans on racks.

Variation
Substitute macadamia nuts for the walnuts.

Double Chocolate Chunkies

This is a traditional chocolate chip cookie with an edgy twist. Always one to buck tradition (as I did when I proposed to my husband — but that's another story), I figured that a double dose of chocolate (after all, this is a chocolate book), with some pecans and raisins thrown in for good measure, would make one delicious cookie. Lo and behold, I was right. I'm really having too much fun with this!

TIP

To toast pecans: Preheat oven to 350°F (180°C). Spread pecans on baking sheet, lined with parchment paper, and bake for 8 to 10 minutes or until lightly browned.

Preheat oven to 350°F (180°C)
Baking sheets, lined with parchment paper

2$\frac{1}{2}$ cups	all-purpose flour	625 mL
$\frac{1}{2}$ cup	unsweetened Dutch-process cocoa powder, sifted	125 mL
1 tsp	ground cinnamon	5 mL
$\frac{1}{2}$ tsp	baking soda	2 mL
$\frac{1}{2}$ tsp	salt	2 mL
1$\frac{1}{2}$ cups	packed light brown sugar	375 mL
1 cup	unsalted butter, at room temperature	250 mL
1	egg	1
1 tbsp	vanilla	15 mL
2 cups	semisweet chocolate chips	500 mL
1$\frac{1}{2}$ cups	pecan halves, broken or coarsely chopped, toasted (see Tip, at left)	375 mL
$\frac{1}{2}$ cup	raisins	125 mL

1. In a medium bowl, mix together flour, cocoa powder, cinnamon, baking soda and salt.

2. In a large bowl, using electric mixer, beat brown sugar and butter until light and fluffy. Beat in egg and vanilla, beating until smooth. Add flour mixture, mixing just until blended. Stir in chocolate chips, pecans and raisins.

3. Scoop batter with $\frac{1}{4}$-cup (50 mL) measure and, using your hands, roll into balls. Place on prepared baking sheets, about 3 inches (7.5 cm) apart. Bake in preheated oven for 15 to 20 minutes or until puffed and firm around edges but still slightly soft to the touch. Let cool on baking sheets on racks until almost cool. Transfer to rack and let cool completely.

Triple Chocolate Chip Cookies

MAKES ABOUT 24 LARGE COOKIES

With a triple chocolate punch, this cookie is a knockout. They didn't even last the first round out of the oven at my house. My children thought that they were "the bomb" and ate them by the handful.

TIP

For smaller cookies, scoop the batter by tablespoons (15 mL) instead of a 1/4-cup (50 mL) measure, placing about 2 inches (5 cm) apart and reducing the baking time to 8 to 10 minutes or until puffed and lightly golden (they will still be soft to the touch in the center and look somewhat undercooked).

Baking sheets, lined with parchment paper

2 1/4 cups	all-purpose flour	550 mL
1 tsp	baking soda	5 mL
1/2 tsp	salt	2 mL
1 cup	unsalted butter, melted and cooled slightly	250 mL
3/4 cup	packed light brown sugar	175 mL
3/4 cup	granulated sugar	175 mL
2 tsp	vanilla	10 mL
2	eggs	2
1 cup	semisweet chocolate chips	250 mL
5 oz	milk chocolate, coarsely chopped	150 g
5 oz	white chocolate, coarsely chopped	150 g

1. In a medium bowl, mix together flour, baking soda and salt.

2. In a large bowl, beat together melted butter, light brown and granulated sugars and vanilla. Add eggs, one at a time, beating well after each addition. Add flour mixture and beat just until combined. Fold in chocolate chips and milk and white chocolates. Refrigerate dough for 30 minutes.

3. Preheat oven to 350°F (180°C). Scoop batter with 1/4-cup (50 mL) measure or ice cream scoop and place on prepared baking sheets, about 3 inches (7.5 cm) apart.

4. Bake in preheated oven for 14 to 16 minutes or until cookies are puffed and lightly golden (they will still be soft to the touch in the center and look somewhat undercooked). Let cookies cool completely on baking sheets on racks.

Raspberry Chocolate Chip Cookies

MAKES ABOUT
38 COOKIES

These cookies are delicate, slightly sweet and make a perfect accompaniment to afternoon tea. At home, we call them Sydney Janes because the above adjectives describe my daughter, Sydney, to a tee.

TIP
These cookies freeze well for about 1 month in resealable freezer bags.

Preheat oven to 350°F (180°C)
Baking sheets, lined with parchment paper

1 cup	unsalted butter, at room temperature	250 mL
$2/3$ cup	granulated sugar	150 mL
1 tsp	almond extract	5 mL
$1/2$ tsp	vanilla	2 mL
2 cups	all-purpose flour	500 mL
$1/4$ cup	raspberry jam	50 mL
	Semisweet chocolate chips	
	Confectioner's (icing) sugar	

1. In a large bowl, using electric mixer, beat butter and sugar until light and fluffy. Add almond extract and vanilla, beating until well mixed. Add flour and mix until incorporated.

2. Drop by tablespoonfuls (15 mL) or with $1^{1}/_{4}$-inch (3 cm) cookie scoop on prepared baking sheets, about 2 inches (2.5 cm) apart. (If using a spoon, roll scoops into balls in the palms of your hands.) Using your thumb or the end of a wooden spoon, make a well in the center of each cookie (pressing down three-quarters of the way through cookie). Using two small spoons, fill wells with jam and sprinkle three chocolate chips on top of each.

3. Bake in preheated oven for 15 minutes or until slightly firm to the touch but still somewhat pale in color. Let cool completely on pans on racks. Dust cooled cookies lightly with confectioner's sugar.

Variation
Substitute apricot jam for the raspberry.

Pumpkin Chocolate Chip Cookies

MAKES ABOUT 48 COOKIES

These cookies are my son Noah's absolute favorite. We used to make them every Halloween but decided that they were too delicious to enjoy only once a year. There's only one trick for making these cookies year-round: maintain a supply of canned pumpkin in your pantry.

TIP

I love parchment paper! It's a grease- and heat-resistant paper used to line baking pans. It keeps your baked goods from sticking and burning and makes cleanup a breeze.

Preheat oven to 350°F (180°C)
Baking sheets, lined with parchment paper

2 cups	all purpose-flour	500 mL
2 tsp	ground cinnamon	10 mL
1 tsp	baking soda	5 mL
1/8 tsp	salt	0.5 mL
1 cup	unsalted butter, at room temperature	250 mL
1 cup	granulated sugar	250 mL
1/2 cup	packed light brown sugar	125 mL
1	egg	1
1 cup	canned pumpkin purée (not pie filling)	250 mL
1 tsp	vanilla	5 mL
2 cups	semisweet chocolate chips	500 mL
	Granulated sugar, for rolling	

1. In a medium bowl, combine flour, cinnamon, baking soda and salt.

2. In a large bowl, using electric mixer, beat butter and granulated and brown sugars until fluffy. Beat in egg, mixing well. Add pumpkin and vanilla until blended. Add flour mixture and beat just until combined. Stir in chocolate chips.

3. Scoop dough by tablespoons (15 mL) and roll in sugar. Place balls on prepared baking sheets, about 2 inches (5 cm) apart. Bake in preheated oven for 10 to 12 minutes or until cookies are set around edges. Let cool completely on pans on racks.

Variation
Add 3/4 cup (175 mL) coarsely chopped walnuts.

Double Chocolate Mint Chunkers

MAKES ABOUT 30 COOKIES

I have watched people clamber over each other for these cookies. A dark chocolate butter cookie studded with semisweet and mint chocolate chips makes for a treat that's worth fighting for.

TIPS

These cookies are best the day they are made. They don't freeze particularly well.

You can find mint baking chips in most well-stocked grocery stores. If you can't find them, substitute chocolate mint chips.

Preheat oven to 350°F (180°C)
Baking sheets, lined with parchment paper

2 cups	all-purpose flour	500 mL
1¼ cups	unsweetened Dutch-process cocoa powder, sifted	300 mL
1 tsp	baking powder	5 mL
¼ tsp	salt	1 mL
1¼ cups	unsalted butter, at room temperature	300 mL
2 cups	granulated sugar	500 mL
2	eggs	2
2 tsp	vanilla	10 mL
1 tsp	peppermint extract	5 mL
1½ cups	semisweet chocolate chips	375 mL
1½ cups	mint baking chips (see Tips, left)	375 mL

1. In a medium bowl, combine flour, cocoa powder, baking powder and salt.

2. In a large bowl, using electric mixer, beat butter and sugar until light and fluffy. Add eggs, one at a time, beating well after each addition. Add vanilla and peppermint extract, mixing well. Add flour mixture and beat just until blended. Stir in chocolate and mint chips.

3. Using 2-tbsp (25 mL) or ⅛-cup (25 mL) measure or ice cream scoop, drop dough on prepared baking sheets, about 3 inches (7.5 cm) apart. Bake in preheated oven for 16 to 17 minutes or until cookies are puffed and starting to crack. They will still be soft to the touch in the center and look somewhat undercooked. Let cool completely on pans on racks.

Variation
Substitute semisweet chocolate chips for the mint baking chips.

Chocolate Chip Butterscotch Cookies

Although this recipe makes a lot of cookies, they freeze beautifully so that you always have cookies at the ready. But they're so melt-in-your-mouth good, they'll probably never make it to the freezer. We named these cookies Jay's Addiction at our bakery because my husband, Jay, can never get enough of them!

TIP

Make sure you don't overbake the cookies as they really do need to be slightly underbaked for the best results.

Preheat oven to 350°F (180°C)
Baking sheets, lined with parchment paper

3 1/3 cups	all-purpose flour	825 mL
2 tsp	ground cinnamon	10 mL
1 tsp	ground ginger	5 mL
1 tsp	baking soda	5 mL
1/2 tsp	ground nutmeg	2 mL
3/4 cup	unsalted butter, at room temperature	175 mL
1 cup	packed light brown sugar	250 mL
2/3 cup	granulated sugar	150 mL
2	eggs	2
2 tsp	vanilla	10 mL
1 1/2 cups	semisweet chocolate chips	375 mL
2/3 cup	butterscotch chips	150 mL
2 cups	confectioner's (icing) sugar	500 mL

1. In a medium bowl, combine flour, cinnamon, ginger, baking soda and nutmeg.

2. In a large bowl, using electric mixer, beat butter and brown and granulated sugars until light and fluffy. Add eggs, one at a time, beating well after each addition. Beat in vanilla. Add flour mixture, beating just until combined. Fold in chocolate and butterscotch chips.

3. Scoop dough by tablespoons (15 mL) and roll in confectioner's sugar. Place cookies on prepared baking sheets, about 2 inches (5 cm) apart. Bake in preheated oven for 12 to 14 minutes or until puffed and pale golden. They will still be soft to the touch in center and look somewhat undercooked. Let cool completely on pans on racks.

> **Variation**
> Omit the butterscotch baking chips, increasing semisweet chocolate chips to 2 cups (500 mL).

Julie's Chocolate Chip Espresso Cookies

I find myself craving these cookies as much as I crave my morning coffee. Caffeine lovers, beware! This one haunts me in my dreams.

TIP

When measuring, always remember to spoon your dry ingredients into the cup and level the top by scraping across it with the flat side of a knife or skewer. This will give you an accurate measurement.

Preheat oven to 350°F (180°C)

Baking sheets, lined with parchment paper

3 cups	all-purpose flour	750 mL
1 tbsp	ground cinnamon	15 mL
$1/2$ tsp	baking soda	2 mL
$1/4$ tsp	salt	1 mL
$1 1/2$ cups	packed light brown sugar	375 mL
1 cup	unsalted butter, at room temperature	250 mL
2 tsp	vanilla	10 mL
1 tsp	grated orange zest	5 mL
1	egg	1
4 tsp	instant espresso or coffee granules	20 mL
2 cups	semisweet chocolate chips or chunks	500 mL

1. In a medium bowl, mix together flour, cinnamon, baking soda and salt. Set aside.

2. In a large bowl, using electric mixer, beat brown sugar and butter until light and fluffy. Beat in vanilla and orange zest. Add egg and instant espresso, beating until smooth. Add flour mixture, mixing just until blended. Stir in chocolate chips.

3. Scoop batter with $1/4$-cup (50 mL) measure or ice cream scoop and, using your hands, roll into balls. Place on prepared baking sheets, about 3 inches (7.5 cm) apart. Using the heel of your hand, lightly flatten tops. Bake in preheated oven for 15 to 20 minutes or until puffed but still slightly soft to the touch. Let cookies cool on baking sheets on racks until almost cool to the touch. Transfer to racks and let cool completely.

Chocolate Cappuccino Chip Cookies

Need to add some octane to your day? Here's your coffee disguised in another form. These cookies are rich, sweet and a tasty treat — perfect when you need an afternoon pick-me-up.

TIPS

Cocoa powder needs to be sifted before use because it can be very lumpy, which makes it difficult to incorporate. Use a fine-meshed sieve to remove any lumps before adding cocoa powder to other dry ingredients.

To bring cold butter to room temperature in a hurry, use a microwave oven. I usually set it on Medium (50%) for 10 to 20 seconds, making sure not to melt the butter.

Preheat oven to 350°F (180°C)
Baking sheets, lined with parchment paper

2¹⁄₂ cups	all-purpose flour	625 mL
¹⁄₂ cup	unsweetened Dutch-process cocoa powder, sifted	125 mL
1¹⁄₂ tbsp	ground cinnamon	22 mL
1 tbsp	instant coffee granules	15 mL
2 tsp	finely ground espresso or French-roast coffee	10 mL
1 tsp	baking powder	5 mL
1 tsp	baking soda	5 mL
¹⁄₄ tsp	salt	1 mL
1 cup	unsalted butter, at room temperature	250 mL
1¹⁄₂ cups	granulated sugar	375 mL
1 cup	packed light or medium brown sugar	250 mL
1 tsp	vanilla	5 mL
2	eggs	2
2 cups	semisweet chocolate chips	500 mL

1. In a medium bowl, combine flour, cocoa powder, cinnamon, instant coffee granules, finely ground coffee, baking powder, baking soda and salt.

2. In a large bowl, using electric mixer, beat butter and granulated and brown sugars until light and fluffy. Beat in vanilla. Add eggs, one at a time, beating well after each addition. Add flour mixture and beat just until combined. Fold in chocolate chips.

3. Scooping dough with a ¹⁄₄-cup (50 mL) ice cream scoop or by heaping tablespoons (15 mL), place dough on prepared baking sheets, about 3 inches (7.5 cm) apart. Bake in preheated oven for 12 minutes or until cookies are puffed and just slightly firm to the touch. They will still look somewhat undercooked. Let cool completely on pans on racks.

Slice-and-Bake Chocolate Chip Almond Cookies

MAKES ABOUT 60 COOKIES

These are fantastic to have on hand in the freezer. My husband, Jay, loves them for midnight snacks, but I love them for quick after-school treats or desserts.

TIP

To toast almonds: Preheat oven to 350°F (180°C). Spread nuts on a baking sheet lined with foil or parchment. Bake for 5 to 7 minutes or until light brown and fragrant.

Baking sheets, lined with parchment paper

2 1/4 cups	all-purpose flour	550 mL
1 tsp	baking soda	5 mL
1/4 tsp	salt	1 mL
1 cup	unsalted butter, at room temperature	250 mL
1 cup	granulated sugar	250 mL
1/2 cup	packed light brown sugar	125 mL
2	eggs	2
2 tsp	vanilla	10 mL
2 cups	semisweet chocolate chips	500 mL
1 cup	almonds, toasted and chopped (see Tip, at left)	250 mL
1/2 cup	sweetened flaked coconut	125 mL

1. In a medium bowl, combine flour, baking soda and salt.

2. In a large bowl, using electric mixer, beat butter and granulated and brown sugars until light and fluffy. Add eggs, one at a time, beating well after each addition. Beat in vanilla. Add flour mixture. Beat just until combined. Stir in chocolate chips, almonds and coconut.

3. Scrape out dough onto a work surface lined with plastic wrap. With lightly floured hands, form into 3 logs. Roll up individually in plastic wrap, then wrap in layer of foil. Freeze until firm. Dough can be frozen for up to 2 months.

4. When ready to bake, preheat oven to 350°F (180°C). Unwrap dough and slice into 1/2-inch (1 cm) thick rounds. Place on prepared baking sheets. Bake for 11 minutes or until light golden brown around edges and still pale and soft to the touch in the center. Let cool on pans on rack.

Variation
Substitute chopped macadamia nuts for the almonds.

Cowgirl Cookies

Cowgirls of the world, unite! This recipe is for you. Soft and chewy, these cookies are full of oats, raisins, chocolate chips and crisp rice cereal. Buckaroos will enjoy them, too.

TIP

I love parchment paper! It's a grease- and heat-resistant paper used to line baking pans. It keeps your baked goods from sticking and burning and makes cleanup a breeze.

Preheat oven to 350°F (180°C)
Baking sheets, lined with parchment paper

1½ cups	all-purpose flour	375 mL
1 tsp	baking powder	5 mL
¼ tsp	salt	1 mL
1 cup	unsalted butter, melted and cooled slightly	250 mL
1 cup	packed light brown sugar	250 mL
½ cup	granulated sugar	125 mL
2	eggs	2
1 tsp	vanilla	5 mL
2½ cups	old-fashioned rolled oats	625 mL
2 cups	semisweet chocolate chips	500 mL
1½ cups	crisp rice cereal	375 mL
1 cup	raisins	250 mL

1. In a small bowl, combine flour, baking powder and salt.

2. In a large bowl, using electric mixer, beat melted butter and brown and granulated sugars until blended. Add eggs, one at a time, beating well after each addition. Beat in vanilla. Add flour mixture and beat just until combined. Stir in oats, chocolate chips, cereal and raisins.

3. Drop by ¼-cup (50 mL) measure on prepared baking sheets, about 2 inches (5 cm) apart. Bake in preheated oven for 14 to 16 minutes or until puffed, light golden and somewhat soft to the touch. Let cool completely on pans on racks.

Variation
Substitute dried cranberries for the raisins.

White Chocolate Chunk Fudge Cookies

This is a delicious chocolaty treat. The cookies look like snowballs and stack perfectly on a cookie platter or dessert tray.

TIPS

To bring cold butter to room temperature in a hurry, use a microwave oven. I usually set it on Medium (50%) for 10 to 20 seconds, making sure not to melt the butter.

Use a cookie scoop for both consistency and a professional appearance. Your scones, cookies and muffins will bake more evenly if they are all the same size.

Preheat oven to 350°F (180°C)
Baking sheets, lined with parchment paper

2 cups	all-purpose flour	500 mL
1¼ cups	unsweetened Dutch-process cocoa powder, sifted	300 mL
1 tsp	baking powder	5 mL
¼ tsp	salt	1 mL
2 cups	granulated sugar	500 mL
1¼ cups	unsalted butter, at room temperature	300 mL
2	eggs	2
1 tbsp	vanilla	15 mL
1½ tsp	finely ground espresso or French-roast coffee	7 mL
9 oz	white chocolate, coarsely chopped	270 g
6 oz	semisweet chocolate, coarsely chopped	175 g
2 cups	confectioner's (icing) sugar, sifted	500 mL

1. In a medium bowl, mix together flour, cocoa powder, baking powder and salt.

2. In a large bowl, using electric mixer, beat sugar and butter until light and fluffy. Add eggs, one at a time, beating well after each addition. Add vanilla and ground coffee, beating well. Add flour mixture, beating just until flour is incorporated. Stir in white and semisweet chocolates.

These cookies are at their best the day they're made.

If baking more than one pan at a time, rotate the pans halfway through baking. Baking will take slightly longer. Adjust your baking time accordingly, relying on visual signs of doneness; generally, you will need to bake about 5 minutes longer.

3. Place confectioner's sugar in a bowl. Scoop batter with $\frac{1}{4}$-cup (50 mL) measure or ice cream scoop and, using your hands, roll into balls. Drop balls into confectioner's sugar. Coat balls well and place on prepared baking sheets, about 3 inches (7.5 cm) apart.

4. Bake in preheated oven for 16 to 17 minutes or until cookies are just puffed and starting to crack (they will still be soft to the touch in the center and look somewhat undercooked). Do not overbake. Let cool completely on baking sheet on a rack.

Variation
Substitute all white chocolate or semisweet chocolate for the chopped white and semisweet chocolates.

Chocolate Almond Drops

MAKES ABOUT
60 SMALL
COOKIES

These cookies are fabulous served with vanilla bean ice cream or a cup of espresso. The recipe goes together in a snap and yields a richly flavored cookie. As you can see, this makes a large batch of cookies. They freeze so well that I always keep some on hand. Louie, this one's for you.

TIPS

If you prefer a smaller quantity of cookies, you can easily cut the recipe in half.

To toast almonds: Preheat oven to 350°F (180°C). Spread nuts on a baking sheet lined with foil or parchment. Bake for 5 to 7 minutes or until light brown and fragrant.

Preheat oven to 350°F (180°C)
Baking sheets, lined with parchment paper

3 cups	whole almonds, toasted (see Tip, at left)	750 mL
1¼ cups	granulated sugar	300 mL
1 cup	semisweet chocolate chips	250 mL
4	egg whites	4
2 tsp	almond extract	10 mL

1. In a food processor fitted with a metal blade, grind almonds and sugar. Add chocolate chips and pulse until finely ground. Add egg whites and almond extract. Blend until smooth.

2. Drop by tablespoons (15 mL) or 1¼-inch (3 cm) cookie scoop onto prepared baking sheets, about 2 inches (5 cm) apart. Bake in preheated oven for 35 minutes or until firm, puffed and slightly cracked. Let cookies cool completely on pans on racks.

Chocolate Almond Chews

MAKES ABOUT 29 COOKIES

When I was a child, there was an ice cream shop called Will Wright's that had the best chewy almond macaroons. The longer the cookies sat, the better they got. If there was moisture in the air, the crust got soft yet maintained a chewy consistency. I crave these cookies regularly, but unfortunately the shop closed years ago. This is my chocolate version of the cookies, made entirely from memory, which I think, this time, served me well.

TIPS

These cookies will be somewhat soft to the touch.

Store cookies in an airtight container at room temperature for up to 2 days.

Preheat oven to 350°F (180°C)

Baking sheets, lined with parchment paper

4 oz	bittersweet or semisweet chocolate	125 g
7 oz	almond paste	210 g
1/3 cup	confectioner's (icing) sugar	75 mL
1/3 cup	granulated sugar	75 mL
1 tbsp	all-purpose flour	15 mL
1/2 tsp	almond extract	2 mL
2	egg whites	2

1. In a microwave-safe bowl, microwave chocolate on Medium (50%) for 1 to $1\frac{1}{2}$ minutes, stirring every 30 seconds, or until chocolate is soft and almost melted. Stir until completely melted and smooth. Let cool slightly.

2. In a food processor fitted with a metal blade, process almond paste until floury. Add confectioner's and granulated sugars, flour and almond extract and pulse several times. Add melted chocolate, pulsing until blended. Add egg whites and process until smooth.

3. Scoop batter by heaping tablespoons (15 mL) or with small ice cream scoop and place on prepared baking sheets, about 2 inches (5 cm) apart. With a lightly moistened fingertip, smooth tops of cookies. Bake in preheated oven for 15 minutes or until puffed, cracked and still soft to the touch in the center. Let cookies cool completely on baking sheets on racks.

Hazelnut Chocolate Cookies

MAKES ABOUT
22 COOKIES

This is a fantastic wheat-free cookie. It's perfect for those who cannot tolerate wheat or for Passover, when no wheat (unless kosher for Passover) is eaten. I love them with a cup of tea or as a garnish for sorbet.

TIPS

To toast hazelnuts: Place hazelnuts in a single layer on a foil or parchment-lined baking sheet. Bake in center of preheated 350°F (180°C) oven for 10 to 15 minutes or until lightly browned and skins are blistered. Wrap nuts in a clean dry kitchen towel and let stand for 1 minute. Rub nuts in towel to remove loose skins (it's okay if you can't remove all of them). Let nuts cool completely.

If you prefer a crunchier cookie, bake 1 or 2 minutes longer. If you prefer a chewier cookie, bake 1 or 2 minutes less.

Preheat oven to 325°F (160°C)
Baking sheets, lined with parchment paper

1 cup	chopped hazelnuts, toasted (see Tip, at left)	250 mL
2/3 cup	granulated sugar	150 mL
2 oz	bittersweet or semisweet chocolate, chopped	60 g
1/4 tsp	salt	1 mL
1	egg	1

1. In a food processor fitted with a metal blade, pulse nuts, sugar, chocolate and salt until finely chopped. Add egg, pulsing until mixture forms a coarse paste.

2. Scoop batter by tablespoons (15 mL) or with small ice cream scoop and place on prepared baking sheets, about 2 inches (5 cm) apart. Lightly press down tops of cookies.

3. Bake in preheated oven for 15 to 20 minutes or until cookies are puffed, cracked and just slightly firm to the touch. Let cookies cool completely on baking sheet on a rack.

Variation
Substitute other nuts for the hazelnuts, such as pistachios or almonds.

Cinnamon Chocolate Crisps

MAKES ABOUT
40 COOKIES

One of the great things about baking from scratch is that you serve desserts that are unavailable in any store. I hear many heartfelt moans and sighs when people sink their teeth into these cookies. I live for those sounds. Make this recipe and you'll know what I'm talking about.

TIPS

For a beautiful hostess gift, break cookies into chunks and place in a cellophane bag and tie with a beautiful ribbon.

Make sure to store cookies in a cool place, as the chocolate will melt and become messy if it gets too warm.

Keep cookies in an airtight container in a cool place until ready to serve.

Pizzelle iron, preheated
Baking sheets, lined with parchment paper

1 1/2 cups	all-purpose flour	375 mL
1/4 cup	unsweetened Dutch-process cocoa powder, sifted	50 mL
2 tsp	baking powder	10 mL
1/2 tsp	ground cinnamon	2 mL
3	eggs	3
3/4 cup	granulated sugar	175 mL
1/2 cup	unsalted butter, melted and cooled slightly	125 mL
2 tsp	vanilla	10 mL
12 oz	semisweet chocolate, chopped	375 g

1. In a small bowl, mix together flour, cocoa powder, baking powder and cinnamon.

2. In a large bowl, whisk together eggs and sugar. Add butter and vanilla, whisking well. Whisk in flour mixture just until blended.

3. Scoop batter by tablespoons (15 mL) onto preheated pizzelle iron. Cook according to manufacturer's directions, 20 to 60 seconds per batch. Remove hot cookies and immediately place on a rack and let cool.

4. In a microwave-safe bowl, microwave chocolate on Medium (50%) for 1 to 2 minutes, stirring every 30 seconds, or until chocolate is soft and almost melted. Stir until completely melted and smooth.

5. When cookies are cool and crisp, spread melted chocolate on half of the cookies. Top with remaining cookies and place on prepared baking sheets. Place baking sheets in refrigerator until chocolate has hardened and is firm to the touch. Break cookies into medium–size pieces before serving.

Ginger Chocolate Molasses Cookies

I've made thousands of these cookies at my bakery, and this recipe has never let me down. Sweet, spicy and chewy, with a granulated sugar topping, this cookie's a star. Ginger lovers, this one's for you!

TIPS

Try crumbling these cookies over chocolate pudding.

Line your baking sheets with parchment paper for blissful baking. It will keep your baked goods from sticking, making cleanup a snap.

Preheat oven to 350°F (180°C)
Baking sheets, lined with parchment paper

2 cups	all-purpose flour	500 mL
1 tbsp	ground ginger	15 mL
2 tsp	baking soda	10 mL
1 tsp	ground cinnamon	5 mL
1 tsp	ground allspice	5 mL
1/2 tsp	salt	2 mL
4 oz	unsweetened chocolate, chopped	125 g
1 cup	granulated sugar	250 mL
3/4 cup	vegetable oil	175 mL
1/4 cup	fancy molasses	50 mL
1	egg	1
1/2 cup	finely chopped candied ginger	125 mL

Topping

1 1/2 cups	granulated sugar	375 mL

1. In a medium bowl, mix together flour, ground ginger, baking soda, cinnamon, allspice and salt.

2. In a microwave-safe bowl, microwave chocolate on Medium (50%) for 1 to 1 1/2 minutes, stirring every 30 seconds, or until chocolate is soft and almost melted. Stir until completely melted and smooth. Let cool slightly.

TIPS

Make sure your cookies and scones are evenly spaced on the pan to allow room for spreading and rising. Place them 2 to 3 inches (5 to 7.5 cm) apart.

Let your baking pans cool thoroughly before reusing for your next batch.

3. In a large bowl, beat together sugar, oil and molasses. Beat in melted chocolate. Stir in egg. Add flour mixture, beating until smooth. Add candied ginger, mixing until smooth.

4. Scoop batter by heaping tablespoons (15 mL) and, using your hands, roll into balls.

5. *Topping:* Roll balls in sugar. Place on prepared baking sheets, about 2 inches (5 cm) apart. Bake in preheated oven for 15 minutes or until puffed and cracked on tops. Let cookies cool completely on baking sheets on racks.

Variation
For a spicier cookie, increase the ground ginger to 2 tbsp (25 mL).

Chocolate Salt and Pepper Cookies

- -

MAKES ABOUT 24 LARGE COOKIES

Okay, stop scratching your head wondering why you would make cookies with salt and pepper. The answer lies, of course, in the psyche of your palate. The salt counterbalances the sweetness of the chocolate, and the pepper gives the cookies just a bit of a bite that will send your taste buds into a tizzy. Trust me that no one will be able to guess the secret ingredients. I am constantly getting requests for this recipe.

TIP

You can increase or decrease the pepper depending on your taste. If you like slightly less bite, decrease the white pepper to 1 tsp (5 mL). If you like more of a bite, you can increase the black pepper by $^1/_2$ to 1 tsp (2 to 5 mL). These cookies are best eaten the day they're made.

Preheat oven to 350°F (180°C)
Baking sheets, lined with parchment paper

2 cups	all-purpose flour	500 mL
$1^1/_4$ cups	unsweetened Dutch-process cocoa powder, sifted	300 mL
2 tsp	finely ground white pepper	10 mL
1 tsp	finely ground black pepper	5 mL
1 tsp	baking powder	5 mL
$^3/_4$ tsp	salt	4 mL
$1^3/_4$ cups	packed light brown sugar	425 mL
$1^1/_4$ cups	unsalted butter, at room temperature	300 mL
2 tsp	vanilla	10 mL
2	eggs	2
2 cups	semisweet chocolate chips	500 mL

1. In a medium bowl, mix together flour, cocoa powder, white and black peppers, baking powder and salt.

2. In a large bowl, using electric mixer, beat brown sugar and butter until light and fluffy. Add vanilla, mixing well. Add eggs, one at a time, beating well after each addition. Add flour mixture, beating just until blended. Stir in chocolate chips.

3. Scoop batter with $^1/_4$-cup (50 mL) measure or ice cream scoop and place on prepared baking sheets, about 3 inches (7.5 cm) apart. Bake in preheated oven for 15 to 17 minutes or until cookies are puffed and starting to crack (they will still be soft to the touch in the center and look somewhat undercooked). Let cool completely on baking sheets on racks.

Variation

Substitute white chocolate chips for the semisweet chocolate chips.

Chocolate Coconut Clouds

These chocolate cookies are the perfect size when you want something big and chocolaty. I like to serve them for dessert, lightly dusted with confectioner's sugar. But even without the dusting their taste and texture is so light and airy, just like a cloud. Alternatively, you can make these much smaller, scooping them by the teaspoon.

TIPS

Don't make these cookies on a rainy day, as the moisture will affect the cookies (they won't be crisp, but will be sticky instead). These cookies are best eaten the day they're made.

Do not remove these cookies from the baking sheets until they are completely cool. They are quite fragile and will break if you try to lift them off the parchment paper too early.

Preheat oven to 350°F (180°C)
Baking sheets, lined with parchment paper

8 oz	bittersweet chocolate, chopped	250 g
4	egg whites	4
3/4 cup	granulated sugar	175 mL
2 cups	packed sweetened flaked coconut	500 mL

1. In a microwave-safe bowl, microwave chocolate, uncovered, on Medium (50%) for 1 to 2 minutes, stirring every 30 seconds, or until chocolate is soft and almost melted. Stir until completely melted and smooth. Let cool slightly.

2. In a large bowl, using electric mixer, whip egg whites until soft peaks form. Gradually add sugar, whipping until stiff peaks form. Gently fold into chocolate just until blended. Fold in coconut.

3. Scoop batter with 1/4-cup (50 mL) measure and mound on prepared baking sheets, about 3 inches (7.5 cm) apart. Bake in preheated oven for 15 to 18 minutes or until puffed, cracked and lightly firm to the touch. Let cool completely on baking sheets on racks.

Chocolate-Dipped Coconut Macaroons

Imagine the Alps sitting on a river of chocolate and you will get an idea of what this cookie looks like — a huge mound of coconut perched atop a foundation of chocolate. It's like your favorite candy bar, but better!

TIP

Store macaroons in an airtight container at cool room temperature so the chocolate won't melt.

Preheat oven to 350°F (180°C)

Baking sheets, lined with parchment paper

3 cups	packed shredded sweetened coconut (about 15 oz/435 g)	750 mL
1/2 cup	granulated sugar	125 mL
6 tbsp	all-purpose flour	90 mL
4	egg whites	4
2 tsp	vanilla	10 mL
1/2 cup	semisweet chocolate chips	125 mL
10 oz	semisweet or bittersweet chocolate, chopped	300 g

1. In a large bowl, using electric mixer, combine coconut, sugar and flour. Add egg whites and vanilla, beating until well mixed. Stir in chocolate chips.

2. Using a 2-inch (5 cm) diameter ice cream scoop or 1/4-cup (50 mL) measure, place mounds of dough on prepared baking sheets, about 2 inches (5 cm) apart. Bake in preheated oven for 15 to 18 minutes or until tops are puffed and golden brown. Cookies will still be moist in center. Let cool completely on pans on racks.

3. In a microwave-safe bowl, microwave chopped chocolate on Medium for 3 to 4 minutes, stirring often, until melted, smooth and warm. Do not overheat. Dip bottoms of cooled macaroons into melted chocolate. Place on baking sheets lined with parchment paper or waxed paper. Refrigerate until chocolate is set.

Chocolate Mint Sandwich Cookies

MAKES ABOUT 24 COOKIE SANDWICHES

These rustic-looking cookie sandwiches are absolutely delightful. Not too sweet, yet full of bittersweet chocolate mint flavor, they are well worth the effort.

TIP

These cookies are best eaten the day they are made but will keep, frozen, for up to 3 weeks.

Preheat oven to 350°F (180°C)
Baking sheets, lined with parchment paper

1$\frac{1}{2}$ cups	all-purpose flour	375 mL
$\frac{3}{4}$ cup	unsweetened Dutch-process cocoa powder, sifted	175 mL
$\frac{1}{4}$ tsp	salt	1 mL
$\frac{3}{4}$ cup	unsalted butter, at room temperature	175 mL
1 cup	granulated sugar	250 mL
1	egg	1
1 tsp	vanilla	5 mL
	Granulated sugar for topping	

Filling

$\frac{1}{4}$ cup	whipping (35%) cream	50 mL
1 cup	semisweet chocolate chips	250 mL
$\frac{1}{2}$ tsp	peppermint extract	2 mL

1. In a medium bowl, combine flour, cocoa powder and salt.

2. In a large bowl, using electric mixer, beat butter and sugar until light and fluffy. Add egg and vanilla, beating until smooth. Add flour mixture and beat just until blended.

3. Drop by tablespoons (15 mL) or 1$\frac{1}{4}$-inch (3 cm) cookie scoop on prepared baking sheets, about 2 inches (5 cm) apart. Dip the heel of your hand in sugar and lightly flatten cookies into 2-inch (5 cm) rounds. Bake in preheated oven for 12 to 15 minutes or until dry to the touch. Let cool completely on pans on racks.

4. *Filling:* In a microwave-safe bowl, combine cream and chocolate chips. Microwave on High for 1 to 1$\frac{1}{2}$ minutes, stirring every 30 seconds, until chocolate is shiny and almost melted. Stir until smooth. Stir in peppermint extract. Set aside to cool slightly.

5. Spread filling on half of the cookies. Top with remaining cookies. Refrigerate until filling is firm, about 20 minutes.

Ice Cream Cookie Cups

Homemade ice cream cups are easy and fun and will inspire you to concoct your own favorite filling. They are fabulous cookies even without the ice cream or filled with chocolate mousse. You have to use a pizzelle iron for this recipe. Look for pizzelle irons in kitchen, home or department stores or on the Internet. You might even find one in your grandmother's cupboard.

TIP

I love parchment paper! It's a grease- and heat-resistant paper used to line baking pans. It keeps your baked goods from sticking and burning and makes cleanup a breeze.

Pizzelle iron, preheated
Baking sheets, lined with parchment paper

1³/₄ cups	all-purpose flour	425 mL
2 tsp	baking powder	10 mL
3	eggs	3
³/₄ cup	granulated sugar	175 mL
¹/₂ cup	unsalted butter, melted and cooled slightly	125 mL
1 tsp	vanilla	5 mL
¹/₂ tsp	almond extract	2 mL
12 oz	bittersweet or semisweet chocolate, chopped	375 g
	Ice cream	

1. In a small bowl, mix together flour and baking powder.

2. In a large bowl, whisk together eggs and sugar. Add butter, vanilla and almond extract, whisking well. Whisk in dry ingredients until blended.

3. Scoop batter by tablespoons (15 mL) onto preheated pizzelle iron. Cook according to manufacturer's directions, 20 to 60 seconds per batch. Remove hot cookies and immediately drape over an upside-down small bowl or cup. Transfer slightly cooled and shaped cookie cups to a rack and let cool completely.

Before dipping them in chocolate, you can freeze these cups in an airtight container for up to 2 days. Wrap them carefully, as they are very fragile.

I also like to twist the hot cookies into cones. Dip the bottoms into the melted chocolate, let harden and serve filled with chocolate ice cream or mousse.

The cookie cups are best served the day they're made.

4. In a microwave-safe bowl, microwave chocolate on Medium (50%) for 1 to 2 minutes, stirring every 30 seconds, or until chocolate is soft and almost melted. Stir until completely melted and smooth. Drizzle cooled cookie cups with melted chocolate and place on prepared baking sheets. Place baking sheets in refrigerator until chocolate has hardened. Keep cookie cups in an airtight container in a cool place until ready to serve. Fill with a scoop of ice cream just before serving.

Variation
Instead of drizzling chocolate over the cups, spread a blob of melted chocolate in the bottom of each cup, creating a chocolate-bottom cookie cup.

Chocolate Cappuccino Creams

I can never get enough chocolate and cappuccino. Here, you can have them both all swirled up into one. I love to serve these for dessert — they're a really fun twist on a childhood favorite.

TIPS

Cocoa powder needs to be sifted before use because it can be very lumpy, which makes it difficult to incorporate. Use a fine-meshed sieve to remove any lumps before adding cocoa powder to other dry ingredients.

To bring cold butter to room temperature in a hurry, use a microwave oven. I usually set it on Medium (50%) for 10 to 20 seconds, making sure not to melt the butter.

Preheat oven to 350°F (180°C)
Baking sheets, lined with parchment paper or greased

1 1/2 cups	all-purpose flour	375 mL
3/4 cup	unsweetened Dutch-process cocoa powder, sifted	175 mL
1/4 tsp	salt	1 mL
1 1/3 cups	granulated sugar	325 mL
3/4 cup	unsalted butter, at room temperature	175 mL
1	egg	1
1 tsp	vanilla	5 mL

Filling

1 cup	unsalted butter, at room temperature	250 mL
1 cup	confectioner's (icing) sugar, sifted	250 mL
1 tbsp	instant coffee granules	15 mL
1 tsp	vanilla	5 mL
1 tsp	milk	5 mL

1. In a medium bowl, mix together flour, cocoa powder and salt. Set aside.

2. In a large bowl, using electric mixer, beat sugar and butter until light and fluffy. Add egg and vanilla and beat until smooth. Add dry ingredients and beat just until smooth.

3. Scoop batter by tablespoons (15 mL) and, using your hands, roll into balls. Place on prepared baking sheets, about 2 inches (5 cm) apart. Using the heel of your hand, lightly flatten each cookie into 2-inch (5 cm) rounds. Bake in preheated oven for about 15 minutes or until cookies are dry to the touch. Let cookies cool completely on baking sheets on racks.

If you don't eat these all
at once, refrigerate them
in an airtight container
for up to 2 days.

Either an electric or a
hand mixer will work just
fine to make the filling.

4. *Filling:* In a medium bowl, using electric mixer, whip butter and confectioner's sugar until light and creamy.

5. In a very small bowl, mix together instant coffee, vanilla and milk. Add to butter mixture and whip until fluffy.

6. Spread half of cookies with filling. Top with remaining cookies. Refrigerate for 20 minutes or until centers are firm.

Variation
For a vanilla filling, omit the instant coffee.

Double Chocolate Dips

MAKES 12 DIPS

Milk is not the only thing to dip your chocolate sandwich cookies in. This very simple sweet can be assembled at the drop of a hat. I always stock the ingredients for this recipe in my pantry (along with loads of chocolate) so that I'm ready to go at a moment's notice.

TIPS

When toasting a small amount of nuts, I like to use a nonstick skillet. Toast them in the pan over medium heat, stirring often, for 3 to 5 minutes or until lightly toasted.

These cookies are best eaten the day they're made.

Baking sheet, lined with parchment paper

6 oz	semisweet chocolate, chopped	175 g
12	chocolate sandwich cookies	12
1/3 cup	sliced almonds, lightly toasted (see Tip, at left)	75 mL

1. In a large microwave-safe bowl, microwave chocolate, uncovered, on Medium (50%) for 1 to 2 minutes, stirring every 30 seconds, or until chocolate is soft and almost melted. Stir until completely melted and smooth.

2. Dip half of each sandwich cookie into melted chocolate. Place dipped cookies on prepared baking sheet. Sprinkle nuts over melted chocolate.

3. Refrigerate cookies for 1 hour or until chocolate is firm.

Variation

Substitute bittersweet or white chocolate for the semisweet chocolate.

Another fun twist is to substitute peanut butter sandwich cookies for the chocolate cookies.

Chocolate Chip Madeleines

Vive la France for sharing these infamous little cake-like cookies, made popular by Marcel Proust in his *Remembrance of Things Past.* You won't have to travel to France to find these gems, because these madeleines are imported right from your kitchen. Look for madeleine pans in kitchen stores and catalogs.

TIP

This dough will keep very well in the refrigerator for up to 1 week, so bake only what you need and refrigerate the rest. Cookies are best eaten the day they are made. Store in an airtight container.

Preheat oven to 350°F (180°C)
Madeleine pans, greased

1 cup	unsalted butter, at room temperature	250 mL
2 1/4 cups	confectioner's (icing) sugar, sifted	550 mL
4	eggs	4
1 tbsp	grated orange zest	15 mL
1/2 tsp	vanilla	2 mL
1/2 tsp	almond extract	2 mL
1 2/3 cups	all-purpose flour	400 mL
3/4 cup	semisweet chocolate chips	175 mL
	Confectioner's (icing) sugar, for dusting	

1. In a large bowl, using electric mixer, beat butter and sugar until light and fluffy (this might take a few minutes). Add eggs, one at a time, beating well after each addition. Add orange zest, vanilla and almond extract, beating until combined. Add flour, beating just until combined.

2. Scoop dough by scant tablespoons (15 mL) into prepared pans. Sprinkle each with about 1 tsp (5 mL) of the chocolate chips. Bake in preheated oven for 10 minutes or until just barely firm to the touch. Cookies will be very pale in color.

3. Unmold cookies onto a sheet of parchment or waxed paper, either by carefully flipping over the pan or by gently using a wooden skewer (the chips might stick a bit when unmolding, but don't worry about this). Separate cookies and let cool completely. Dust with confectioner's sugar.

Chocolate Tea Cakes

This cookie is a blend of delicate, buttery shortbread, toasted chopped hazelnuts and chocolate. Three words sum this one up — yum, yum and yum! Although this recipe makes a lot of cookies, they all fit on two baking sheets. This is a great cookie to make around the holidays or when you need cookies for a crowd.

TIPS

To toast hazelnuts: Place hazelnuts in a single layer on a foil or parchment-lined baking sheet. Bake in center of preheated 350°F (180°C) oven for 10 to 15 minutes or until lightly browned and skins are blistered. Wrap nuts in a clean dry kitchen towel and let stand for 1 minute. Rub nuts in towel to remove loose skins (it's okay if you can't remove all of them). Let nuts cool completely.

These cookies freeze very well in an airtight container or resealable bag for up to 1 month.

Preheat oven to 350°F (180°C)
Baking sheets, lined with parchment paper

2$\frac{1}{2}$ cups	all-purpose flour	625 mL
1 cup	finely chopped hazelnuts, toasted (see Tip, at left)	250 mL
$\frac{1}{2}$ tsp	salt	2 mL
1$\frac{1}{2}$ cups	confectioner's (icing) sugar	375 mL
1 cup	unsalted butter, at room temperature	250 mL
1 tsp	vanilla	5 mL
4 oz	bittersweet or semisweet chocolate, finely chopped	125 g

Topping

1 cup	confectioner's (icing) sugar, sifted	250 mL

1. In a medium bowl, mix together flour, hazelnuts and salt.

2. In a large bowl, using electric mixer, beat confectioner's sugar and butter. Beat in vanilla. Add flour mixture, beating well. The dough will be very thick and somewhat dry. Mix in chopped chocolate.

3. Scoop batter by tablespoons (15 mL) and, using your hands, roll into balls. Place on prepared baking sheets, about 2 inches (5 cm) apart. Bake in preheated oven for 12 to 14 minutes or until puffed and slightly cracked on top. They will be fragile and still somewhat soft to the touch. Let cool on baking sheets on racks for 10 minutes.

4. *Topping:* Working with one warm cookie at a time, roll in confectioner's sugar and place on a clean tray or baking sheet. Let cool completely.

Variation
Substitute almonds for the hazelnuts.

Chocolate Chip Meringues

These crisp little gems are low in both fat and calories. They are delicious, with melt-in-your-mouth goodness, and completely addictive for all the right reasons.

TIPS

For a decorative look that's also delicious, lightly dust meringues with unsweetened cocoa powder or ground cinnamon before baking. Also, I like these cookies when they are crisp on the outside and just slightly soft and chewy in the center. To achieve crispy yet soft meringues, slightly underbake the cookies by a few minutes.

Store meringues in an airtight container for several days.

Preheat oven to 300°F (150°C)
Baking sheets, lined with parchment paper

4	egg whites	4
1/4 tsp	cream of tartar	1 mL
1 cup	granulated sugar	250 mL
3/4 cup	miniature semisweet chocolate chips	175 mL

1. In a large bowl, using electric mixer, beat egg whites and cream of tartar at high speed until soft peaks form. Add sugar, 1 tbsp (15 mL) at a time, beating until peaks are stiff and glossy. Fold in chocolate chips.

2. Drop by rounded tablespoons (15 mL) on prepared baking sheets, about 2 inches (5 cm) apart. Bake in preheated oven for 40 to 45 minutes or until crisp. Let cookies cool completely on pans on racks.

Brown Sugar Shortbread

These crunchy little cookies make a great accompaniment to a cup of tea or a bowl of ice cream. When I am in the mood for something crunchy and lightly sweet, these fit the bill.

TIPS

I love parchment paper! It's a grease- and heat-resistant paper used to line baking pans. It keeps your baked goods from sticking and burning and makes cleanup a breeze.

To bring cold butter to room temperature in a hurry, use a microwave oven. I usually set it on Medium (50%) for 10 to 20 seconds, making sure not to melt the butter.

Preheat oven to 350°F (180°C)
Baking sheets, lined with parchment paper

2 cups	all-purpose flour	500 mL
1/4 tsp	salt	1 mL
1 cup	unsalted butter, at room temperature	250 mL
1 cup	packed light brown sugar	250 mL
1	egg yolk	1
2 tsp	vanilla	10 mL
3/4 cup	semisweet chocolate chips	175 mL
1/2 cup	coarsely chopped walnuts	125 mL
	Granulated sugar, for rolling	

1. In a small bowl, combine flour and salt.

2. In a large bowl, using electric mixer, beat butter and brown sugar until fluffy. Beat in egg yolk and vanilla. Add flour mixture and beat until smooth. Stir in chocolate chips and walnuts.

3. Using a small cookie scoop or tablespoon (15 mL), scoop dough into balls. Roll in granulated sugar. Place sugared cookies on prepared baking sheets, about 2 inches (5 cm) apart. Using the heel of your hand, press down lightly on top of each cookie, flattening into a disk. Don't worry if they aren't perfectly flat; this adds to their rustic appearance. Bake in preheated oven for 15 to 17 minutes or until light golden brown and firm to the touch. Let cool on pans on rack.

Variations
You can omit the walnuts or substitute pecans, if you prefer.

Ginger Chocolate Shortbread

MAKES
36 COOKIES

Chocolate chips and candied ginger make excellent additions to traditional shortbread. Cut into small bars, they are a perfect accompaniment to sorbet. My mother has become addicted to these cookies, so I have to keep her freezer stocked with a ready supply.

TIP

You can freeze the cookies in an airtight container or resealable plastic bag for up to 1 month. They will also keep at room temperature in an airtight container for up to 3 days.

Preheat oven to 350°F (180°C)

9-inch (2.5 L) square metal baking pan, greased

1¾ cups	all-purpose flour	425 mL
¼ cup	cornstarch	50 mL
¼ tsp	salt	1 mL
1 cup	unsalted butter, at room temperature	250 mL
½ cup	granulated sugar	125 mL
1 cup	semisweet chocolate chips	250 mL
¾ cup	candied ginger, diced	175 mL

1. In a small bowl, mix together flour, cornstarch and salt.

2. In a large bowl, using electric mixer, beat butter and sugar until light and fluffy. Add flour mixture, beating just until smooth. Stir in chocolate chips and candied ginger.

3. Spread batter in prepared pan, smoothing top. Bake in preheated oven for 40 to 50 minutes or until golden brown on top and somewhat firm to the touch. A slight indentation should be left when you touch the top of the cookies.

4. Let cool completely in pan on a rack. Invert pan onto a cutting board and cut into 36 bars.

Variation
Drizzle cooled cookies with melted chocolate.

Chocolate Cherry Biscotti

Over the years, I have developed many recipes for biscotti (there are no bad biscotti), but this is one of my favorites. This version was created for an article I wrote on biscotti in *Cooking Light* magazine.

TIP

When measuring, always remember to spoon your dry ingredients into the cup and level the top by scraping across it with the flat side of a knife or skewer. This will give you an accurate measurement.

Preheat oven to 350°F (180°C)
Baking sheets, lined with parchment paper

3 cups	all-purpose flour	750 mL
2 tsp	baking powder	10 mL
1/4 tsp	salt	1 mL
1 cup	granulated sugar	250 mL
3	eggs	3
2 tbsp	vegetable oil	25 mL
2 tsp	vanilla	10 mL
1 1/2 tsp	almond extract	7 mL
1 cup	semisweet chocolate chips	250 mL
2/3 cup	dried sour cherries	150 mL

1. In a medium bowl, combine flour, baking powder and salt.

2. In a large bowl, using electric mixer, beat sugar and eggs until thickened and pale, about 4 minutes. Add oil, vanilla and almond extract, beating just until blended. Add flour mixture, beating on low speed just until blended. Stir in chocolate chips and cherries.

3. Divide dough in half. Turn out dough onto prepared baking sheets. Shape each half into a 10-inch (25 cm) long log and flatten to 1-inch (2.5 cm) thickness. Bake in preheated oven for 25 to 30 minutes or until lightly browned. Transfer logs to rack. Let cool for 10 minutes. Reduce oven temperature to 325°F (160°C).

4. Transfer logs to a cutting board. Cut each log diagonally into 1/2-inch (1 cm) slices. Place slices, cut side down, on baking sheet. Bake for 15 to 20 minutes longer or until golden and toasted. The biscotti will be slightly soft in center but will harden as they cool. Transfer to racks and let cool completely.

Variations

If you don't have dried cherries, dried cranberries work really well. You can also add 1/2 cup (125 mL) chopped toasted almonds, if desired.

Chocolate Chip Orange Biscotti

MAKES ABOUT 30 BISCOTTI

These biscotti are a very popular item in our gift baskets. Orange and chocolate leave an everlasting impression on the taste buds. My buds are partial to this combo. Properly stored in an airtight container, they will last for 2 months.

TIP

All of the recipes in this book were tested using large eggs. Using medium or extra-large eggs may adversely affect the outcome of the recipe.

Preheat oven to 350°F (180°C)
Baking sheets, lined with parchment paper

2¾ cups	all-purpose flour	675 mL
1 cup	granulated sugar	250 mL
2 tsp	baking powder	10 mL
1 tbsp	vegetable oil	15 mL
1 tbsp	orange extract	15 mL
2 tsp	grated orange zest	10 mL
1 tsp	vanilla	5 mL
3	eggs	3
1 cup	semisweet chocolate chips	250 mL

1. In a medium bowl, combine flour, sugar and baking powder.

2. In a large bowl, using electric mixer, beat oil, orange extract, orange zest, vanilla and eggs until blended. Add flour mixture, beating until well blended. Stir in chocolate chips.

3. Divide dough in half. Turn out dough onto prepared baking sheets. Shape each half into 10-inch (25 cm) long logs and flatten to 1-inch (2.5 cm) thickness. Bake in preheated oven for 25 to 30 minutes or until lightly browned. Transfer logs to a rack. Let cool for 10 minutes. Reduce oven temperature to 325°F (160°C).

4. Transfer logs to cutting board. Cut each log diagonally into ½-inch (1 cm) slices. Place slices, cut side down, on baking sheet. Bake for 15 to 20 minutes longer or until golden and toasted. The biscotti will be soft in center but will harden as they cool. Transfer to racks and let cool completely.

Snickerdoodle Chip Biscotti

This is a variation of a recipe that I created for *Cooking Light* magazine. It has a nice vanilla flavor to it, with a light cinnamon-sugar coating and, of course, chocolate chips. This is the ultimate cookie for dunking and munching.

TIP

I love parchment paper! It's a grease- and heat-resistant paper used to line baking pans. It keeps your baked goods from sticking and burning and makes cleanup a breeze.

Preheat oven to 350°F (180°C)
Baking sheet, lined with parchment paper

2³/₄ cups	all-purpose flour	675 mL
2 tsp	baking powder	10 mL
¹/₄ tsp	salt	1 mL
1 cup plus 2 tbsp	granulated sugar, divided	275 mL
1 tbsp	vegetable oil	15 mL
1 tsp	vanilla	5 mL
3	eggs	3
1 cup	semisweet chocolate chips	250 mL
1 tsp	ground cinnamon	5 mL
1	egg white	1

1. In a medium bowl, combine flour, baking powder and salt.

2. In a large bowl, using electric mixer, beat 1 cup (250 mL) of the sugar, oil, vanilla and eggs until blended. Add flour mixture. Beat until combined. Stir in chocolate chips.

3. Divide dough in half. Turn out dough onto prepared baking sheet. Shape each half into 10-inch (25 cm) long log and flatten to 1-inch (2.5 cm) thickness. Combine remaining sugar and cinnamon. Gently brush tops of logs with egg white and sprinkle with cinnamon-sugar topping.

4. Bake in preheated oven for 25 to 30 minutes or until lightly browned. Transfer logs to rack. Let cool for 10 minutes. Reduce oven temperature to 325°F (160°C).

5. Transfer logs to cutting board. Cut each diagonally into ¹/₂-inch (1 cm) slices. Place biscotti, cut side down, on baking sheet. Bake for 15 to 20 minutes longer or until golden and toasted. Biscotti will be slightly soft in center but will harden as they cool. Transfer to racks and let cool completely.

White Chocolate Almond Chunk Biscotti

This biscotti teams together white chocolate, almonds and coconut. They are so incredibly delicious that even tasters who dislike white chocolate will love them. I could eat a whole batch with a pot of tea.

TIPS

To toast almonds: Preheat oven to 350°F (180°C). Spread nuts on a baking sheet lined with foil or parchment. Bake for 5 to 7 minutes or until light brown and fragrant.

To toast coconut: Place coconut in a nonstick skillet over medium heat and cook, stirring constantly, for 3 to 5 minutes or until lightly browned. Be careful not to let it burn. Transfer to a plate and let cool.

Store these cookies in an airtight container for up to 5 days. You can also freeze them for up to 1 month.

Preheat oven to 350°F (180°C)
Baking sheets, lined with parchment paper or lightly greased

2½ cups	all-purpose flour	625 mL
2 tsp	baking powder	10 mL
¼ tsp	salt	1 mL
½ cup	unsalted butter, at room temperature	125 mL
1 cup	granulated sugar	250 mL
2 tsp	almond extract	10 mL
3	eggs	3
6 oz	white chocolate, coarsely chopped	175 g
1 cup	almonds, toasted (see Tip, at left)	250 mL
½ cup	packed sweetened flaked coconut, toasted (see Tip, at left)	125 mL

1. In a medium bowl, mix together flour, baking powder and salt.

2. In a large bowl, using electric mixer, beat butter until light and creamy. Add sugar and almond extract, beating well. Add eggs, one at a time, beating well after each addition. Gradually add flour mixture, beating well. Stir in chocolate, almonds and coconut.

3. Divide dough in half. Turn out dough onto prepared baking sheets. Shape each half into a 10-inch (25 cm) long log and flatten to 1-inch (2.5 cm) thickness. Bake in preheated oven for 25 to 30 minutes or until lightly golden and firm to the touch. Let logs cool on baking sheets on racks, but keep the oven on.

4. Transfer logs to a cutting board. With a serrated knife, cut each log diagonally into ¾-inch (2 cm) slices. Place slices, cut side down, on baking sheet. Bake for 10 minutes longer or until lightly toasted. Transfer to racks and let cool completely.

Vegan Chocolate Espresso Brownies

**MAKES
12 BROWNIES**

I developed this recipe for my friend Heather. She is vegan, so I am always trying to come up with dessert recipes that she can enjoy. This one works really well; not just for vegans but also for anyone who loves dark, chocolaty, decadent desserts. It's also a boon for anyone allergic to eggs or dairy.

TIP

A great ratio for strong brewed coffee is 2 tbsp (25 mL) finely ground French-roast coffee or espresso for every ¾ cup (175 mL) water.

Preheat oven to 350°F (180°C)
8-inch (2 L) square metal baking pan, greased

¼ cup	vegetable oil	50 mL
4 oz	unsweetened chocolate (dairy-free), chopped	125 g
1 cup	all-purpose flour	250 mL
2 tsp	finely ground espresso or French-roast coffee	10 mL
1 tsp	baking powder	5 mL
	Powdered egg replacer for 2 eggs (see Tip, opposite)	
1 cup	packed light brown sugar	250 mL
¼ cup	granulated sugar	50 mL
1 tbsp	strong brewed coffee, cooled (see Tip, at left)	15 mL
1 tsp	vanilla	5 mL
¼ tsp	almond extract	1 mL
½ cup	semisweet chocolate chips (dairy-free)	125 mL

1. In a microwave–safe bowl, combine oil and unsweetened chocolate. Microwave, uncovered, on Medium (50%) for 1 to 1½ minutes, stirring every 30 seconds, or until chocolate is soft and almost melted. Stir until chocolate is melted and mixture is smooth. Set aside and let cool slightly.

2. In a small bowl, mix together flour, ground coffee and baking powder.

TIP

I like to use Ener-G Egg Replacer, made by Ener-G Foods, Inc. in Seattle, Washington (see Sources, page 369). It's a natural product that contains, among other ingredients, potato starch, tapioca flour and leavening. Ener-G Egg Replacer is available at many health food stores. Follow the instructions on the box to substitute for 2 eggs. Do not use liquid egg replacements, as they contain eggs. Also, some vegans will not consume white cane sugar. You can substitute $1\frac{1}{4}$ cups (300 mL) unbleached cane sugar or beet sugar for the granulated and brown sugars.

3. In a large bowl, mix together egg replacer, brown and granulated sugars, brewed coffee, vanilla and almond extract. Stir in cooled chocolate mixture, mixing until smooth. Stir in flour mixture, mixing until smooth.

4. Spread batter in prepared pan, smoothing top. Sprinkle chocolate chips over top, lightly pressing into surface. Bake in preheated oven for 20 to 30 minutes or until puffed, slightly cracked and top springs back a bit when touched. Let cool completely in pan on a rack before cutting into squares.

Variation
Substitute coarsely chopped walnuts for the chocolate chips. Fold them into the batter before spreading in the prepared pan.

Double Fudge
Espresso Brownies

MAKES 12
BROWNIES

This is a great recipe when you want an awesome brownie but don't want to have to go to a lot of work. They're very fast to make, so you can satisfy that chocolate craving in no time.

TIP

For a decorative garnish, lightly dust cooled cut brownies with confectioner's (icing) sugar.

Preheat oven to 350°F (180°C)

13- by 9-inch (3 L) metal baking pan, lined with parchment paper, greased

1 cup	all-purpose flour	250 mL
3/4 cup	unsweetened Dutch-process cocoa powder, sifted	175 mL
2 tsp	finely ground espresso or French-roast coffee	10 mL
1 1/2 tsp	baking powder	7 mL
1 tsp	instant coffee granules	5 mL
1/4 tsp	salt	1 mL
1 cup	unsalted butter, melted	250 mL
1 cup	granulated sugar	250 mL
1 cup	packed light brown sugar	250 mL
3	eggs	3
1 1/2 tsp	vanilla	7 mL
1/2 tsp	almond extract	2 mL
1 cup	semisweet chocolate chips	250 mL

1. In a medium bowl, combine flour, cocoa powder, ground coffee, baking powder, instant coffee granules and salt.

2. In a large bowl, using electric mixer, beat melted butter and granulated and brown sugars until blended. Add eggs, one at a time, beating well after each addition. Beat in vanilla and almond extract. Add flour mixture and beat until blended.

3. Spread batter in prepared pan. Sprinkle with chocolate chips, lightly pressing into surface. Bake in preheated oven for 30 minutes or until still somewhat soft to the touch and a tester inserted into center has moist crumbs clinging to it. Let cool completely in pan on rack. Invert onto a cutting board to remove from pan and peel off parchment paper. Cut into squares.

Rum Raisin Spoon Brownies

These are small individual brownie cookies, about the size of a teaspoon. Though bite-size, they're packed with the punch of rum, raisins and chocolate.

TIP

All of the recipes in this book were tested using large eggs. Using medium or extra-large eggs may adversely affect the outcome of the recipe.

Preheat oven to 350°F (180°C)
Baking sheets, lined with parchment paper

8 oz	unsweetened chocolate, chopped	250 g
2 cups	semisweet chocolate chips, divided	500 mL
6 tbsp	unsalted butter	90 mL
3/4 cup	raisins	175 mL
1/4 cup	dark rum	50 mL
1/2 cup	all-purpose flour	125 mL
1/2 tsp	baking powder	2 mL
4	eggs	4
1 1/2 cups	granulated sugar	375 mL
1 tsp	vanilla	5 mL

1. In a microwave-safe bowl, combine unsweetened chocolate, 1 cup (250 mL) of the chocolate chips and butter. Microwave on High for 2 minutes, stirring every 30 seconds, until chocolate is shiny and almost melted. Stir until smooth. Let cool slightly.

2. In a small microwave-safe bowl, combine raisins and rum. Microwave on High for 1 minute. Set aside to cool.

3. In a small bowl, mix together flour and baking powder.

4. In a large bowl, using electric mixer, beat eggs, sugar and vanilla until well combined. Add chocolate mixture, beating well. Add flour mixture and blend until smooth. Stir in raisin mixture. Stir in remaining chocolate chips. Refrigerate dough for 30 minutes to thicken.

5. Drop by tablespoons (15 mL) or with 1 1/4-inch (3 cm) cookie scoop on prepared pans, about 2 inches (5 cm) apart. Bake in preheated oven for 10 minutes or until puffed and cracked. Cookies will firm up when cool; do not overbake. Let cool completely on pans on racks.

Banana Blondies with Chocolate Chips and Walnuts

My kids like to call these Monkey Bars. The bananas bring out the best in their behavior. These bars are a superb combination of banana bread and chocolate chip cookie. They are an ideal alternative to traditional brownies.

TIP

For a more intense walnut flavor, toast the nuts before adding to the batter. Simply spread the nuts on a rimmed baking sheet and bake in a preheated 350°F (180°C) oven until lightly browned and fragrant, about 8 to 10 minutes. Let cool before mixing into batter.

Preheat oven to 350°F (180°C)

13- by 9-inch (3 L) metal baking pan, lined with foil, greased

2 cups	all-purpose flour	500 mL
2 tsp	baking powder	10 mL
1/4 tsp	salt	1 mL
3/4 cup	unsalted butter, at room temperature	175 mL
2/3 cup	granulated sugar	150 mL
2/3 cup	packed light brown sugar	150 mL
1 tsp	vanilla	5 mL
1	egg	1
1 cup	mashed ripe bananas (about 2 large)	250 mL
2 cups	semisweet chocolate chips	500 mL
1 cup	walnut pieces (see Tip, at left)	250 mL

1. In a medium bowl, combine flour, baking powder and salt.

2. In a large bowl, using electric mixer, beat butter and granulated and brown sugars until light and fluffy. Beat in vanilla. Add egg and bananas, beating well. Add flour mixture and beat just until combined. Fold in chocolate chips and walnuts.

3. Spread batter in prepared pan. Bake in preheated oven for 30 to 35 minutes or until light golden brown and starting to pull away from sides of pan. The center will still be slightly soft to the touch. Let cool completely in pan on rack. Invert onto a cutting board to remove from pan and peel off foil. Cut into bars.

Variations

You can substitute pecans for the walnuts. Or, if you're not a nut fan, omit them altogether.

Butterscotch Pecan Chocolate Chip Blondies

Let's raise the bar a few notches. This scrumptious cookie bar is easy to prepare and the results are above one's personal best. Try it and see for yourself.

TIPS

Butterscotch extract can be found at specialty food stores and some well-stocked grocery and health food stores.

To toast pecans: Preheat oven to 350°F (180°C). Spread pecans on baking sheet, lined with parchment paper, and bake for 8 to 10 minutes or until lightly browned.

Preheat oven to 350°F (180°C)
13- by 9-inch (3 L) metal baking pan, lined with parchment paper, greased

2½ cups	all-purpose flour	625 mL
1 tbsp	baking powder	15 mL
¼ tsp	salt	1 mL
1 cup	unsalted butter, melted	250 mL
3 cups	packed light brown sugar	750 mL
2 tsp	butterscotch extract (see Tips, left)	10 mL
1 tsp	vanilla	5 mL
4	eggs	4
2 cups	semisweet chocolate chips	500 mL
1 cup	coarsely chopped pecans, toasted (see Tips, left)	250 mL

1. In a medium bowl, combine flour, baking powder and salt.

2. In a large bowl, using electric mixer, beat melted butter and brown sugar until smooth. Add butterscotch extract and vanilla, beating well. Add eggs, one at a time, beating well after each addition. Add flour mixture and beat just until combined. Fold in chocolate chips and pecans.

3. Spread batter in prepared pan. Bake in preheated oven for 40 to 45 minutes or until browned and starting to pull away from sides of pan. Center will still be slightly soft to the touch. Let cool completely in pan on rack. Invert onto a cutting board to remove from pan and peel off parchment paper. Cut into bars.

Variation

Substitute walnuts for pecans or omit nuts altogether, if desired.

Chocolate Brittle Bars

These bars are more confection than cookie. "To die for" is an understatement when describing the flavor and sensation of these treats. Making them is a lot of fun, too. I always let my artistic expression emerge when drizzling chocolate.

TIPS

Look for 10-oz (300 g) bags of English toffee bits in the baking section of the grocery store.

To toast almonds: Preheat oven to 350°F (180°C). Spread nuts on a baking sheet lined with foil or parchment. Bake for 5 to 7 minutes or until light brown and fragrant.

Preheat oven to 350°F (180°C)
17- by 11-inch (45 by 28 cm) rimmed baking sheet, lined with parchment paper

2 cups	all-purpose flour	500 mL
1/4 tsp	salt	1 mL
1 cup plus 1 tbsp	unsalted butter, at room temperature	265 mL
1 cup	lightly packed light brown sugar	250 mL
1 tsp	vanilla	5 mL
1 1/2 cups	English toffee bits (see Tip, at left)	375 mL
2 1/2 cups	semisweet chocolate chips	625 mL
1 1/2 cups	almonds, toasted and chopped (see Tip, at left)	375 mL

1. In a medium bowl, combine flour and salt.

2. In a large bowl, beat butter and sugar. Beat in vanilla. Stir in flour mixture just until dough is smooth. Stir in English toffee bits.

3. Press dough onto prepared baking sheet. Bake in preheated oven for 25 to 30 minutes or until dark golden brown. Let cool on pan on rack for 5 minutes. Sprinkle top with chocolate chips. When chocolate chips look soft and shiny, spread them over surface with a spatula. Sprinkle with chopped almonds. Refrigerate until chocolate is firm, then break into pieces.

Variation
Substitute shelled pistachios for the almonds.

Oat Bars

When you are in the mood for something sweet, buttery and full of chocolate but don't want to expend much effort, these are the cookies for you. They are a one-bowl wonder.

TIP

To make these bars even easier, melt the butter in a microwave-safe mixing bowl or glass dish. Then add the remaining ingredients to the same dish.

Preheat oven to 350°F (180°C)
13- by 9-inch (3 L) metal baking pan, lined with parchment paper, greased

1 cup	packed dark brown sugar	250 mL
3/4 cup	unsalted butter, melted	175 mL
3 tbsp	light corn syrup	45 mL
1/2 tsp	vanilla	2 mL
1/4 tsp	salt	1 mL
3 cups	old-fashioned rolled oats	750 mL
1 cup	semisweet chocolate chips	250 mL

1. In a large bowl, combine brown sugar, melted butter, corn syrup, vanilla and salt. Add oats and chocolate chips, mixing well.

2. Press dough into prepared pan. Bake in preheated oven for 20 to 25 minutes or until browned but not too dark. It will still be soft to the touch but will harden when it cools. Let cool completely in pan on rack. Invert onto a cutting board to remove from pan and peel off parchment paper. Cut into bars.

Chocolate Chip Cherry Bars

MAKES 16 BARS

Fred and Ginger, Dean and Jerry, John and Yoko, and chocolate and cherries. Can you mention one of these without including the other? I think not. This recipe pairs these inseparable partners for yet another encore with award-winning results. They make a great after-school snack.

TIP

To bring cold butter to room temperature in a hurry, use a microwave oven. I usually set it on Medium (50%) for 10 to 20 seconds, making sure not to melt the butter.

Preheat oven to 350°F (180°C)
13- by 9-inch (3 L) metal baking pan, lined with parchment paper, greased

2¹/₄ cups	all-purpose flour	550 mL
³/₄ tsp	baking soda	4 mL
³/₄ tsp	baking powder	4 mL
¹/₂ tsp	ground cinnamon	2 mL
¹/₄ tsp	salt	1 mL
³/₄ cup	unsalted butter, at room temperature	175 mL
2¹/₄ cups	packed light brown sugar	550 mL
3	eggs	3
1 tbsp	vanilla	15 mL
4¹/₂ cups	old-fashioned rolled oats	1.125 L
2 cups	semisweet chocolate chips	500 mL
1 cup	dried sour cherries	250 mL

1. In a medium bowl, combine flour, baking soda, baking powder, cinnamon and salt.

2. In a large bowl, using electric mixer, beat butter and sugar until light and fluffy. Add eggs, one at a time, beating well after each addition. Beat in vanilla. Stir in flour mixture. Add oats, mixing until moistened. Stir in chocolate chips and cherries.

3. Spread batter in prepared pan. Bake in preheated oven for 25 to 30 minutes or until golden and starting to pull away from sides of pan. Center will still be slightly soft to the touch. Let cool completely in pan on rack. Invert onto a cutting board to remove from pan and peel off parchment paper. Cut into bars.

Variation
Substitute raisins or dried cranberries for the cherries.

Raspberry
Chocolate Chip Bars

This is a recipe that I developed for an article in *Cooking Light* magazine. If you cut the bars into 16 portions, you have a decadent but virtuous snack. Personally, I prefer a larger bar, despite the extra calories.

TIPS
I love parchment paper! It's a grease- and heat-resistant paper used to line baking pans. It keeps your baked goods from sticking and burning and makes cleanup a breeze.

Preheat oven to 375°F (190°C)
8-inch (2 L) square baking pan, lined with parchment paper, greased

1 cup	all-purpose flour	250 mL
1 cup	quick-cooking rolled oats	250 mL
1/2 tsp	baking soda	2 mL
1/2 tsp	salt	2 mL
1/3 cup	unsalted butter, at room temperature	75 mL
3/4 cup	packed light brown sugar	175 mL
3/4 cup	semisweet chocolate chips	175 mL
1	jar (10 oz/300 mL) seedless raspberry jam (1 1/4 cups/300 mL)	1

1. In a medium bowl, combine flour, oats, baking soda and salt.

2. In a large bowl, using electric mixer, beat butter and sugar until light and fluffy. Add flour mixture and beat until well blended (mixture will be crumbly).

3. Transfer 3/4 cup (175 mL) of the dough to a bowl. Toss with chocolate chips and set aside. Press remaining dough into prepared pan. Spread evenly with jam. Sprinkle with chocolate chip mixture. Bake in preheated oven for 30 minutes or until golden brown. Let cool completely in pan on rack. Invert onto a cutting board to remove from pan and peel off parchment paper. Cut into squares.

Variation
Add 1/2 cup (125 mL) sliced almonds with chocolate chips.

Chocolate Chip Spice Bars with Maple Glaze

MAKES 16 BARS

These bars are tasty to the nth degree. Don't let the ingredient list deter you. The flavors will continue to enhance the bars hours after baking. The combination of spices, chocolate and a maple glaze makes this cookie quite the taste sensation. Light and dark brown sugars add a deeper, more complex flavor.

TIP

A great ratio for strong brewed coffee is 2 tbsp (25 mL) finely ground French-roast coffee or espresso for every $3/4$ cup (175 mL) water.

Preheat oven to 350°F (180°C)
13- by 9-inch (3 L) metal baking pan, greased

$1^3/_4$ cups	all-purpose flour	425 mL
2 tsp	ground cinnamon	10 mL
2 tsp	ground ginger	10 mL
1 tsp	ground allspice	5 mL
$3/_4$ tsp	baking soda	4 mL
$3/_4$ tsp	baking powder	4 mL
$1/_2$ tsp	ground nutmeg	2 mL
$1/_4$ tsp	salt	1 mL
$1/_2$ cup	unsalted butter, at room temperature	125 mL
$3/_4$ cup	packed light brown sugar	175 mL
$1/_2$ cup	packed dark brown sugar	125 mL
$1/_4$ cup	strong brewed coffee, cooled to room temperature (see Tip, at left)	50 mL
2	eggs	2
1 cup	raisins	250 mL
$3/_4$ cup	semisweet chocolate chips	175 mL

Glaze

$1^1/_2$ cups	confectioner's (icing) sugar, sifted	375 mL
$1/_3$ cup	milk	75 mL
$1/_2$ tsp	maple extract	2 mL

1. In a small bowl, combine flour, cinnamon, ginger, allspice, baking soda, baking powder, nutmeg and salt.

2. In a large bowl, using electric mixer, beat butter and light and dark brown sugars until light and fluffy. Stir in coffee. Add eggs, one at a time, beating well after each addition. Add flour mixture, beating on low speed until combined. Stir in raisins and chocolate chips.

TIP

When measuring, always remember to spoon your dry ingredients into the cup and level the top by scraping across it with the flat side of a knife or skewer. This will give you an accurate measurement.

3. Spread batter in prepared pan. Bake in preheated oven for 25 minutes or until top is just firm to the touch. Let cool in pan on rack.

4. *Glaze:* In a small bowl, combine confectioner's sugar, milk and maple extract, whisking until smooth. When bars are almost cool, spread glaze over top. Let cool until glaze is set. Cut into bars.

Variation
If you prefer, you can omit the raisins.

White Chocolate Sesame Shortbread Bars

Toasted sesame and white chocolate joined together. How long can this relationship last? Indefinitely! This is a perfect shortbread to serve as a finale with Asian or Mediterranean food, or just for nibbling with tea.

TIPS

If shortbread puffs up during baking, lightly prick top again with a fork.

Baked shortbread freezes very well. Store it in a resealable plastic freezer bag or an airtight container for up to 1 month.

To toast sesame seeds: Place sesame seeds in a nonstick skillet over medium heat. Cook, stirring constantly, for 3 minutes or just until sesame seeds start to turn light golden. Be careful not to let them burn. Transfer to a plate and let cool.

Preheat oven to 300°F (150°C)

9-inch (2.5 L) square metal baking pan, greased

1 cup	unsalted butter, at room temperature	250 mL
1 cup	granulated sugar	250 mL
2 cups	all-purpose flour	500 mL
2/3 cup	sesame seeds, toasted (see Tips, left)	150 mL
1/4 tsp	salt	1 mL
6 oz	white chocolate, coarsely chopped	175 g

1. In a large bowl, beat together butter and sugar until creamy. Add flour, sesame seeds and salt, beating until smooth. Stir in white chocolate.

2. Press dough into prepared pan, smoothing top. Prick top of shortbread with a fork. Bake in preheated oven for 55 to 60 minutes or until just firm to the touch and lightly golden brown.

3. Let cool completely in pan on a rack. When cookies are cool, invert pan onto a cutting board and cut into bars.

Variation

Substitute chopped bittersweet chocolate for the white chocolate.

Chocolate Almond Bars

MAKES 20 BARS

This is a deliciously rich, crunchy, nutty and slightly chewy bar. All the fun adjectives apply here, yet these bars have a delicate flavor that is perfect as a garnish over ice cream. This recipe is inspired by a recipe from *Mary Engelbreit's Home Companion* magazine.

TIP

These bars are best eaten the day they're made.

Preheat oven to 350°F (180°C)
13- by 9-inch (3 L) metal baking pan, greased

1³/₄ cups	all-purpose flour	425 mL
¹/₃ cup	unsweetened Dutch-process cocoa powder, sifted	75 mL
¹/₂ tsp	salt	2 mL
1 cup	unsalted butter, at room temperature	250 mL
1 cup	granulated sugar	250 mL
1 tsp	vanilla	5 mL
1 cup	sliced almonds	250 mL
³/₄ cup	semisweet chocolate chips	175 mL

1. In a small bowl, mix together flour, cocoa powder and salt.

2. In a large bowl, using electric mixer, beat butter, sugar and vanilla until light and fluffy. Add flour mixture, beating just until blended. Stir in almonds and chocolate chips.

3. Spread batter in prepared pan, smoothing top. Bake in preheated oven for 20 to 25 minutes or until almost firm to the touch and crisp around the edges. Let cool completely in pan on a rack. Cut into bars or break into pieces.

Almond Caramel Bars

MAKES 24 BARS

If you love buttery flavor, nutty crunch, chewy caramel and chocolate chip sensations all in one bite, then you will love these bars! Take heed: they are dangerously habit-forming.

TIPS

Wait until the crust has been baking in the oven for 10 to 15 minutes before preparing the caramel. Otherwise the caramel will thicken too quickly to spread on the baked crust.

For true caramel lovers, you can double the filling for an extra-gooey bar.

Preheat oven to 350°F (180°C)
13- by 9-inch (3 L) metal baking pan, lined with parchment paper, greased
Candy thermometer

2 cups	all-purpose flour	500 mL
3/4 cup	unsalted butter, at room temperature	175 mL
1/2 cup	packed light brown sugar	125 mL
1/2 tsp	vanilla	2 mL
1/4 tsp	salt	1 mL
2 cups	coarsely chopped almonds	500 mL
Filling		
6 tbsp	unsalted butter	90 mL
3/4 cup	packed light brown sugar	175 mL
3/4 cup	light corn syrup	175 mL
Pinch	salt	Pinch
Topping		
2 cups	semisweet chocolate chips	500 mL

1. In a food processor fitted with a metal blade, combine flour, butter, brown sugar, vanilla and salt. Process until mixture comes together and just starts to form a ball. Press evenly into prepared pan. Sprinkle almonds over dough. Bake in preheated oven for 20 to 25 minutes or until golden brown.

2. *Filling:* In a heavy saucepan over medium heat, melt butter. Stir in brown sugar, corn syrup and salt. Simmer, stirring often, for about 5 minutes or until it reaches the soft-ball stage, 240°F (116°C) on a candy thermometer. Pour over baked crust, spreading evenly.

3. *Topping:* Sprinkle chocolate chips over caramel. Let cool and refrigerate until caramel is firm. (This also makes cutting easier.) Invert onto a cutting board to remove from pan and peel off parchment paper. Cut into bars.

Variation

Substitute coarsely chopped macadamia nuts or walnuts for the almonds.

Chocolate Almond Graham Bars

MAKES
16 SQUARES

I'm not sure if this recipe appeals more to adults or children. But whatever the case, it is utterly delicious! Look for graham cracker cereal in grocery stores.

TIPS

Be sure to line and grease your pan, as this recipe will really stick. It is best eaten within 1 day after it is made.

To toast almonds: Preheat oven to 350°F (180°C). Spread nuts on a baking sheet lined with foil or parchment. Bake for 5 to 7 minutes or until light brown and fragrant.

8-inch (2 L) square glass baking dish, bottom lined with parchment paper, greased

8 oz	semisweet chocolate, chopped	250 g
1 cup	graham cracker cereal	250 mL
1 1/2 cups	miniature marshmallows	375 mL
1/2 cup	almonds, toasted and coarsely chopped (see Tip, at left)	125 mL
1/2 cup	semisweet chocolate chips	125 mL

1. In a microwave-safe bowl, microwave chopped chocolate, uncovered, on Medium (50%) for 1 to 2 minutes, stirring every 30 seconds, or until chocolate is soft and almost melted. Stir until completely melted and smooth.

2. Stir in graham cracker cereal, marshmallows, almonds and chocolate chips. Press mixture into prepared pan.

3. Refrigerate for 2 hours or overnight, until chocolate is firm. Using a knife, loosen edges of mixture and cut into squares.

Variation
Increase the chocolate in the recipe to 10 to 12 oz (300 to 375 g) for a thicker, more chocolaty bar.

Chocolate Caramel Bars

· ·

MAKES 16 BARS

I was trying to come up with a name for these bars when my daughter suggested that I just call them "the best cookie that you will ever taste." How's that for an introduction? They are a fantastic combo of an oatmeal shortbread crust, walnuts, caramel and a chocolate chip streusel top. Wow, what a cookie! And, even better, they are very easy to prepare.

TIP

Store chocolate in a cool, dry place for up to one year. Chocolate will sometimes develop a white "bloom," or coating, when it gets too warm, causing the cocoa butter to separate. The chocolate is still fine to use in recipes or for melting.

Preheat oven to 350°F (180°C)

9-inch (2.5 L) square metal baking pan, lined with parchment paper, greased

Crust

1 cup	all-purpose flour	250 mL
1 cup	old-fashioned rolled oats (not quick-cooking oats)	250 mL
¾ cup	packed light brown sugar	175 mL
½ tsp	baking soda	2 mL
¼ tsp	salt	1 mL
¾ cup	unsalted butter, melted	175 mL
¾ cup	walnut pieces	175 mL

Filling

½ cup	packed light brown sugar	125 mL
½ cup	unsalted butter	125 mL
2 tbsp	whipping (35%) cream	25 mL
Pinch	salt	Pinch

Topping

5 oz	semisweet chocolate, coarsely chopped	150 g

1. *Crust:* In a medium bowl, mix together flour, oats, brown sugar, baking soda and salt. Stir in melted butter, mixing until combined. Press half of mixture into bottom of prepared pan. Set aside remaining oat mixture. Bake crust in preheated oven for 12 to 15 minutes or until your finger leaves a slight indentation on top when touched. Remove pan from oven and sprinkle walnuts over crust. Return pan to oven for 5 minutes longer.

· · · · · · · · · · · · · · · · ·

2. *Filling:* Meanwhile, in a saucepan over medium-high heat, combine brown sugar, butter, cream and salt. Bring to a boil, stirring occasionally. When mixture comes to a boil, increase heat to high and boil for 1 minute. Remove from heat and stir until smooth.

3. Pour filling evenly over walnuts on crust.

4. *Topping:* Mix chopped chocolate into reserved oat mixture and sprinkle evenly over filling.

5. Return pan to oven and bake an additional 20 minutes or until edges are medium brown and filling is bubbling up through top like hot lava. Let cool completely in pan on a rack. When cool, refrigerate for 30 minutes. Invert onto a cutting board to remove from pan and peel off parchment paper. Cut into squares.

Variation
Substitute almonds for the walnuts.

Chocolate Macaroon Bars

MAKES 16 BARS

Make these bars early in the day, cut them into squares, then take them on a picnic. You'll be glad you did. They are best eaten the day they're made.

TIP

Store chocolate in a cool, dry place for up to one year. Chocolate will sometimes develop a white "bloom," or coating, when it gets too warm, causing the cocoa butter to separate. The chocolate is still fine to use in recipes or for melting.

Preheat oven to 350°F (180°C)
9-inch (2.5 L) square metal baking pan, greased

2 cups	packed sweetened shredded or flaked coconut	500 mL
1/2 cup	granulated sugar	125 mL
1/4 cup	all-purpose flour	50 mL
1/4 tsp	salt	1 mL
5	egg whites	5
1/2 tsp	almond extract	2 mL
3/4 cup	semisweet chocolate chunks or chips	175 mL
1/2 cup	sliced almonds	125 mL
4 oz	semisweet chocolate, chopped	125 g

1. In a large bowl, stir together coconut, sugar, flour and salt. Add egg whites and almond extract, mixing to combine. Fold in the 3/4 cup (175 mL) chocolate chunks and almonds. Spread mixture in prepared pan.

2. Bake in preheated oven for 35 to 40 minutes or until golden brown. Let cool completely in pan on a rack.

3. In a microwave-safe bowl, microwave the 4 oz (125 g) chocolate on Medium (50%) for 1 to 1 1/2 minutes, stirring every 30 seconds, or until chocolate is soft and almost melted. Stir until completely melted and smooth. Drizzle over top of bars. Refrigerate until chocolate is firm before cutting into bars.

Variation
Substitute milk chocolate for the semisweet.

Six-Layer Bars

MAKES 12
TO 16 BARS

My brother, Jon, and I grew up on these bars. Although there are many versions of this recipe, I like mine with chocolate, coconut and almonds. These are extremely easy to make — the perfect project for children or when you want dessert in a jiffy.

TIPS

Store any leftover sweetened condensed milk in a covered container in the refrigerator. Try stirring it into coffee or tea for a real treat.

To toast almonds: Preheat oven to 350°F (180°C). Spread nuts on a baking sheet lined with foil or parchment. Bake for 5 to 7 minutes or until light brown and fragrant.

Preheat oven to 350°F (180°C)
9-inch (2.5 L) square metal baking pan, greased

$3/4$ cup	butter, melted	175 mL
$1^1/_2$ cups	graham cracker crumbs, cinnamon or regular	375 mL
$1^1/_3$ cups	sweetened condensed milk	325 mL
$1^1/_2$ cups	sweetened flaked coconut	375 mL
$1^1/_2$ cups	almonds, toasted and coarsely chopped (see Tip, at left)	375 mL
$1^1/_2$ cups	semisweet chocolate chips	375 mL

1. Pour butter into prepared baking dish and sprinkle with graham cracker crumbs. Drizzle sweetened condensed milk over crumbs (spreading with a spatula, if necessary). Top with coconut, almonds and chocolate chips. With a spatula, press down lightly on top of bars to pack down ingredients.

2. Bake in preheated oven for 30 minutes or until lightly browned. Let cool completely in pan on rack. Cut into bars.

Variation
Substitute chopped macadamia nuts for the almonds.

Vancouver Bars

MAKES 16 BARS

Okay, so there is no such thing as a Vancouver Bar. But I first fell in love with Nanaimo bars over 20 years ago while living in Vancouver and felt obliged to give something back. This version has an almond crust, chocolate espresso filling and a bittersweet chocolate topping. Outstanding!

TIP

To make almond meal: Finely grind about ²/₃ cup (150 mL) unsalted whole blanched or unblanched almonds (raw or toasted) in a food processor with a metal blade until finely ground. Do not overprocess or you will wind up with almond butter.

Preheat oven to 350°F (180°C)
8-inch (2 L) square metal baking pan, bottom and sides greased, then bottom lined with parchment paper

Crust

³/₄ cup	all-purpose flour	175 mL
³/₄ cup	almond meal or finely ground almonds (see Tip, at left)	175 mL
¹/₂ cup	granulated sugar	125 mL
¹/₄ tsp	salt	1 mL
¹/₂ cup	unsalted butter, at room temperature	125 mL
1 tsp	almond extract	5 mL

Filling

2 oz	unsweetened chocolate, chopped	60 g
¹/₄ cup	whipping (35%) cream	50 mL
2 tbsp	instant coffee granules	25 mL
1 tbsp	coffee liqueur	15 mL
2 cups	confectioner's (icing) sugar, sifted	500 mL
¹/₄ cup	unsalted butter, at room temperature	50 mL
2 tbsp	custard powder or vanilla pudding powder	25 mL

Topping

4 oz	bittersweet or semisweet chocolate, chopped	125 g
1 tbsp	unsalted butter	15 mL

1. *Crust:* In a food processor fitted with a metal blade, pulse flour, almond meal, sugar and salt until combined. Add butter and almond extract, pulsing until dough just comes together. Press dough into prepared pan, smoothing top. Bake in preheated oven for about 20 minutes or until lightly golden brown and firm to the touch. Place pan on a rack and let cool completely.

TIP
Store bars in resealable
plastic bags in the
refrigerator or freezer
for up to 2 weeks.

2. *Filling:* In a microwave-safe bowl, combine unsweetened chocolate and cream. Microwave, uncovered, on Medium (50%) for 1 minute, stirring every 30 seconds, or until smooth.

3. In a small bowl, whisk together instant coffee and 2 tsp (10 mL) hot water. Whisk in liqueur. Add to chocolate mixture, whisking well. Whisk in confectioner's sugar, butter and custard powder until smooth. Spread chocolate mixture evenly over cooled crust. Refrigerate for 15 minutes.

4. *Topping:* In a small microwave-safe bowl, combine chocolate and butter. Microwave, uncovered, on Medium (50%) for 1 minute, stirring every 30 seconds, or until chocolate is soft and almost melted. Stir until chocolate is melted and smooth. Spread over filling in pan. Refrigerate until chocolate is firm. Invert onto a cutting board to remove from pan and peel off parchment paper. Cut into bars.

Candies, Snacks and Other Treats

Quick-Mix Chocolate Fudge *238*

White Chocolate Lemon Fudge *239*

Whiskey Fudge *240*

Double Chocolate Lollipops *241*

Dark Chocolate Truffles *242*

Chocolate Cherry Truffles *243*

Chocolate Rum Balls *244*

Crispy Chocolate Drops *245*

Chocolate Cherry Drops *246*

Chocolate Mints *247*

Rocky Roads *248*

Chocolate Halvah Mounds *249*

Chocolate-Dipped Sesame Almond Candy *250*

Almond Chocolate Ginger Bark *251*

Chocolate Salami *252*

Chocolate-Dipped Fruit Skewers *253*

Milk Chocolate S'mores *254*

Hip Chip Trail Mix *255*

Chocolate Potato Chips *256*

Chocolate-Dipped Pretzels *257*

Chocolate Toffee Crackers *258*

Chocolate Crunchies *259*

Chocolate Matzo *260*

Matzo Pizza *261*

Quick-Mix Chocolate Fudge

**MAKES
16 SQUARES**

This fudge is delectable, known to make even the most jaded fudge lovers swoon. Until this recipe, I was never a huge fudge lover. Now I am president of the fudge fan club.

TIP

Store chocolate in a cool, dry place for up to one year. Chocolate will sometimes develop a white "bloom," or coating, when it gets too warm, causing the cocoa butter to separate. The chocolate is still fine to use in recipes or for melting.

8-inch (2 L) square baking pan, greased

2¹/₂ cups	semisweet chocolate chips	625 mL
3 oz	unsweetened chocolate, chopped	90 g
1¹/₃ cups	sweetened condensed milk	325 mL
¹/₄ tsp	salt	1 mL
¹/₄ cup	Galliano liqueur	50 mL

1. In a medium saucepan, combine chocolate chips, unsweetened chocolate, sweetened condensed milk and salt. Cook over medium–low heat, stirring constantly. Chocolate mixture will be very thick and hard to stir, but keep stirring so that chocolate doesn't burn.

2. When chocolate is almost melted, turn off burner. Continue stirring over warm burner until chocolate is completely melted. Stir in liqueur, mixing until smooth.

3. Spread chocolate mixture in prepared pan, smoothing top with a spatula. Cover and refrigerate for about 2 hours or until firm. Cut into 16 squares.

Variation
Substitute your favorite liqueur for the Galliano.

White Chocolate Lemon Fudge

All I can say is that this recipe is devilishly delish, almost like the frosting on a carrot cake. You know, the kind of frosting you pull the cake layers off to get at. If you like lemons, you'll love this very different fudge. Make sure to keep it refrigerated because it's perishable.

TIPS

Look for pure lemon oil in well-stocked grocery or health food stores. Do not substitute lemon extract for the oil, as it will not taste the same. Lemon oil tastes like fresh lemons, and it is worthwhile seeking this product out. You can also order it directly from Boyajian (see Sources, page 369).

Store in an airtight container in the refrigerator for up to 2 days.

8-inch (2 L) square glass baking dish, greased

9 oz	white chocolate, chopped	270 g
7 oz	cream cheese, softened (see Tip, page 100)	210 g
3 cups	confectioner's (icing) sugar	750 mL
1/4 tsp	lemon oil (see Tip, at left)	1 mL

1. In a microwave-safe bowl, microwave white chocolate, uncovered, on Medium (50%) for 1 to 2 minutes, stirring every 30 seconds, or until chocolate is soft and almost melted. Stir until completely melted and smooth.

2. In a large bowl, using an electric mixer, beat cream cheese until smooth. Add confectioner's sugar, beating well. Mix in lemon oil, stirring well.

3. Add melted white chocolate, beating only until smooth. Spread in prepared pan and refrigerate until firm. Cut fudge into squares once firm.

Whiskey Fudge

**MAKES
16 SQUARES**

While we were living in Idaho, someone slipped me a recipe for whiskey fudge. Sounded good, so I anxiously gave it a try. But try as I might, the recipe just wouldn't come out right. So I took the whiskey idea and adapted it to my tried-and-true recipe for fudge. I have family members that will kill for this fudge. It's so good that it's hard to eat just one piece.

TIP

Store fudge in a resealable bag and refrigerate. It keeps really well in the refrigerator for at least 1 week.

8-inch (2 L) square baking dish, greased

19 oz	bittersweet chocolate, chopped	570 g
1	can (14 oz/398 mL) sweetened condensed milk	1
⅓ cup	whiskey	75 mL

1. In a saucepan over medium-low heat, combine chocolate and sweetened condensed milk. Cook, stirring continuously, for 5 minutes or until chocolate is almost melted.

2. Remove from heat and add whiskey, stirring until mixture is smooth.

3. Spread fudge evenly in prepared pan. Cover and refrigerate overnight or until firm before cutting into squares.

Variation
Stir in 1 cup (250 mL) walnuts or pecans along with the whiskey.

Chocolate Fruit Tarts (page 168)

Butterscotch Pecan Chocolate Chip Blondies (page 219),
The Quintessential Chocolate Chip Cookie (page 177)
and Chocolate-Dipped Coconut Macaroons (page 198)

Six-Layer Bars (page 233)

Old-Fashioned Dark Chocolate Pudding (page 266)
and Chocolate Cherry Biscotti (page 210)

Chocolate Espresso Cups (page 275)

Banana Chocolate Ice Cream (page 289)

Chocolate Tiramisu (page 282)

Double Chocolate Lollipops

Chocolate lollipops are super easy to make. Not only do kids and adults alike love them but they also make great gifts and party favors. My son, Noah, even found that they make great bargaining chips in the lunchroom at school.

TIP

The lollipops are best served the day they're made but will keep, covered, in a cool place for up to 2 days.

Baking sheet, lined with parchment paper
6 ice pop sticks or $4^1/_2$-inch (11 cm) skewers

5 oz	milk chocolate, chopped	150 g
2 oz	white chocolate, chopped	60 g

1. In a small microwave-safe bowl, microwave milk chocolate, uncovered, on Medium (50%) for 1 to $1^1/_2$ minutes, stirring every 30 seconds, or until chocolate is soft and almost melted. Stir until completely melted and smooth.

2. Place ice pop sticks on prepared baking sheet. Spoon chocolate into a circle over top 2 inches (5 cm) of each stick. Refrigerate for 30 minutes to 1 hour or until chocolate is firm.

3. While lollipops are chilling, place white chocolate in a small microwave-safe bowl. Microwave, uncovered, on Medium (50%) for 30 to 60 seconds, stirring every 30 seconds, or until chocolate is soft and almost melted. Stir until completely melted and smooth.

4. Using the back of a teaspoon, decoratively swirl a layer of white chocolate over top of each firm lollipop. Chill lollipops again until firm. Store chocolate lollipops in an airtight container in a cool place until ready to serve.

Variation
Substitute bittersweet or semisweet chocolate for the white chocolate.

Dark Chocolate Truffles

**MAKES ABOUT
25 TRUFFLES**

Wine and bittersweet chocolate are sinfully tantalizing together, so I just couldn't resist combining the two in a rich, decadent truffle. And because the recipe calls for only 2 tbsp (25 mL), it's a perfect excuse to crack open a bottle of wine to enjoy with dinner. If you don't have red wine on hand, you can substitute your favorite liqueur.

TIP

This recipe can be doubled to make a large quantity of truffles. Refrigerate any uneaten truffles in an airtight container in the refrigerator for up to 2 weeks.

½ cup	whipping (35%) cream	125 mL
6 oz	bittersweet chocolate, chopped	175 g
2 tbsp	unsalted butter	25 mL
2 tbsp	red wine, such as Cabernet Sauvignon	25 mL
1 tbsp	superfine sugar (see Tip, page 289)	15 mL
1 cup	unsweetened Dutch-process cocoa powder, sifted	250 mL

1. In a large microwave-safe bowl, microwave cream, chocolate and butter, uncovered, on Medium (50%) for 1 to 2 minutes or until cream is hot and chocolate is soft and almost melted. Whisk until completely melted and smooth.

2. Whisk in red wine and sugar. Refrigerate for 2 to 3 hours or until firm.

3. Place cocoa powder in a dish. Scoop chilled truffle mixture into small balls. Roll scoops of truffle mixture in cocoa powder until well coated.

4. Chill truffles for at least 2 hours or until firm. Serve chilled.

Chocolate Cherry Truffles

You no longer have to go to fancy chocolate shops when you yearn for truffles. This very easy and decadent recipe will have you making truffles year-round. And for an added bonus, they make a fabulous hostess gift.

TIP

Store in a covered container for up to 1 week.

Baking sheet, lined with parchment paper

2 cups	semisweet chocolate chips	500 mL
³/₄ cup	whipping (35%) cream	175 mL
³/₄ cup	dried sour cherries, finely chopped	175 mL
2 tbsp	kirsch (cherry brandy)	25 mL
¹/₂ cup	unsweetened Dutch-process cocoa powder, sifted	125 mL

1. In a microwave-safe bowl, combine chocolate chips and cream. Microwave on High for 2 to 2¹/₂ minutes, stirring every 30 seconds, until chocolate is shiny and almost melted. Stir until smooth.

2. Add dried cherries and kirsch, stirring well. Refrigerate until firm.

3. Scoop the chilled mixture by tablespoons (15 mL) and form into balls. Roll in unsweetened cocoa powder. Place on prepared baking sheet.

4. Refrigerate truffles until ready to serve.

Chocolate Rum Balls

MAKES ABOUT
60 BALLS

These rum balls were
a huge hit last holiday
season. After I served
them to friends, my
phone began to ring off
the hook with demands
for the recipe. We like to
eat them year-round.

TIP

Store rum balls in an
airtight container at room
temperature for up to
1 week.

12 oz	vanilla wafer cookies (about 86 cookies)	375 g
1 cup	walnuts	250 mL
1 cup	semisweet chocolate chips	250 mL
3/4 cup	dried apricots	175 mL
1/2 cup	confectioner's (icing) sugar, sifted	125 mL
1/2 cup	dark rum	125 mL
3 tbsp	light corn syrup	45 mL
2 tbsp	unsweetened Dutch-process cocoa powder	25 mL
	Unsweetened Dutch-process cocoa powder, sifted	
	Confectioner's (icing) sugar, sifted	

1. In a food processor fitted with a metal blade, process cookies until finely ground. Transfer to a large bowl. Add walnuts and chocolate chips to processor, pulsing until finely chopped. Add to cookie crumbs. Process dried apricots in processor until finely chopped. Add to cookie mixture.

2. Add confectioner's sugar, rum, corn syrup and cocoa powder to cookie mixture, stirring well.

3. Scoop dough with a spoon and form into 1-inch (2.5 cm) balls. Roll in unsweetened cocoa powder. Before serving, roll in confectioner's sugar.

Variation
Substitute pecans for the walnuts and dried cranberries for the apricots.

Crispy Chocolate Drops

My son, Noah, is crazy
for chocolate bars with
crisp rice, and I love the
crunching-munching
noises he makes while
he dives into these treats.
This is a quick-mix,
one-pan recipe. The only
difficulty is not eating
them all in one sitting!

TIPS

Don't use puffed rice cereal
in this recipe as it's not
crisp enough.

Store drops in an airtight
container or resealable
plastic bag in a cool place
or the refrigerator for up
to 2 days.

Baking sheet, lined with parchment paper

10 oz	milk chocolate, chopped	300 g
1 cup	crisp rice cereal (see Tip, at left)	250 mL

1. In a large microwave-safe bowl, microwave chocolate, uncovered, on Medium (50%) for 1 to 2 minutes, stirring every 30 seconds, or until chocolate is soft and almost melted. Stir until completely melted and smooth.

2. Stir in cereal. Using two teaspoons, drop chocolate mixture onto prepared baking sheet.

3. Refrigerate chocolate drops until firm.

Variation
Substitute bittersweet chocolate for the milk chocolate.

Chocolate Cherry Drops

MAKES ABOUT
22 DROPS

This is a very sophisticated candy that makes a beautiful gift for the holidays. I love chocolate and cherries together, but add to that the toasted almonds and this combo is a winner. Your popularity will increase each time you make these drops.

TIPS

To toast almonds: Preheat oven to 350°F (180°C). Spread nuts on a baking sheet lined with foil or parchment. Bake for 5 to 7 minutes or until light brown and fragrant.

Lightly dust chocolates with confectioner's sugar just before serving, if desired, for a fancier presentation.

Store the chocolates in a covered airtight container in a cool place for up to 2 days.

Baking sheet, lined with parchment paper

10 oz	bittersweet chocolate, chopped	300 g
3/4 cup	whole almonds, toasted (see Tip, at left)	175 mL
1/2 cup	dried sour cherries	125 mL

1. In a microwave-safe bowl, microwave chocolate, uncovered, on Medium (50%) for 1 to 2 minutes, stirring every 30 seconds, or until chocolate is soft and almost melted. Stir until completely melted and smooth.

2. Stir in toasted almonds and dried cherries. Drop by teaspoons (5 mL) onto prepared baking sheet.

3. Refrigerate chocolates until firm to the touch.

Variation
Substitute chopped dried apricots for the cherries or toasted hazelnuts for the almonds.

Chocolate Mints

Here's a fun, easy dessert recipe. Bittersweet chocolate pairs beautifully with the hint of peppermint in this chocolate sweet. They cool the palate and leave your breath minty fresh.

TIP

Store mints in an airtight container or resealable bag in a cool place or the refrigerator for up to 2 days.

Baking sheet, lined with parchment paper

8 oz	bittersweet chocolate, chopped	250 g
$\frac{1}{2}$ tsp	peppermint extract	2 mL

1. In a small microwave-safe bowl, microwave chocolate, uncovered, on Medium (50%) for 1 to 2 minutes, stirring every 30 seconds, or until chocolate is soft and almost melted. Stir until melted and smooth. Stir in peppermint extract.

2. Using two teaspoons, drop chocolate in dollops onto prepared baking sheet, about 2 inches (5 cm) apart. Use back of spoon to lightly swirl each dollop into a small circle.

3. Refrigerate chocolates for 1 hour or until firm to the touch.

Variation
Add broken pieces of candy cane for extra crunch. Stir into melted chocolate along with the extract.

Rocky Roads

MAKES ABOUT 30 CANDIES

I love the fact that you can make these gems in 5 minutes flat. If you are in a really big hurry (with only a few minutes before your guests arrive), place Rocky Roads in the freezer instead of the refrigerator. Freeze for about 15 minutes or until firm.

TIPS

To toast almonds: Preheat oven to 350°F (180°C). Spread nuts on a baking sheet lined with foil or parchment. Bake for 5 to 7 minutes or until light brown and fragrant.

Store in an airtight container for up to 2 days.

Baking sheet, lined with parchment paper

2³⁄₄ cups	semisweet chocolate chips	675 mL
2 tbsp	shortening	25 mL
1 cup	almonds, toasted (see Tip, at left)	250 mL
6 oz	miniature marshmallows (about 5 cups/1.25 L)	175 g

1. In a large microwave-safe bowl, combine chocolate chips and shortening. Microwave on High for 2 to 2½ minutes, stirring every 30 seconds, until chocolate is shiny and almost melted. Stir until smooth. If chocolate mixture is hot, let cool until slightly warm.

2. Stir almonds and marshmallows into chocolate mixture. Using two spoons, scoop mounds of mixture onto prepared baking sheet.

3. Refrigerate until chocolate is firm.

Variations

Substitute toasted hazelnuts for almonds.

You can also add ½ cup (125 mL) dried sour cherries to the Rocky Roads.

Chocolate Halvah Mounds

Chocolate halvah is a delicious dessert to serve after a Mediterranean or Middle Eastern dinner or on its own with a cup of espresso. I can always tell when a recipe is a winner because I watch my husband sneak it out of the kitchen until it's gone. Well, this is one of those recipes! Halvah is made from ground sesame seeds.

TIPS

You can find halvah in well-stocked grocery and health food stores or Middle Eastern and ethnic markets. Sometimes you'll find it marbled with chocolate, scented with vanilla or studded with pistachios. They're all great in this recipe.

Store the chocolates in an airtight container in a cool place for up to 2 days.

2 baking sheets, lined with parchment paper

7 oz	bittersweet chocolate, chopped	210 g
12 oz	halvah (any kind except chocolate-covered), coarsely chopped (see Tip, at left)	375 g
1/3 cup	shelled pistachios, toasted (see Nuts, page 14)	75 mL
	Confectioner's (icing) sugar for dusting (optional)	

1. In a large microwave-safe bowl, microwave chocolate, uncovered, on Medium (50%) for 1 to 2 minutes, stirring every 30 seconds, or until chocolate is soft and almost melted. Stir until completely melted and smooth.

2. Fold in halvah and pistachios. Drop chocolate mixture by tablespoons (15 mL) onto prepared baking sheets. Let stand in a cool place until chocolates are hardened. To speed up this process, you can refrigerate the chocolates briefly until firm.

3. Lightly dust with confectioner's sugar, if using, just before serving.

Chocolate-Dipped
Sesame Almond Candy

I love sesame candy. One day a piece of my candy inadvertently slipped into some melted dark chocolate. The next thing you know, I toasted some sesame seeds and almonds, enrobed them in a honey caramel syrup and then dipped the whole thing in bittersweet chocolate. I love it when inspiration takes hold and won't let go. This candy is best eaten the day it's made.

TIPS

To toast the sesame seeds and almonds, place in a large skillet over medium heat. Toast the seeds and nuts, stirring often, for 5 to 10 minutes or until golden.

Don't make this on a rainy or humid day or else the candy will be too sticky.

To shortcut this recipe, purchase sesame candy from a Middle Eastern grocery or health food store. Break the bars into chunks and dip into melted chocolate.

2 baking sheets, 1 greased and 1 lined with parchment paper
Candy thermometer (optional)

½ cup	light-colored liquid honey	125 mL
½ cup	granulated sugar	125 mL
1 cup	sesame seeds, lightly toasted (see Tip, at left)	250 mL
½ cup	sliced almonds, lightly toasted (see Tip, at left)	125 mL
6 oz	bittersweet or semisweet chocolate, chopped	175 g

1. In a saucepan over medium heat, combine honey, sugar and 2 tbsp (25 mL) water. Bring to a boil, stirring, just until sugar is dissolved. Let boil until syrup reaches 320°F (160°C) or until ½ tsp (2 mL) of the syrup drizzled into cold water separates into hard threads (it will turn a darker caramel color).

2. Remove from heat and quickly stir in toasted sesame seeds and almonds, stirring until seeds are well coated.

3. Pour syrup mixture onto greased baking sheet and, using a greased offset spatula or metal spoon, spread out into an 11- by 9-inch (28 by 23 cm) rectangle, about ¼ inch (0.5 cm) thick. Place baking sheet on rack and let cool. When cool but not hard, remove candy from pan and place on wire rack. Let cool completely. When completely cool, break into about 30 pieces.

4. In a microwave-safe bowl, microwave chocolate, uncovered, on Medium (50%) for 1 to 2 minutes, stirring every 30 seconds, or until chocolate is soft and almost melted. Stir until completely melted and smooth. Dip ends of sesame candies in melted chocolate. Place candies on parchment paper–lined baking sheet. Refrigerate for 30 minutes or until chocolate is firm.

5. Candies are best eaten the day they're made. Store them in a single layer in an airtight container (do not stack them or they will stick together) in a cool place for up to 1 day.

Almond Chocolate Ginger Bark

Calling all ginger lovers! If you love ginger as much as I do, then this is for you. Here, melted bittersweet chocolate is combined with crunchy bits of toasted almonds and candied ginger. Quick, easy and, of course, delicious!

TIPS

To toast almonds: Preheat oven to 350°F (180°C). Spread nuts on a baking sheet lined with foil or parchment. Bake for 5 to 7 minutes or until light brown and fragrant.

Store the bark in a resealable plastic bag in the refrigerator for 2 days.

Baking sheet, lined with parchment paper

11 oz	bittersweet chocolate, chopped	330 g
3 oz	candied ginger pieces, chopped into little bits ($\frac{1}{2}$ cup/125 mL)	90 g
$\frac{3}{4}$ cup	almonds, toasted and coarsely chopped (see Tip, at left)	175 mL

1. In a large microwave-safe bowl, microwave chocolate, uncovered, on Medium (50%) for 1 to 2 minutes, stirring every 30 seconds, or until chocolate is soft and almost melted. Stir until completely melted and smooth.

2. Fold in candied ginger and almonds. Using a spatula, spread mixture out to a rough rectangle about 12 by 9 inches (30 by 23 cm) on prepared baking sheet. Refrigerate for 1 hour or until chocolate is firm. Break chocolate into pieces.

Variations

For a slightly lighter ginger flavor, you can reduce the ginger to 2 oz (60 g), about $\frac{1}{3}$ cup (75 mL), chopped.

You can also substitute macadamia nuts for the almonds.

Chocolate Salami

SERVES 12

MAKES 1 LARGE SALAMI, 20 TO 24 SLICES

I got the idea for this fun chocolate dessert while shopping in a gourmet market. There was actually something called chocolate salami, which I believe was from Portugal. I immediately ran home and started trying to come up with my own version. This tastes almost like a truffle, but with broken cookies and dried cherries. I love to serve this on a platter with fresh and dried fruit and slices of baguette so that it looks like I'm serving a real salami (it looks so cool!).

TIP

The chocolate salami will keep, refrigerated, for up to 1 week.

Baking sheet

6 oz	semisweet or bittersweet chocolate, chopped	175 g
1/3 cup	whipping (35%) cream	75 mL
1 cup	coarsely broken butter cookies, shortbread or ladyfingers	250 mL
1/2 cup	dried cherries	125 mL
2 tbsp	dark rum	25 mL
	Confectioner's (icing) sugar	

1. In a microwave-safe bowl, microwave chocolate and cream, uncovered, on Medium (50%) for 1 to 2 minutes, stirring every 30 seconds, or until cream is hot and chocolate is soft and almost melted. Stir until completely melted and smooth. Stir in cookies, dried cherries and rum. Let cool until slightly thickened but still pourable.

2. Scoop chocolate mixture onto plastic wrap. Roughly shape into a 10-inch (25 cm) long log. Wrap plastic wrap around chocolate. Using your hands, shape plastic-wrapped chocolate into a log (it won't be perfect because the chocolate is still too soft). Wrap log in a layer of foil and place on a tray or baking sheet in refrigerator for 1 hour or until chocolate is partly firm. Remove foil (but not plastic wrap) and, using your hands, shape into a more refined, smoother log. Return to refrigerator and chill for 1 hour longer or until firm.

3. When ready to serve, remove log from refrigerator and lightly dust with confectioner's (icing) sugar. Serve it on a small cutting board or plate with a sharp knife for cutting into slices. Let everyone cut some off as desired.

Variations

Substitute dried cranberries for the cherries.

You can also reduce the broken cookies to 1/2 cup (125 mL), adding 1/2 cup (125 mL) chopped almonds or hazelnuts.

Chocolate-Dipped Fruit Skewers

MAKES
6 SKEWERS

Nothing could be simpler than this recipe. Simply skewer dried fruit and dip in melted chocolate for a very impressive dessert. Most dried fruits, such as pineapple, apricots, peaches, cherries and mangoes, will work beautifully. Dried orange peel, bananas and figs also work well. Use your imagination and develop your own unique creations.

TIP

I used 4¹/₂-inch (11 cm) skewers when developing this recipe. If your skewers are 8 to 9 inches (20 to 23 cm) long, just double the amount of fruit on each skewer and the amount of melted chocolate and dip the top 4 to 6 inches (10 to 15 cm) into the chocolate.

Baking sheet, lined with parchment paper
6 skewers

12	dried apricot halves	12
6	dried pitted dates	6
4 oz	bittersweet chocolate, chopped	125 g

1. Thread two apricots and one date onto each skewer, leaving enough room on bottom of skewer to be able to grasp it.

2. In a microwave-safe bowl, microwave chocolate on Medium (50%) for 1 to 1½ minutes, stirring every 30 seconds, or until chocolate is soft and almost melted. Stir until completely melted and smooth.

3. Dip top 2 to 3 inches (5 to 7.5 cm) of skewer in chocolate and place on prepared baking sheet. Alternatively, drizzle skewers with melted chocolate. Refrigerate skewers for 30 minutes or until chocolate is firm to the touch.

Variation
Stuff dried figs or dates with almond paste or marzipan before skewering.

Milk Chocolate S'mores

MAKES
8 S'MORES

S'mores are a camping tradition and the first thing that most campers pack. Personally, I prefer access to them year-round, which is why I've devised a foolproof, no-fire-needed s'more.

TIP

These sandwiches are best eaten the day they're made, but if not eating them right away, keep s'mores flat in an airtight container in a cool place for up to 1 day.

Baking sheet, lined with parchment paper

4 oz	milk chocolate, chopped	125 g
8	large marshmallows	8
8	whole graham crackers, preferably cinnamon-flavored, broken into 16 halves	8

1. In a large microwave–safe bowl, microwave chocolate, uncovered, on Medium (50%) for 1 to $1\frac{1}{2}$ minutes, stirring every 30 seconds, or until chocolate is soft and almost melted. Stir until completely melted and smooth.

2. Lightly flatten each marshmallow. Using a fork, stab one marshmallow and roll into melted chocolate, covering completely. Place coated marshmallow on one graham cracker half. Top with a second graham cracker half. Continue with remaining marshmallows, chocolate and crackers.

3. Place s'mores on prepared baking sheet and refrigerate for 1 hour or until chocolate is firm.

Variation

Substitute bittersweet chocolate for the milk chocolate.

Hip Chip Trail Mix

MAKES ABOUT
3½ CUPS
(875 ML)

Whip up this delicious combination of caramelized pecans, salted almonds, chocolate chips and tangy dried apricots in a jiffy. Try not to make it too far in advance of serving as the caramelized nuts can get sticky. Serve with mint tea or strong coffee.

TIPS

Kitchen shears are a great way to slice dried apricots (or any dried fruit, for that matter).

Trail mix is best served the day it is made (it tends to get too sticky).

Baking sheet, lined with parchment paper or foil

1 cup	whole pecans	250 mL
⅓ cup	granulated sugar	75 mL
1 cup	dry-roasted salted almonds	250 mL
1 cup	dried apricots, snipped into slivers (see Tip, at left)	250 mL
½ cup	semisweet chocolate chips	125 mL
Pinch	salt	Pinch

1. In a large nonstick skillet over medium–high heat, toast pecans, stirring often, until they just start to turn golden, about 5 minutes.

2. Reduce heat to medium–high. Add sugar, stirring or shaking the pan as necessary, until sugar is melted, about 5 minutes. If sugar or nuts start to burn, reduce heat to low.

3. Spread caramelized nuts on prepared baking sheet, separating pecans with a fork as necessary. Be careful not to burn your fingers as caramel is very hot. Let pecans cool completely on pan on rack.

4. In a medium bowl, combine cooled pecans, almonds, dried apricots and chocolate chips. Sprinkle with salt and serve.

Chocolate Potato Chips

**MAKES
6 SERVINGS**

I know, potato chips and chocolate sound weird. But let me assure you that this is a match made in heaven. It's that combo of salty and sweet that is so irresistible.

TIPS

Try to use unbroken chips in this recipe. It can be doubled or tripled for a crowd.

Ideally, serve chips the same day they're dipped. But if you're not eating them right away, keep covered in a cool place for up to 2 days.

2 baking sheets, lined with parchment paper

4 oz	bittersweet or semisweet chocolate, chopped	125 g
2 cups	ruffled plain potato chips (about 2 oz/60 g)	500 mL

1. In a microwave-safe bowl, microwave chocolate, uncovered, on Medium (50%) for 1 to $1\frac{1}{2}$ minutes, stirring every 30 seconds, or until chocolate is soft and almost melted. Stir until completely melted and smooth.

2. Dip ends of chips into melted chocolate. Place dipped chips on prepared baking sheet and refrigerate for 30 minutes to 1 hour or until chocolate is firm.

> **Variation**
> Instead of dipping the chips, drizzle the melted chocolate over tops of chips in a decorative pattern.

Chocolate-Dipped Pretzels

**MAKES
12 PRETZELS**

I love to get children involved in the kitchen. This is a perfect cooking project because it's easy to do, gives quick results and tastes great. My children use these as bartering chips at school.

TIP

Store in an airtight container at room temperature for up to 2 days.

Baking sheet, lined with parchment paper

1 cup	semisweet chocolate chips	250 mL
1 tbsp	shortening	15 mL
12	pretzel rods	12
	Assorted sprinkles, candies or chopped nuts for sprinkling	

1. In a microwave-safe bowl, combine chocolate chips and shortening. Microwave on High for 1 to 2 minutes, stirring every 30 seconds, until chocolate is shiny and almost melted. Stir until smooth.

2. Dip top halves of pretzel rods in melted chocolate. Place on prepared baking sheet. Sprinkle chocolate-covered halves with sprinkles, candies or nuts.

3. Refrigerate until chocolate is hardened.

Variation
Substitute dried fruit or unseasoned potato chips for the pretzels.

Chocolate Toffee Crackers

This recipe was given to me by my mother, who got it from her friend Mary Jo. This is my adaptation of the original. It has been given two very enthusiastic thumbs up from everyone who has tried it. A word of warning, though: this dessert is very habit-forming!

TIP

Store in an airtight container for up to 3 days.

Preheat oven to 350°F (180°C)
Rimmed baking sheet, lined with foil, greased

35 to 40	saltine soda crackers	35 to 40
1 cup	butter	250 mL
1 cup	packed light brown sugar	250 mL
2 cups	semisweet chocolate chips	500 mL
2 tbsp	shortening	25 mL

1. Arrange crackers in rows on prepared baking sheet right next to each other. The amount you use will depend upon dimensions of pan.

2. In a microwave-safe bowl, microwave butter on High until melted, about $1\frac{1}{2}$ minutes. Add brown sugar and stir. Microwave for 3 minutes longer, whisking every 30 seconds, until sugar is dissolved.

3. Whisk butter mixture until smooth and pour over crackers in pan. Bake in preheated oven until bubbling but not burning, about 14 to 17 minutes.

4. In a separate microwave-safe bowl, combine chocolate chips and shortening. Microwave on High for 2 to $2\frac{1}{2}$ minutes, stirring every 30 seconds, until chocolate is shiny and almost melted. Stir until smooth. Drizzle over cooled crackers. Refrigerate for 1 hour. Break into pieces.

Variation
Sprinkle chopped nuts over the chocolate.

Chocolate Crunchies

· ·

**MAKES ABOUT
30 CRUNCHIES**

Ellen Bloom shared this recipe with my brother, Jon, who then passed it on to me. She says that these no-bake treats are her family's favorite. Taste them and you will see why.

TIP

Store in an airtight container in the refrigerator if the weather is warm so the chocolate doesn't melt.

Baking sheet, lined with parchment paper

2 cups	semisweet chocolate chips	500 mL
2 tbsp	shortening	25 mL
8 oz	Chinese noodles	250 g
1 cup	English toffee candy bits	250 mL
1/2 cup	raisins (optional)	125 mL
	Confectioner's (icing) sugar	

1. In a large microwave-safe bowl, combine chocolate chips and shortening. Microwave on High for 2 to 2 1/2 minutes, stirring every 30 seconds, until chocolate is shiny and almost melted. Stir until smooth. Mix in Chinese noodles, toffee bits and raisins, if using. Mix well.

2. Using two spoons, drop mounds of chocolate mixture on prepared baking sheet, 1 to 2 inches (2.5 to 5 cm) apart. Sprinkle lightly with confectioner's sugar.

3. Refrigerate chocolate mounds until firm. When hardened, carefully peel off waxed paper.

Variation
Substitute 2 crushed peanut butter candy bars for the English toffee bits.

· · · · · · · · · · · · · · · · · · · CANDIES, SNACKS AND OTHER TREATS **259**

Chocolate Matzo

This is a delicious dessert for Passover, but it's also great any time of the year. Plain matzo is a perfect foil for sweet chocolate. Go ahead and get creative with it as well. Top the melted chocolate with a sprinkle of toffee bits, toasted coconut or mini marshmallows.

TIPS

To toast hazelnuts: Place hazelnuts in a single layer on a foil or parchment-lined baking sheet. Bake in center of preheated 350°F (180°C) oven for 10 to 15 minutes or until lightly browned and skins are blistered. Wrap nuts in a clean dry kitchen towel and let stand for 1 minute. Rub nuts in towel to remove loose skins (it's okay if you can't remove all of them). Let nuts cool completely.

Store matzo in an airtight container or resealable plastic bag in a cool place for up to 2 days.

2 baking sheets, lined with parchment paper

6 oz	bittersweet or semisweet chocolate, chopped	175 g
3	sheets matzo	3
2 oz	milk chocolate, chopped	60 g
2 oz	white chocolate, chopped	60 g
2/3 cup	coarsely chopped hazelnuts or almonds, toasted (see Tip, at left)	150 mL

1. In a small microwave-safe bowl, microwave bittersweet chocolate, uncovered, on Medium (50%) for 1 to 2 minutes, stirring every 30 seconds, or until chocolate is soft and almost melted. Stir until melted and smooth. Using an offset spatula, spread chocolate over matzo. Refrigerate for 1 hour or until chocolate is firm.

2. While matzo is chilling, melt milk chocolate in a small microwave-safe bowl, uncovered, on Medium (50%) for 30 to 60 seconds, stirring every 30 seconds, or until chocolate is soft and almost melted. Stir until melted and smooth. Remove matzo from refrigerator and drizzle tops with melted milk chocolate. Refrigerate again for 30 minutes or until chocolate is firm.

3. In a small microwave-safe bowl, microwave white chocolate, uncovered, on Medium (50%) for 30 to 60 seconds, stirring every 30 seconds, or until chocolate is soft and almost melted. Stir until melted and smooth. Remove matzo from refrigerator and drizzle tops with melted white chocolate. Sprinkle chopped nuts over white chocolate. Refrigerate for 30 minutes or until chocolate is firm. Break into pieces and serve.

Matzo Pizza

MAKES ABOUT 30 PIECES

I developed this recipe about seven years ago, when I needed an incredible Passover dessert. I tried many variations before hitting upon this final recipe. This is no ordinary matzo. It's covered with rich, crisp toffee, drizzled with melted chocolate and topped with chocolate chips. The toffee portion of the recipe is adapted from a recipe by Natalie Haughton. Although this recipe may look complicated, it is very easy and truly irresistible.

TIP

Do not make this recipe on a rainy or humid day — the toffee doesn't harden properly and will be sticky. Also don't try to double this recipe, because it won't work well. If you're making it for a crowd, just make several batches of the recipe, one after another. I do this often, as I give it as gifts at the holidays. It goes very quickly as long as everything is premeasured and ready to go.

2 baking sheets, lined with parchment paper
Candy thermometer

1 cup	butter	250 mL
1 cup	granulated sugar	250 mL
3 tbsp	water	45 mL
1 tbsp	light corn syrup	15 mL
5	sheets matzo	5
4 oz	semisweet or milk chocolate, chopped	125 g
3/4 cup	semisweet chocolate chips	175 mL

1. In a large heavy saucepan over medium heat, combine butter, sugar, water and corn syrup. Cook until butter is melted, stirring often. Increase heat to medium-high. Boil without stirring until syrup reaches 250°F (120°C) on candy thermometer. Once beyond this point, stir often until mixture reaches 300°F (150°C). Adjust stove temperature as necessary to prevent scorching.

2. Place matzos on prepared baking sheets. Once temperature reaches 300°F (150°C), carefully pour toffee over matzo. Working quickly, use an offset spatula or back of a spoon to evenly spread poured toffee over matzo. Don't worry if toffee looks a bit blobby when you spread it. Let toffee stand for 20 to 30 minutes to harden and cool.

3. In a large microwave-safe bowl, microwave chopped chocolate, uncovered, on Medium (50%) for 1 to 1½ minutes, stirring every 30 seconds, or until chocolate is soft and almost melted. Stir until completely melted and smooth.

4. Drizzle melted chocolate over toffee-covered matzo. Sprinkle chocolate chips over chocolate. Refrigerate for 1 hour or until chocolate is firm. Break matzo into pieces.

Variation
Omit the chocolate chips or substitute white chocolate chips or thinly sliced dried apricots for them.

Puddings and Mousses

Better-Than-Store-Bought Chocolate Pudding Mix *264*

Quick Chocolate Pudding *265*

Old-Fashioned Dark Chocolate Pudding *266*

Café au Lait Pudding *267*

Chocolate Butterscotch Pudding *268*

Chocolate Tapioca for Grown-Ups *269*

White Chocolate Almond Rice Pudding *270*

Chocolate Chip Bread Pudding with Irish Cream *271*

Chocolate Banana Bread Pudding *272*

Pumpkin Chip Bread Pudding *273*

Ricotta Puddings *274*

Chocolate Espresso Cups *275*

Strawberry Cheesecake Mousse Parfaits *276*

Cookie Parfaits *277*

Dark Chocolate Mousse *278*

Chocolate Chip Raspberry Clafouti *279*

Chocolate Chip Trifle *280*

Chocolate Cherry Terrine *281*

Chocolate Tiramisu *282*

Chocolate Soup *283*

Better-Than-Store-Bought Chocolate Pudding Mix

· ·

When I was growing up, my mother would always have a big container of homemade pudding mix on hand. It is amazing how simple and quick it is to put this together. Plus, there aren't any preservatives, colors or other additives in this mix.

TIP
When making the pudding with this mix, the recipe can be doubled.

Pudding Mix

4 cups	nonfat dry milk	1 L
1³/₄ cups	granulated sugar	425 mL
1¹/₂ cups	unsweetened Dutch-process cocoa powder, sifted	375 mL
1¹/₂ cups	cornstarch	375 mL
³/₄ tsp	salt	4 mL
2 cups	semisweet chocolate chips	500 mL

Pudding

2 cups	milk, divided	500 mL
1 cup	pudding mix	250 mL
¹/₂ tsp	vanilla	2 mL

1. *Pudding Mix:* In a large bowl, whisk together dry milk, sugar, cocoa powder, cornstarch and salt. Stir in chocolate chips.

2. Transfer to an airtight container or glass jar. Store at room temperature for up to 6 months.

3. *Pudding:* In a bowl, whisk ¹/₂ cup (125 mL) of the milk with pudding mix. Set aside. In a medium saucepan, heat remaining milk until steaming and very warm to the touch. Gradually whisk in pudding mixture. Cook, whisking constantly, until thickened and bubbling.

4. Remove from heat and stir in vanilla. Pour pudding into a serving bowl or scoop into individual dessert bowls. Let stand for 15 minutes before serving. Alternatively, cover and refrigerate cooled pudding and serve chilled.

Variations
Sprinkle a little ground cinnamon into the warm pudding.

For a richer taste, whisk 1 tbsp (15 mL) butter into hot pudding.

Quick Chocolate Pudding

Ever had a craving for something quick, rich, creamy and chocolaty? If your answer is no, you'd better pinch yourself out of your dietary slumber. This recipe will satisfy all of these yearnings. Serve the pudding warm or cold.

TIPS

To toast almonds: Preheat oven to 350°F (180°C). Spread nuts on a baking sheet lined with foil or parchment. Bake for 5 to 7 minutes or until light brown and fragrant.

You can also layer the pudding and whipped cream parfait-style in glasses.

2½ cups	store-bought chocolate milk, divided	625 mL
¼ cup	granulated sugar	50 mL
⅓ cup	cornstarch	75 mL
⅛ tsp	salt	0.5 mL
4 oz	semisweet chocolate, chopped	125 g

Topping

½ cup	whipping (35%) cream	125 mL
1 tbsp	confectioner's (icing) sugar	15 mL
¼ cup	sweetened flaked coconut, toasted (see Tip, at left)	50 mL

1. In a saucepan over medium heat, heat 2 cups (500 mL) chocolate milk and sugar just until warm to the touch.

2. In a small bowl, whisk together remaining chocolate milk, cornstarch and salt. Whisk into warm milk mixture, whisking continuously until thick. Remove from heat and whisk in chocolate until melted and smooth. Spoon pudding into a bowl and place plastic wrap directly on surface. Let pudding cool for 20 minutes to serve warm, or refrigerate to chill further.

3. *Topping:* In a small bowl, using electric mixer, whip together cream and confectioner's sugar until soft peaks form. Spoon whipped cream over chocolate pudding. Serve in bowls with a sprinkling of coconut.

Variation
Substitute milk chocolate for the semisweet chocolate.

Old-Fashioned Dark Chocolate Pudding

SERVES 6

You will love the old-fashioned chocolate hominess of this dessert. Just the name conjures images of comfort in Bubbie's kitchen.

TIP

You will find it easiest to cook this pudding in a heavy-bottomed nonstick saucepan.

1/2 cup	unsweetened Dutch-process cocoa powder, sifted	125 mL
1/3 cup	cornstarch	75 mL
1/4 tsp	salt	1 mL
2 cups	milk	500 mL
2 cups	half-and-half (10%) cream	500 mL
3/4 cup	granulated sugar	175 mL
1 cup	semisweet chocolate chips	250 mL
2 tsp	vanilla, divided	10 mL
1 cup	whipping (35%) cream	250 mL
2 tbsp	confectioner's (icing) sugar	25 mL

1. In a small bowl, combine cocoa powder, cornstarch and salt.

2. In a large saucepan over medium–high heat, heat milk, half-and-half and sugar until sugar is dissolved. Quickly whisk in cocoa powder mixture until completely dissolved with no lumps. Reduce heat to medium and cook, stirring constantly, until thickened. Continue cooking and stirring for 2 minutes longer or until thickened. Remove from heat. Stir in chocolate chips and 1 tsp (5 mL) of the vanilla. Pour pudding into large bowl or six individual dishes.

3. Press a sheet of plastic wrap directly on surface of pudding to prevent a skin from forming. Let cool for 20 minutes. Refrigerate for several hours or until chilled, or overnight.

4. Meanwhile, in a small bowl, using electric mixer, whip together cream, confectioner's sugar and remaining vanilla until soft peaks form.

5. Remove plastic wrap. Serve pudding with whipped cream.

Café au Lait Pudding

SERVES 6

As a huge coffee fan, I am always inventing new ways to enjoy my cup o' joe. This pudding hits the spot, with a light coffee flavor and a nuance of white chocolate.

TIP

Garnish pudding with a dollop of whipped cream and chocolate-covered espresso beans, if desired.

¾ cup	granulated sugar	175 mL
⅓ cup	cornstarch	75 mL
2	egg yolks	2
3 cups	milk	750 mL
1 cup	whipping (35%) cream	250 mL
2 tbsp	instant coffee granules	25 mL
2 oz	white chocolate, chopped	60 g
½ tsp	vanilla	2 mL

1. In a saucepan, mix together sugar and cornstarch.

2. In a large bowl, whisk together egg yolks, milk, cream and instant coffee. Add to sugar mixture, whisking well to dissolve sugar and eliminate any lumps.

3. Cook over medium heat, stirring constantly, for 10 minutes or until the mixture has thickened. Whisk in white chocolate and vanilla until melted and smooth.

4. Eat warm or transfer pudding to a bowl and place plastic wrap directly on surface. Let stand until cool before refrigerating. Refrigerate until chilled, or for up to 2 days.

Variation
Substitute milk chocolate for the white chocolate.

Chocolate Butterscotch Pudding

SERVES 4 TO 6

Wow, this pudding is a taste sensation! The combo of butterscotch, milk chocolate and Scotch really plays with your taste buds. For a fun dessert, you can serve this dressed up in china teacups.

TIP

This pudding is best served the day it's made but is still delicious and will keep, refrigerated, for several days.

½ cup	packed dark brown sugar	125 mL
¼ cup	cornstarch	50 mL
¼ tsp	salt	1 mL
3	egg yolks	3
2 cups	milk	500 mL
1 cup	whipping (35%) cream	250 mL
4 oz	milk chocolate, chopped	125 g
2 tbsp	unsalted butter, softened	25 mL
2 tbsp	Scotch	25 mL

1. In a saucepan, mix together brown sugar, cornstarch and salt.

2. In a medium bowl, whisk together egg yolks, milk and cream. Add to the sugar mixture, whisking well to dissolve the sugar and eliminate lumps.

3. Cook over medium heat, stirring constantly, for 10 minutes or until the mixture has thickened. Remove from heat. Whisk in chocolate, butter and Scotch until melted and smooth.

4. Transfer pudding to a bowl and place plastic wrap directly on surface. Let stand until cool before refrigerating. Refrigerate until chilled.

Chocolate Tapioca
for Grown-Ups

I love comforting tapioca pudding. I call this recipe a grown-up version because it has a swift kick of Irish cream — sure to help cure what ails ya!

TIPS
You will find it easiest to cook this pudding in a heavy-bottomed nonstick saucepan. A great way to serve the pudding is in martini glasses garnished with a dollop of freshly whipped cream.

Small, airline-size bottles of liqueur are exactly ¼ cup (50 mL).

3 cups	milk	750 mL
½ cup	granulated sugar	125 mL
3 tbsp plus 1 tsp	quick-cooking tapioca	50 mL
2	egg yolks	2
1 cup	semisweet chocolate chips	250 mL
¼ cup	Irish cream liqueur	50 mL
½ tsp	vanilla	2 mL

1. In a large saucepan, whisk together milk, sugar, tapioca and egg yolks. Let stand for 5 minutes.

2. Place saucepan over medium–high heat and cook, stirring constantly, until mixture is thickened and comes to a boil (it will look like bubbling lava). Cook for 2 minutes longer. Remove from heat and stir in chocolate chips, Irish cream liqueur and vanilla.

3. Scoop pudding into a large bowl or individual cups. Press a sheet of plastic wrap directly on surface to prevent a skin from forming. Let cool for 20 minutes. Refrigerate until chilled.

4. Remove plastic wrap. Serve pudding warm or chilled. The pudding will continue to thicken as it chills. It is best eaten the day it is made.

Variation
Substitute another sweet liqueur for the Irish cream. Try amaretto or Kahlúa for an equally pleasing flavor.

White Chocolate Almond Rice Pudding

SERVES 6 TO 8

This pudding is inspired by a recipe from the *Los Angeles Times*. It's delectably different and a great sweet to serve for dessert.

TIPS

When toasting a small amount of nuts, I like to use a nonstick skillet. Toast them in the pan over medium heat, stirring often, for 3 to 5 minutes or until lightly toasted.

Don't try to fold the whipped cream into warm pudding, because the cream will melt from the heat, making a drippy mess.

1 cup	medium-grain white rice, such as Calrose (do not rinse)	250 mL
2 cups	milk	500 mL
1/2 cup	granulated sugar	125 mL
3 oz	white chocolate, chopped	90 g
1 tsp	almond extract	5 mL
3/4 cup	whipping (35%) cream	175 mL
2 tbsp	sliced almonds, toasted (see Tip, at left)	25 mL

1. In a saucepan over medium heat, combine 2 cups (500 mL) water and rice and bring to a boil. Reduce heat to low and simmer, covered, for 15 minutes or until most of the liquid is absorbed. Remove from heat and let stand, covered, for 5 minutes.

2. Return saucepan to low heat. Stir in milk and sugar. Cook, stirring continuously, for 15 minutes or until very thick and creamy and rice is soft. Remove from heat and, stirring occasionally, let stand for 5 minutes. Stir in white chocolate and almond extract until melted. Let cool completely.

3. In a small bowl, using electric mixer, whip cream until soft peaks form. Fold into rice pudding. Garnish with almonds.

Variation
Fold 2 to 4 tbsp (25 to 60 mL) chopped candied ginger into the rice pudding along with the whipped cream for a ginger version.

Chocolate Chip Bread Pudding with Irish Cream

Irish cream makes an unbelievably delicious bread pudding. My friend Susan Bussel proclaimed this dessert a "10." I just know that once I start eating this pudding, I can't stop. It's comfort food at its best!

TIP

All of the recipes in this book were tested using large eggs. Using medium or extra-large eggs may adversely affect the outcome of the recipe.

Preheat oven to 350°F (180°C), with rack placed in center of oven

13- by 9-inch (3 L) baking dish, greased

8 cups	loosely packed bread cubes (preferably egg bread)	2 L
9	eggs	9
3 $^1/_3$ cups	milk	825 mL
1 cup	whipping (35%) cream	250 mL
$^3/_4$ cup	packed light brown sugar	175 mL
$^3/_4$ cup	granulated sugar	175 mL
$^1/_2$ cup	Irish cream liqueur	125 mL
1 cup	semisweet chocolate chips	250 mL

1. Place bread cubes in prepared dish. Set aside.

2. In a large bowl, whisk eggs well. Whisk in milk, cream, brown sugar, granulated sugar and liqueur. Pour mixture over bread cubes and let stand for 10 minutes so that bread absorbs liquid. With a spatula, press down bread cubes into liquid once or twice. Sprinkle chocolate chips over top, pressing them in with a fork.

3. Bake in preheated oven until custard is set but still slightly wobbly in the center, about 45 minutes. Let cool on a rack.

Chocolate Banana Bread Pudding

Being a huge fan of chocolate and banana, I love the flavors in this bread pudding. The bananas almost have a roasted flavor, which is divine in this not-so-traditional pudding.

TIP

Serve this dessert warm with a scoop of vanilla ice cream, if desired.

Preheat oven to 350°F (180°C)
8-inch (2 L) square glass baking dish, greased

4$\frac{1}{2}$ cups	loosely packed bread cubes	1.125 L
1$\frac{1}{2}$	medium bananas, sliced $\frac{1}{4}$ inch (0.5 cm) thick	1$\frac{1}{2}$
$\frac{1}{3}$ cup	semisweet chocolate chips	75 mL
3	eggs	3
2	egg yolks	2
$\frac{3}{4}$ cup	packed light brown sugar	175 mL
2$\frac{1}{2}$ cups	milk	625 mL
1 tsp	vanilla	5 mL
2 tbsp	bourbon (optional)	25 mL

1. Place bread cubes in prepared dish. Scatter banana slices over top. Sprinkle with chocolate chips.

2. In a large bowl, whisk together eggs and egg yolks. Whisk in brown sugar. Add milk, vanilla and bourbon, if using, whisking well. Pour mixture over banana slices.

3. Bake in preheated oven for about 50 minutes or until pudding is puffed and center is firm to the touch. Let cool slightly before serving.

Pumpkin Chip Bread Pudding

This dessert is a cross between pumpkin pie and bread pudding — delicious and comforting year-round. For an extra treat, drizzle caramel sauce across the top.

TIP

To make your own nonstick pan release, whip together $1/3$ cup (75 mL) vegetable or canola oil, $1/3$ cup (75 mL) vegetable shortening and $1/3$ cup (75 mL) all-purpose flour. (I use a mini food processor for this.) Store in an airtight container in the refrigerator (it will last several months).

Preheat oven to 350°F (180°C)
13- by 9-inch (3 L) glass baking dish, greased

6 cups	lightly packed bread cubes (about 8 standard slices)	1.5 L
4	eggs	4
$2^1/_2$ cups	milk	625 mL
$1^3/_4$ cups	pumpkin purée (not pie filling)	425 mL
$3/_4$ cup	granulated sugar	175 mL
$1/_4$ cup	packed dark brown sugar	50 mL
1 tsp	ground cinnamon	5 mL
$1/_2$ tsp	ground allspice	2 mL
1 tsp	vanilla	5 mL
$3/_4$ cup	semisweet chocolate chips	175 mL

1. Place bread cubes in prepared dish and set aside.

2. In a large bowl, whisk together eggs, milk, pumpkin, granulated sugar, brown sugar, cinnamon, allspice and vanilla until combined. Pour mixture over bread cubes and sprinkle with chocolate chips. With a spatula, lightly press bread cubes and chocolate chips into custard mixture to coat.

3. Bake in preheated oven for 50 minutes or until top is puffed and center is firm to the touch. Let cool slightly before serving.

Ricotta Puddings

SERVES 4

Here's a fantastic quickie that's as delicious as it is quick to prepare. This recipe is inspired by something that I tasted at Joan's on Third in Los Angeles, a fabulous little gourmet shop. To showcase fresh ricotta cheese, it's drizzled with honey and a sprinkle of ground espresso. I took it a touch further and added chopped bittersweet chocolate and served it in a martini glass.

TIP

You can make this dessert up to 1 hour ahead. Just make sure to refrigerate it, and don't drizzle on the honey and espresso until just before serving.

4 martini glasses

2 cups	ricotta cheese	500 mL
2 oz	bittersweet chocolate, grated or finely chopped	60 g
¼ cup	liquid honey	50 mL
2 tsp	finely ground espresso	10 mL

1. In a small bowl, mix together ricotta cheese and chocolate.
2. Divide ricotta mixture equally among martini glasses.
3. Drizzle honey over top. Sprinkle with espresso and serve immediately.

Variation

Fold chopped cherries into the ricotta along with the chocolate.

Chocolate Espresso Cups

This fabulously rich and mouth-watering dessert is a cross between a mousse, a pudding and a truffle. I refer to these cups as my magic trick — they instantly disappear, without sleight of hand. They're that good!

TIP

My daughter thinks that this dessert should be garnished with a small dollop of whipped cream and a chocolate-covered espresso bean.

2 cups	whipping (35%) cream	500 mL
1 tbsp	finely ground espresso	15 mL
8 oz	bittersweet chocolate, chopped	250 g
3 tbsp	superfine sugar (see Tip, page 289)	45 mL
3 tbsp	instant coffee granules	45 mL

1. In a microwave-safe bowl, combine cream and ground coffee. Microwave, uncovered, on High for 2 minutes or until cream is hot.

2. Add chocolate, sugar and instant coffee, whisking until smooth. Strain mixture into a clean bowl, removing any little bits of ground coffee.

3. Ladle or scoop the chocolate mixture into small tea or espresso cups. Chill for 3 hours or until firm. Serve chilled.

Strawberry Cheesecake Mousse Parfaits

A version of this dessert won our bakery the coveted Best Dessert Chef's Affair 2000 award. We serve it in martini glasses with graham cracker crumbs and raspberry sauce.

TIPS

Superfine sugar dissolves very quickly in liquid. It is sometimes labeled as "instant dissolving fruit powdered sugar." If you can't find it in your grocery store, make your own: process granulated sugar in a food processor until very finely ground.

4	whole graham crackers	4
10 oz	frozen unsweetened strawberries, thawed and including liquid (about 2$\frac{1}{2}$ cups/625 mL)	300 g
$\frac{1}{3}$ cup	superfine sugar (see Tip, at left)	75 mL
$\frac{1}{3}$ cup	water	75 mL
1	package (8 oz/250 g) cream cheese, softened	1
1 cup	confectioner's (icing) sugar	250 mL
1$\frac{1}{4}$ cups	whipping (35%) cream	300 mL
1 tbsp	light rum (optional)	15 mL
$\frac{3}{4}$ cup	semisweet chocolate chips	175 mL

1. In a food processor fitted with a metal blade, pulse graham crackers until finely ground. Transfer to a bowl and set aside. Wipe out processor bowl.

2. Place strawberries in clean processor. Pulse just until chunky. Transfer strawberries to a separate bowl. Whisk in sugar and water. Set aside.

3. In a separate bowl, using electric mixer, whip cream cheese until smooth. Add confectioner's sugar, whipping until creamy and smooth. Gradually add cream and rum in a steady stream, beating on low speed. Whisk mixture on high speed until it reaches soft peaks.

4. Place a scoop of the cream cheese mixture in each of six wine glasses. Drizzle with some of the strawberry sauce and sprinkle with chocolate chips. Continue layering cream cheese mixture, strawberry sauce and chocolate chips until glasses are three-quarters full. Top each parfait with about 1 tbsp (15 mL) of the graham cracker crumbs.

Variation
Top the parfaits with chocolate sandwich crumbs instead of graham cracker crumbs, if desired.

Cookie Parfaits

Delicious, delicious, delicious to the nth degree! Imagine a rich and creamy dessert that's quick to throw together and very impressive to serve for dessert. Well, this is that dessert and then some. My son, Noah, gave it a rating of 19.5 on a scale of 1 to 10.

TIPS

The parfaits are best served the day they're made.

You can use juice glasses, wineglasses, martini glasses or water glasses for this dessert.

4 parfait or regular glasses

1 cup	whipping (35%) cream	250 mL
3 tbsp	confectioner's (icing) sugar	45 mL
1/2 tsp	vanilla	2 mL
2 cups	broken chocolate chip cookies	500 mL
2 cups	prepared chocolate pudding, chilled	500 mL

1. In a small bowl, using electric mixer, whip together cream, confectioner's sugar and vanilla until soft peaks form.

2. In a glass, sprinkle a few broken cookies. Top with a layer of chocolate pudding. Spread a small layer of whipped cream, followed by another sprinkle of broken cookies. Repeat with another layer of pudding, whipped cream and cookies.

3. Repeat with remaining glasses, beginning and ending with cookies. Refrigerate parfaits until ready to serve.

Variation
Substitute chocolate sandwich cookies for the chocolate chip cookies.

Dark Chocolate Mousse

I always have unexpected guests, most expecting to be served spectacular desserts. So I like to be armed with a handful of super delicious, make-them-in-minutes desserts. This mousse is one of those recipes, as it can be made almost instantly with ingredients on hand. My brother, Jon, says this is one of his favorite desserts.

TIP

Garnish mousse with fresh raspberries and sprigs of mint.

8 oz	bittersweet chocolate, chopped	250 g
2½ cups	whipping (35%) cream, divided	625 mL
3 tbsp	superfine sugar (see Tip, page 289)	45 mL
2 tsp	vanilla	10 mL

1. In a microwave-safe bowl, combine chocolate and ½ cup (125 mL) cream. Microwave on High for 60 seconds or until cream is hot and chocolate is soft and almost melted. Stir until completely melted and smooth. Let cool slightly.

2. In a medium bowl, using electric mixer, whip remaining cream, sugar and vanilla until stiff peaks form. With a rubber spatula, fold melted chocolate mixture into whipped cream mixture.

3. Scoop mousse into small cups. Chill for several hours before serving.

Variation
Substitute 1 tbsp (15 mL) orange-flavored liqueur for the vanilla extract.

Chocolate Chip Raspberry Clafouti

SERVES 8

Can you say clafouti without smiling? *The Moosewood Restaurant Book of Desserts* inspired this recipe. It is a great dessert that makes me think of summertime.

TIP
All of the recipes in this book were tested using large eggs. Using medium or extra-large eggs may adversely affect the outcome of the recipe.

Preheat oven to 350°F (180°C)
10-inch (25 cm) deep-dish glass pie plate, greased

2 cups	fresh raspberries	500 mL
1/2 cup	semisweet chocolate chips	125 mL
4	eggs	4
3/4 cup	all-purpose flour	175 mL
1/2 cup	granulated sugar	125 mL
1/2 cup	whipping (35%) cream	125 mL
1/2 cup	milk	125 mL
1/2 tsp	almond extract	2 mL

1. Scatter raspberries and chocolate chips in bottom of prepared pie plate.

2. In a blender or using an immersion/stick blender, combine eggs, flour, sugar, cream, milk and almond extract. Blend until smooth.

3. Pour batter over raspberries and chocolate chips. Bake in preheated oven for 55 to 60 minutes or until puffed, golden and a knife inserted into center comes out clean. Let cool for 15 minutes before serving.

Chocolate Chip Trifle

SERVES
ABOUT 20

This is a spectacular dessert that is really quite easy to assemble. Instant pudding tastes homemade with the addition of half-and-half cream and almond syrup. You can prepare this dessert a day ahead of time, which only improves the flavors and textures.

TIPS

If unsweetened raspberries are unavailable, use frozen sweetened raspberries instead, but reduce the amount of sugar in the sauce to taste.

Almond syrup can be found in the coffee aisle of most large supermarkets.

Large glass bowl

12 oz	frozen unsweetened raspberries, thawed and including juice (about 3 cups/750 mL)	375 g
$1/2$ cup	superfine sugar (see Tip, page 276)	125 mL
$2/3$ cup	water	150 mL
2	boxes (each 3.4 oz/192 g) instant vanilla pudding mix	2
2 cups	milk	500 mL
$1 1/2$ cups	half-and-half (10%) cream	375 mL
1 tsp	almond syrup (see Tips, left)	5 mL
8 cups	cake cubes (either pound or angel food cake)	2 L
$1/4$ cup	sherry	50 mL
$1/2$ cup	semisweet chocolate chips	125 mL
1 cup	whipping (35%) cream	250 mL
1 tbsp	confectioner's (icing) sugar	15 mL
$1/2$ tsp	vanilla	2 mL

1. In a food processor fitted with a metal blade, pulse raspberries and sugar until berries are puréed. Strain mixture into a bowl, discarding solids. Whisk in water and set aside.

2. In a large bowl, whisk together instant pudding mixes, milk, half-and-half and almond syrup until smooth.

3. In bottom of a large glass bowl, arrange one-third of the cake cubes. Drizzle cake with one-third of the sherry, then one-third of the raspberry sauce. Sprinkle with one-third of the chocolate chips, then one-third of the custard. Repeat layers twice, ending with custard. Cover and refrigerate for several hours or overnight.

4. Before serving, in a large bowl, with electric mixer or whisk, whip together cream, sugar and vanilla until soft peaks form. Spread on top of custard layer.

Variation
Garnish the trifle with fresh raspberries.

Chocolate Cherry Terrine

Chocolate Paradise would be a better name for this awesome dessert. The brandy-soaked cherries are draped with chocolate cream for a truly grand finale.

TIP

Garnish with a dollop of raspberry sorbet, if desired. For a decorative touch, lightly dust the serving plates with either unsweetened cocoa powder or confectioner's sugar.

9- by 5-inch (2 L) loaf pan, lined with plastic wrap

³/₄ cup	dried sour cherries	175 mL
¹/₄ cup	cherry brandy	50 mL
4 cups	semisweet chocolate chips	1 L
2 oz	unsweetened chocolate, chopped	60 g
2 cups	whipping (35%) cream	500 mL

1. In a microwave-safe bowl, combine dried cherries and cherry brandy. Microwave on High for 40 seconds, just until heated. Set aside.

2. In a large microwave-safe bowl, combine chocolate chips, unsweetened chocolate and cream. Microwave on High for 3 to $3\frac{1}{2}$ minutes, stirring every 30 seconds, until chocolate is shiny and almost melted. Stir until smooth.

3. Whisk reserved cherry mixture into chocolate mixture. Spread in prepared pan. Cover and refrigerate overnight or until firm, or for up to 1 day.

4. Invert terrine onto a serving plate. Slice and serve.

Chocolate Tiramisu

The name of this fabulous Italian dessert means "pick me up." Be forewarned: once you make this dessert for guests, you will forever be known for it. My sister-in-law Meredith loves this dessert so much that she had me make giant ones for her wedding reception.

TIPS

A great ratio for strong brewed coffee is 2 tbsp (25 mL) finely ground French-roast coffee or espresso for every $3/4$ cup (175 mL) water.

This dessert is best made 1 day before serving.

13- by 9-inch (3 L) glass baking dish or large bowl

2	packages (each 8 oz/250 g) cream cheese or mascarpone	2
2 cups	confectioner's (icing) sugar, sifted	500 mL
$2^1/_3$ cups	whipping (35%) cream	575 mL
1 cup	hot strong brewed coffee (see Tip, at left)	250 mL
$3/4$ cup	semisweet chocolate chips	175 mL
$1/4$ cup	dark rum	50 mL
48	crisp ladyfingers, divided	48
	Unsweetened cocoa powder	

1. In a large bowl, using electric mixer, whip cream cheese until smooth. Add confectioner's sugar, whipping until creamy and smooth. With machine on low, gradually add cream in a steady stream. Whip mixture on high speed until it reaches soft peaks.

2. In a medium bowl, whisk together hot coffee, chocolate chips and rum until smooth. Dip half of the ladyfingers in coffee mixture and place in an even layer in bottom of baking dish. Spread half of the cream mixture over ladyfingers. Dip remaining ladyfingers in coffee mixture and place over cream mixture. Spread remaining cream mixture over ladyfingers, smoothing top.

3. Cover and refrigerate tiramisu overnight. Just before serving, lightly dust top with unsweetened cocoa powder.

Chocolate Soup

Years ago there was a restaurant in California called Chocolate Soup. My brother and I would lose our minds when the craving struck. We relentlessly begged our mother to take us there, dreaming of steaming bowls of chocolate soup. All I can say is that from a child's point of view, it was nirvana. Here is a recipe for a dessert that is somewhere between hot chocolate and chocolate pudding.

TIP

Garnish mugs of chocolate soup with a sprinkle of ground cinnamon.

2½ cups	store-bought chocolate milk, divided	625 mL
3 tbsp plus 1 tsp	cornstarch	50 mL
4 oz	milk chocolate, chopped	125 g
1 tsp	vanilla	5 mL

1. In a saucepan over medium heat, heat 2¼ cups (550 mL) chocolate milk.

2. In a small bowl, whisk together remaining chocolate milk and cornstarch. Whisk into hot milk, whisking continuously for 2 to 4 minutes or until thick.

3. Remove from heat and whisk in milk chocolate and vanilla until melted and smooth.

4. Ladle soup into small mugs and serve immediately while hot.

Frozen Desserts

Double Chocolate Cheesecake Ice Cream 286

Chocolate Chip Dream Cream 287

Chocolate Rum Raisin Ice Cream 288

Banana Chocolate Ice Cream 289

Cherry Chocolate Chunk Ice Cream 290

Raspberry Chocolate Ice Cream 291

Pumpkin Chocolate Chip Ice Cream 292

Green Tea White Chocolate Chip Ice Cream 293

Banana Caramel Terrine 294

Banana Chip Foster 295

Affogato 296

Chipwiches 297

Mississippi Mud Pie 298

Frozen Chocolate Mousse 300

Tiramisu Chip Gelato 301

Peppermint Chip Gelato 302

Frozen Chocolate Malt Yogurt 303

Dark Chocolate Sorbet in Frozen Orange Cups 304

Raspberry Chocolate Chip Sorbet 305

Coconut Chip Sorbet 306

Frozen Cappuccino 307

Pomegranate Ice with Dark Chocolate Sauce 308

Mocha Ice 309

Chocolate Chai Snow Cones 310

Chocolate Bonbons 311

Chocolate Cherry Bombs 312

Chocolate Pudding Pops 313

Chocolate Banana Pops 314

Orange Fudge Pops 315

Double Chocolate Cheesecake Ice Cream

MAKES ABOUT
4 CUPS (1 L)

If you love chocolate and you love cheesecake, then this ice cream is for you! Your friends and family will think that this homemade ice cream came from your local gourmet gelato shop — it's that good.

TIPS

Serve with a raspberry or strawberry sauce.

This ice cream is best eaten the day it's frozen. To make ahead: The unfrozen mixture can be refrigerated for a day or two before freezing. When ready to serve, freeze for 20 to 30 minutes in the ice cream maker. Serve immediately or store in the freezer for up to 2 hours.

Ice cream maker

1 cup	whipping (35%) cream	250 mL
3 oz	white chocolate, chopped	90 g
1	package (8 oz/250 g) cream cheese, softened	1
2/3 cup	superfine sugar (see Tip, page 289)	150 mL
1 cup	milk	250 mL
3 oz	bittersweet chocolate, finely chopped	90 g

1. In a microwave-safe bowl, microwave cream, uncovered, on High for 1 to 2 minutes or until steaming. Add white chocolate, stirring until smooth and melted.

2. In a food processor fitted with a metal blade, blend cream cheese and sugar. Add milk and blend until smooth. Add white chocolate mixture and blend again until smooth. Transfer to a bowl, cover and refrigerate until cold.

3. Pour mixture into an ice cream maker and freeze according to manufacturer's directions. Without stopping machine, when ice cream is thick, add bittersweet chocolate. Continue freezing until very thick and frozen.

Variation
Substitute chopped white chocolate for the bittersweet.

Chocolate Chip Dream Cream

This honey-and-cream combo is what dreams are made of. Better REMs are achieved with the addition of chocolate chips! Wake me up before it's all gone.

TIPS

Serve ice cream immediately or freeze in an airtight container for up to 1 day.

The best way to store homemade ice cream is to pack it into a plastic container, press a piece of plastic wrap onto the surface, cover with a tight-fitting plastic lid and freeze. This helps prevent freezer burn.

Be sure to let the frozen ice cream sit at room temperature for a bit to soften slightly before scooping.

Ice cream maker

1$\frac{1}{2}$ cups	whipping (35%) cream	375 mL
1$\frac{1}{2}$ cups	milk	375 mL
$\frac{1}{2}$ cup	liquid honey	125 mL
$\frac{1}{2}$ cup	miniature semisweet chocolate chips	125 mL

1. In a medium bowl, whisk together cream, milk and honey.
2. Pour mixture into ice cream maker and freeze according to manufacturer's directions. When ice cream is thick and almost frozen, add chocolate chips. Continue freezing until very thick and frozen.

Variation

For a vanilla version, omit the honey and substitute $\frac{1}{2}$ cup (125 mL) superfine sugar and 2 tsp (10 mL) vanilla.

Chocolate Rum Raisin Ice Cream

MAKES ABOUT 4 CUPS (1 L)

I have always been a huge fan of rum raisin ice cream. This is my version, with rum-infused raisins and morsels of chocolate chips submerged in dark chocolate ice cream.

TIPS

Homemade ice cream will be somewhat softer in texture than store-bought. It is best served the day that it is made, but can be stored in the freezer for up to 1 day.

The best way to store homemade ice cream is to pack it into a plastic container, press a piece of plastic wrap onto the surface, cover with a tight-fitting plastic lid and freeze. This helps prevent freezer burn.

Be sure to let the frozen ice cream sit at room temperature for a bit to soften slightly before scooping.

Ice cream maker

$1/2$ cup	raisins	125 mL
2 tbsp	dark rum	25 mL
1 cup	semisweet chocolate chips	250 mL
$1 1/2$ cups	whipping (35%) cream, divided	375 mL
$3/4$ cup	milk	175 mL
$1/3$ cup	superfine sugar (see Tip, page 289)	75 mL
1 cup	miniature semisweet chocolate chips	250 mL

1. In a small microwave-safe bowl, combine raisins and rum. Microwave on High for 60 seconds. Set aside to cool for 20 minutes.

2. In a separate microwave-safe bowl, combine chocolate chips and $3/4$ cup (175 mL) of the cream. Microwave on High for 2 minutes, stirring every 30 seconds, until cream is hot and chocolate is shiny and almost melted. Stir until smooth. Whisk until chocolate is completely melted and mixture is smooth.

3. Add remaining cream, milk and sugar to melted chocolate mixture. If mixture is warm, refrigerate or freeze until chilled.

4. Pour mixture into an ice cream maker and freeze according to manufacturer's directions. Without stopping machine, add miniature chocolate chips and raisin mixture when ice cream is thick and almost frozen. Continue freezing until very thick and frozen.

Banana Chocolate Ice Cream

Chocolate and bananas grow in tropical climates and when the two are combined, they complement each other like amicable neighbors. Here's a new take on an old favorite, with some sour cream added for extra flavor and tang. This recipe is dedicated to Erika Novick, who has spent many an afternoon making banana ice cream with me.

TIPS

Superfine sugar dissolves very quickly in liquid. It is sometimes labeled as "instant dissolving fruit powdered sugar." If you can't find it in your grocery store, make your own: Process granulated sugar in a food processor until very finely ground.

Store ice cream in an airtight container with a piece of plastic wrap pressed onto the surface of the ice cream. This will keep it from becoming freezer-burned. Homemade ice cream is best eaten fresh the day it is made but will keep for several days in the freezer.

Ice cream maker

1 cup	hot milk	250 mL
2/3 cup	unsweetened Dutch-process cocoa powder, sifted	150 mL
3/4 cup	superfine sugar (see Tips, left)	175 mL
2	large bananas, divided	2
3/4 cup	sour cream	175 mL
1 cup	whipping (35%) cream	250 mL
3 oz	bittersweet or semisweet chocolate, finely chopped	90 g
1/3 cup	coarsely chopped walnuts	75 mL

1. In a large bowl, whisk together hot milk and cocoa powder until smooth. Whisk in sugar.

2. In a food processor fitted with a metal blade, pulse one banana until finely chopped. Add sour cream, pulsing until smooth. Whisk banana mixture into milk mixture. Whisk in cream. Cover and refrigerate until cold.

3. Pour mixture into an ice cream maker and freeze according to manufacturer's directions, dividing into batches as necessary to prevent overflow. Dice remaining banana. Without stopping machine, when ice cream is thick, add banana, chocolate and walnuts. Continue freezing until very thick and frozen.

Variation
You can substitute white or milk chocolate for the bittersweet.

Cherry Chocolate Chunk Ice Cream

Here's another super quick, ultra delicious ice cream. No need to run down to your local ice cream parlor. Impress your friends with your own gourmet ice cream.

TIPS

Superfine sugar dissolves very quickly in liquid. It is sometimes labeled as "instant dissolving fruit powdered sugar." If you can't find it in your grocery store, make your own: Process granulated sugar in a food processor until very finely ground.

This is fabulous garnished with toasted chopped almonds.

Ice cream maker

1/2 cup	dried pitted cherries, coarsely chopped	125 mL
2 tbsp	cherry liqueur or dark rum	25 mL
2 cups	whipping (35%) cream, chilled	500 mL
1 cup	milk	250 mL
1/2 cup	superfine sugar (see Tip, at left)	125 mL
1 tsp	vanilla	5 mL
1/2 tsp	almond extract	2 mL
3 oz	semisweet chocolate, coarsely chopped	90 g

1. In a microwave-safe bowl, mix together dried cherries and liqueur. Microwave, uncovered, on High for 20 to 30 seconds or until cherries are very warm. Set cherries aside to absorb liqueur.

2. In a medium bowl, whisk together cream, milk, sugar, vanilla and almond extract until smooth.

3. Pour mixture into an ice cream maker and freeze according to manufacturer's directions. Without stopping machine, when ice cream is thick, add reserved cherries with any remaining liqueur and chocolate. Continue freezing until very thick and frozen.

Variation
The almond extract can be omitted or you can substitute vanilla extract. Bittersweet chocolate can be substituted for the semisweet chocolate.

Raspberry Chocolate Ice Cream

**MAKES ABOUT
4 CUPS (1 L)**

I have yet to meet a fruit (except tomatoes) that you can't mix with chocolate. This ice cream is an exceptional union. It's creamy and full-flavored without being too rich.

TIPS

You can prepare the Raspberry Chocolate Sauce up to 2 days ahead, then freeze this dreamy dessert just prior to serving.

Serve with chocolate ice cream or sorbet for a great combo of flavors.

Ice cream maker

1	batch Raspberry Chocolate Sauce (see recipe, page 325)	1
1 cup	whipping (35%) cream	250 mL
1/4 cup	superfine sugar (see Tip, page 290)	50 mL

1. In a medium bowl, whisk together Raspberry Chocolate Sauce, cream and sugar. Cover and refrigerate until cold, if necessary.

2. Pour mixture into an ice cream maker and freeze according to manufacturer's directions. Freeze mixture until very thick and frozen.

Variation

You can add 3 oz (90 g) finely chopped bittersweet chocolate to this ice cream, for an extra special treat.

Pumpkin Chocolate Chip Ice Cream

MAKES ABOUT
4 CUPS (1 L)

Imagine a velvety slice of pumpkin pie with a big dollop of whipped cream. Now picture those flavors swirled together and frozen, with little bits of dark chocolate throughout. You've got the best flavors of autumn rolled into one dessert.

TIP

If you enjoy pumpkin desserts but can only purchase canned pumpkin in the fall, stock up on extra cans. That way, you can enjoy the luscious flavors of fall all year long.

Ice cream maker

1 1/2 cups	whipping (35%) cream	375 mL
1 1/4 cups	canned pumpkin purée (not pie filling)	300 mL
1 cup	milk	250 mL
3/4 cup	superfine sugar (see Tip, page 290)	175 mL
1 tsp	ground cinnamon	5 mL
1 tsp	ground allspice	5 mL
1 tsp	ground ginger	5 mL
3 oz	bittersweet chocolate, finely grated or chopped	90 g

1. In a saucepan over medium heat, whisk together cream, pumpkin, milk, sugar, cinnamon, allspice and ginger. Bring mixture to a simmer, whisking continuously.

2. Strain mixture into a bowl. Let cool until lukewarm, then cover and refrigerate until chilled.

3. Pour mixture into an ice cream maker and freeze according to manufacturer's directions. Without stopping machine, when ice cream is thick, add chocolate. Continue freezing until very thick and frozen.

Variation
For an extra-delicious treat, stir in 1/2 cup (125 mL) coarsely chopped candied ginger along with the chocolate.

Green Tea White Chocolate Chip Ice Cream

Ever been served green tea ice cream after an Asian meal and suddenly your whole meal is complete? This green tea ice cream is a delicacy and will complement any meal. White chocolate, which is chopped into little bits and stirred into this ice cream, is a natural with the green tea flavor.

TIPS

Look for matcha green tea powder in tea shops or well-stocked health food or grocery stores.

To cool the ice cream base quickly and prevent any curdling, place bowl with hot strained ice cream base into a larger bowl filled with ice. Stir constantly for a couple of minutes, then occasionally, to speed up the cooling process. Cover and refrigerate when it becomes lukewarm to the touch.

Ice cream maker

1 tbsp	matcha green tea powder (see Tips, left)	15 mL
2¼ cups	milk, divided	550 mL
1½ cups	whipping (35%) cream	375 mL
¾ cup	granulated sugar	175 mL
2	egg yolks	2
1 tbsp	cornstarch	15 mL
3 oz	white chocolate, finely chopped or grated	90 g

1. In a saucepan over medium-high heat, add green tea powder. Slowly whisk in 2 cups (500 mL) milk and cream until smooth. Bring mixture to a boil.

2. Meanwhile, in a medium bowl, whisk together sugar, egg yolks, cornstarch and remaining milk until smooth.

3. Remove saucepan from heat and gradually whisk 1 cup (250 mL) of the hot milk mixture into egg yolk mixture, whisking continuously.

4. Reduce heat to medium. Whisk mixture back into remaining hot milk mixture in saucepan and cook, stirring constantly, for 2 to 5 minutes or until slightly thickened. Be careful not to let mixture boil or eggs will scramble.

5. Remove from heat and pour hot tea custard through a strainer into a clean bowl. Cover and refrigerate until cold.

6. Pour mixture into an ice cream maker and freeze according to manufacturer's directions. Without stopping machine, when ice cream is thick, add white chocolate. Continue freezing until very thick and frozen.

Banana Caramel Terrine

This is a fun way to serve vanilla ice cream with a fancy flair. Your guests will be eager to dig into the center filling of caramel, chocolate chips, walnuts and bananas.

TIP

Use a warm sharp knife (not wet) to slice the terrine.

9- by 5-inch (2 L) metal loaf pan, lined with plastic wrap

4 cups	vanilla ice cream, slightly softened	1 L
1	banana, chopped into chunks	1
$3/4$ cup	walnuts, coarsely chopped	175 mL
$1/2$ cup	semisweet chocolate chips	125 mL
$2/3$ cup	caramel sauce, store-bought or homemade (see Chocolate Caramel Sauce, Variation, page 320)	150 mL

1. Spread half of the ice cream in bottom of prepared pan. Top with banana chunks. Sprinkle walnuts and chocolate chips over banana. With your hand or a spatula, lightly press top of terrine to pack down ingredients. Spread caramel sauce over walnuts. Carefully spread remaining ice cream over caramel.

2. Place a piece of plastic wrap directly on ice cream to cover. Gently press down on plastic wrap to smooth top. Freeze until frozen solid, preferably overnight.

3. Remove pan from freezer and carefully invert onto a cutting board or serving platter. Slice terrine and serve immediately.

Variations

Use Chocolate Caramel Sauce (see recipe, page 320) in place of the caramel sauce.

You can also substitute chocolate ice cream for the vanilla.

Banana Chip Foster

I could sit and eat a bowl of this right now! Whoever thought bananas could taste this good? Use medium to large bananas, just barely ripe with a touch of green, and you'll see what I mean.

TIP

This recipe is fantastic served over buttermilk pancakes.

$1/2$ cup	unsalted butter	125 mL
$3/4$ cup	packed light brown sugar	175 mL
$1/4$ tsp	salt	1 mL
5	bananas, peeled and cut diagonally into 1-inch (2.5 cm) pieces	5
$1/2$ cup	dark rum	125 mL
2 cups	vanilla ice cream	500 mL
6 tbsp	semisweet chocolate chips	90 mL

1. In a large skillet over medium heat, melt butter. Stir in brown sugar and salt. Heat until foamy. Add bananas, stirring to coat. Cook for 1 minute. Add rum and cook for 5 minutes or until thickened and syrupy. Remove from heat and let cool for 10 minutes.

2. Scoop ice cream into six individual dishes. Spoon banana mixture over top. Sprinkle 1 tbsp (15 mL) of the chocolate chips over each serving. Serve immediately.

Affogato

Tradition abounds in this Italian recipe, the name of which means "drowned ice." It can be thrown together in minutes. It is a perfect summertime dessert but equally appealing at other times of the year.

TIPS

Look for almond syrup and other flavored syrups in the coffee aisle of your grocery store. Or check out local coffeehouses or shops; they usually carry a large selection.

This would be a great dessert to serve with Chocolate Chip Orange Biscotti (see recipe, page 211).

2 cups	vanilla ice cream	500 mL
1/3 cup	semisweet chocolate chips	75 mL
4 tsp	kirsch liqueur	20 mL
4 tsp	almond syrup (see Tip, at left)	20 mL
1 cup	hot strong brewed coffee (see Tip, page 282)	250 mL

1. Divide ice cream among four wine goblets. Sprinkle chocolate chips over ice cream. Drizzle kirsch and almond syrup over top.

2. Pour 1/4 cup (50 mL) of the hot coffee into each glass. Serve immediately.

Chipwiches

SERVES 8

These are better than store-bought ice cream sandwiches and very addictive. In fact, my children have been known to willingly do household chores for these chilly treats. They will keep, frozen in a resealable freezer bag, for a week or two.

TIPS

I find that ice cream sandwiches work best with store-bought ice cream, unless you are going to serve them the day they are made.

You can make these ice cream sandwiches using a tube or roll of store-bought cookie dough. Simply slice or scoop dough into 16 portions and bake according to manufacturer's directions.

Store in the freezer for up to 2 weeks.

Baking sheet, lined with parchment paper

2 cups	vanilla ice cream, slightly softened	500 mL
16	freshly baked and cooled chocolate chip cookies (see The Quintessential Chocolate Chip Cookie, page 177)	16
1 cup	miniature semisweet chocolate chips	250 mL

1. Place a scoop of ice cream on a cookie. Top with another cookie, pressing down lightly so that ice cream spreads almost to edges. Repeat with remaining ice cream and cookies.

2. Place chocolate chips in a bowl. Stand 1 cookie sandwich on edge and roll across chocolate chips so that they adhere to surface of ice cream. Repeat with remaining cookie sandwiches.

3. Freeze sandwiches on prepared baking sheet for several hours or until ice cream is firm.

Variation
Substitute coffee or mint ice cream for the vanilla.

Mississippi Mud Pie

Ice cream pies were all the rage in the '60s and '70s. I thought it was about time for a comeback with a contemporary chocolate chip twist.

TIP

To toast almonds: Preheat oven to 350°F (180°C). Spread nuts on a baking sheet lined with foil or parchment. Bake for 5 to 7 minutes or until light brown and fragrant.

9-inch (23 cm) pie plate, greased

20	cream-filled chocolate sandwich cookies	20
1/4 cup	unsalted butter, melted	50 mL
4 cups	coffee ice cream, softened and divided	1 L
1 cup	chocolate fudge or caramel sauce	250 mL
1 cup	semisweet chocolate chips	250 mL
1 1/2 cups	whipping (35%) cream	375 mL
3 tbsp	confectioner's (icing) sugar, sifted	45 mL
1/2 tsp	vanilla	2 mL
1/3 cup	almonds, toasted and coarsely chopped (see Tip, at left)	75 mL

1. In a food processor fitted with a metal blade, process chocolate sandwich cookies until crumbs form. Add melted butter and process until finely ground. Press mixture into bottom and up side of prepared pie plate. Freeze for 30 minutes or until firm.

2. Spread half of the coffee ice cream over prepared crust. Drizzle evenly with fudge sauce and sprinkle with chocolate chips. Freeze until ice cream hardens slightly. Keep remaining ice cream in the freezer for about 15 minutes, just until the fudge firms up slightly (so that it doesn't ooze into the next ice cream layer). Spread with remaining ice cream.

TIP

Read through the entire recipe before starting. That way, you know both the steps and ingredients in the recipe before you start.

3. In a medium bowl, using electric mixer, combine cream, confectioner's sugar and vanilla. Beat until stiff peaks form.

4. Spread whipped cream over pie and sprinkle with chopped almonds. Freeze for several hours or until completely frozen, or for up to 1 day. If leaving for a day, cover with plastic wrap once it is completely frozen. Let stand at room temperature for 15 minutes before slicing.

Variation

Substitute cookies and cream or mint chip ice cream for the coffee ice cream. If using mint chip ice cream, use fudge sauce, not caramel.

Frozen Chocolate Mousse

**MAKES ABOUT
4 CUPS (1 L)**

This isn't your average ice cream. Children will delight in it, thinking that it is very fancy. You'll delight in the fact that it is so easy to make.

TIPS

Superfine sugar dissolves very quickly in liquid. It is sometimes labeled as "instant dissolving fruit powdered sugar." If you can't find it in your grocery store, make your own: Process granulated sugar in a food processor until very finely ground.

Serve scoops of frozen mousse with a drizzle of Raspberry Sauce (see Variation, page 325).

4-cup (1 L) freezer-safe plastic container with lid

7 oz	bittersweet chocolate, chopped	210 g
2 cups	whipping (35%) cream, divided	500 mL
1 tbsp	instant coffee granules	15 mL
1 tbsp	coffee liqueur	15 mL
3 tbsp	superfine sugar (see Tip, at left)	45 mL
1 tsp	vanilla	5 mL

1. In a microwave-safe bowl, combine chocolate and $\frac{1}{2}$ cup (125 mL) cream. Microwave, uncovered, on Medium (50%) for 1 to 2 minutes, stirring every 30 seconds, or until cream is hot and chocolate is soft and almost melted. Stir until melted and smooth. Let cool slightly.

2. In a small bowl, mix together instant coffee and coffee liqueur.

3. In a large bowl, using electric mixer, whip together remaining cream, sugar, coffee mixture and vanilla until soft peaks form. With mixer on low speed, add melted chocolate mixture, whipping until smooth and mixture almost forms stiff peaks.

4. Scoop mousse into freezer-safe container. Press a piece of plastic wrap onto surface of mousse, cover with container lid and place in freezer. Freeze mousse overnight or until frozen and firm to the touch, or for up to 2 days.

5. When ready to serve, let stand at room temperature for 15 minutes or until mousse is soft enough to scoop like ice cream. Scoop mousse into serving cups and serve immediately.

Variation
Substitute milk chocolate for the bittersweet.

Tiramisu Chip Gelato

**MAKES
4 TO 5 CUPS
(1 TO 1.25 L)**

If you are a tiramisu lover, this gelato will blow your socks off. It contains all the luscious flavors you have come to enjoy, but it's frozen.

TIPS

Serve the gelato immediately or freeze in an airtight container for up to 1 day.

The best way to store homemade ice cream is to pack it into a plastic container, press a piece of plastic wrap onto the surface, cover with a tight-fitting plastic lid and freeze. This helps prevent freezer burn.

Be sure to let the frozen ice cream sit at room temperature for a bit to soften slightly before scooping.

Ice cream maker

2 tbsp	coffee liqueur	25 mL
1 tbsp	instant coffee granules	15 mL
1 cup	whipping (35%) cream	250 mL
1	package (8 oz/250 g) cream cheese, softened	1
1/2 cup	superfine sugar (see Tip, page 300)	125 mL
1 cup	milk	250 mL
1/2 cup	miniature semisweet chocolate chips	125 mL

1. In a small bowl, stir together coffee liqueur and instant coffee granules.

2. In a food processor fitted with a metal blade, combine cream, cream cheese and sugar. Pulse until smooth, scraping down side of bowl as necessary. Add milk and coffee mixture, pulsing until smooth.

3. Pour into ice cream maker and freeze according to manufacturer's directions. When gelato is thick and almost frozen, add chocolate chips. Continue freezing until very thick and firm.

Peppermint Chip Gelato

The flavors in this ice cream are downright refreshing on a hot summer day. The beautiful light pink color brings out the friendly feminine side in each and every one of us. You'll want to start chatting on impact.

TIPS

A quick way to chop the candy canes is in a food processor. If you happen to have a mini processor, it will make the cleanup even easier.

Serve ice cream immediately or freeze in an airtight container for up to 1 day (see Tip, page 301).

Ice cream maker

1 1/4 cups	whipping (35%) cream	300 mL
1 1/4 cups	milk	300 mL
1/2 cup	superfine sugar (see Tip, page 300)	125 mL
1/2 cup	crushed peppermint candies or candy canes	125 mL
1/4 tsp	peppermint extract	1 mL
1/2 cup	miniature semisweet chocolate chips	125 mL

1. In a medium bowl, whisk together cream, milk, sugar, crushed peppermint candies and peppermint extract.

2. Pour mixture into ice cream maker and freeze according to manufacturer's directions. When gelato is thick and almost frozen, add chocolate chips. Continue freezing until very thick and firm. (Homemade ice cream will be somewhat softer in texture than store-bought.)

Frozen Chocolate Malt Yogurt

**MAKES ABOUT
4½ CUPS (1.125 L)**

This frozen dessert is full of deep chocolate flavor, and the yogurt gives it a nice tang that will tickle your tongue. It's also a great way to satisfy your chocolate tooth while getting a hefty dose of calcium.

TIP

Serve with a drizzle of store-bought chocolate sauce.

Ice cream maker

1 cup	whipping (35%) cream	250 mL
½ cup	malted milk powder	125 mL
3 oz	unsweetened chocolate, chopped	90 g
2 cups	plain yogurt (not nonfat)	500 mL
1 cup	superfine sugar (see Tip, page 300)	250 mL

1. In a large microwave-safe bowl, microwave cream, uncovered, on High for 1 to 2 minutes or until steaming.

2. Whisk in malted milk powder and chocolate until smooth. Whisk in yogurt and sugar. Cover and refrigerate until chilled.

3. Pour mixture into an ice cream maker and freeze according to manufacturer's directions. Freeze mixture until very thick and frozen.

Variation
Add ½ cup (125 mL) miniature semisweet chocolate chips to the ice cream maker once frozen yogurt is very thick and almost done.

Dark Chocolate Sorbet in Frozen Orange Cups

3	oranges, cut in half	3
2½ cups	boiling water	625 mL
1 cup	unsweetened Dutch-process cocoa powder, sifted	250 mL
¾ cup	granulated sugar	175 mL
3 oz	unsweetened chocolate, chopped	90 g
2 tbsp	dark rum	25 mL

SERVES 6

Orange cups give this dessert an air of playful sophistication that will always amaze your guests. You can substitute lemon halves for the oranges, if you prefer. I like to make them ahead of time and simply pull them out of the freezer 10 minutes before serving.

TIPS

If you don't have time to make homemade sorbet, substitute store-bought.

The size of each serving will depend on the size of your oranges. So you might wind up with some extra sorbet — either freeze it in a separate container or use an extra orange, increasing the total number of servings to 8.

1. Scoop out fruit from orange halves and reserve for another use. Place orange halves on a plate or baking sheet, cover and place in freezer. Chill overnight, until frozen. Use immediately or transfer to an airtight container and freeze for up to 1 month.

2. In a large bowl, whisk together boiling water, cocoa powder and sugar. Whisk in chocolate and rum until smooth. Cover and refrigerate until chilled.

3. Pour mixture into an ice cream maker and freeze according to manufacturer's directions. Freeze sorbet until very thick and frozen.

4. Scoop sorbet into frozen orange halves. Return orange halves to freezer until ready to serve.

Variation
Fill orange halves with chocolate ice cream.

Raspberry Chocolate Chip Sorbet

MAKES ABOUT 4 CUPS (1 L)

Need a little change in your life? Raspberry, chocolate, wine and lemon blended together and frozen into a remarkable sorbet will cleanse your palate, leaving you feeling fresh and rejuvenated.

TIPS

Superfine sugar dissolves very quickly in liquid. It is sometimes labeled as "instant dissolving fruit powdered sugar." If you can't find it in your grocery store, make your own: Process granulated sugar in a food processor until very finely ground.

Serve the sorbet immediately or freeze in an airtight container for up to 1 day (see Tip, page 306).

Ice cream maker

12 oz	frozen unsweetened raspberries, thawed and including juice (about 3 cups/750 mL)	375 g
1½ cups	water	375 mL
½ cup	superfine sugar (see Tip, at left)	125 mL
2 tbsp	Merlot wine	25 mL
2 tbsp	light corn syrup	25 mL
2 tsp	grated lemon zest	10 mL
⅓ cup	miniature semisweet chocolate chips	75 mL

1. In a food processor fitted with a metal blade, combine thawed raspberries and water. Process until smooth. Strain mixture into a bowl, discarding seeds. Whisk in sugar, wine, corn syrup and lemon zest.

2. Pour mixture into ice cream maker and freeze according to manufacturer's directions. When sorbet is thick and almost frozen, add chocolate chips. Continue freezing until very thick and frozen.

Coconut Chip Sorbet

This sorbet will transport you to the Hawaiian Islands. For a festive touch, you can garnish it with a sprinkle of toasted sweetened coconut.

TIPS

Sorbet gets very hard and icy, so it is best served the day it is made. However, it can be frozen for several days in an airtight container with a piece of plastic wrap pressed onto its surface (this prevents the formation of ice crystals temporarily). Let the sorbet sit at room temperature until soft enough to scoop.

This sorbet is divine with a drizzle of chocolate sauce.

Ice cream maker

2$\frac{1}{2}$ cups	unsweetened coconut milk	625 mL
$\frac{1}{2}$ cup	superfine sugar (see Tip, page 305)	125 mL
$\frac{1}{2}$ cup	water	125 mL
2 tsp	coconut rum	10 mL
$\frac{1}{3}$ cup	miniature semisweet chocolate chips	75 mL

1. In a medium saucepan over medium–high heat, combine coconut milk, sugar and water. Simmer for 5 minutes or until sugar is dissolved. Remove from heat and stir in coconut rum. Pour mixture into a bowl or pitcher and refrigerate until chilled.

2. Pour mixture into ice cream maker and freeze according to manufacturer's directions. When sorbet is thick and almost frozen, add chocolate chips. Continue freezing until very thick and frozen.

Variation
Substitute light rum for the coconut rum.

Frozen Cappuccino

**MAKES ABOUT
4 CUPS (1 L)**

One day my mother called to rave about a sorbet she had had. She went on to describe its flavor, aroma and texture. I never got to taste that sorbet, but I developed this one based entirely upon her colorful description. It is truly heavenly.

TIPS

Serve immediately or freeze in an airtight container for up to 1 day (see Tip, page 306).

This dessert looks great served in espresso cups. Place espresso cups in the freezer for 30 minutes before you're ready to serve the dessert. Remove the cups from the freezer and fill with a scoop of frozen cappuccino. A chocolate chip cookie would make a perfect accompaniment to the sorbet.

Ice cream maker

1 cup	unsweetened Dutch-process cocoa powder, sifted	250 mL
3/4 cup	superfine sugar (see Tip, page 305)	175 mL
1/2 tsp	ground cinnamon	2 mL
2 cups	hot freshly brewed coffee	500 mL
1/2 cup	semisweet chocolate chips	125 mL
1/2 cup	whipping (35%) cream	125 mL
1 tbsp	dark rum	15 mL
1 tsp	grated orange zest	5 mL
1 tsp	vanilla	5 mL
1/3 cup	miniature semisweet chocolate chips	75 mL

1. In a small bowl, whisk together cocoa powder, sugar and cinnamon.

2. In a large bowl or pitcher, combine hot coffee, chocolate chips, cream, rum, orange zest and vanilla. Whisk in cocoa mixture until smooth.

3. Refrigerate mixture until cold. Pour into ice cream maker and freeze according to manufacturer's directions. When mixture is thick, add miniature chocolate chips. Continue freezing until very thick and frozen.

Pomegranate Ice with Dark Chocolate Sauce

This is an easy, easy recipe that is as satisfying as it is simple. You can now find both fresh refrigerated and shelf-stable bottled pomegranate juice in many grocery and health food stores.

TIPS

Superfine sugar dissolves very quickly in liquid. It is sometimes labeled as "instant dissolving fruit powdered sugar." If you can't find it in your grocery store, make your own: Process granulated sugar in a food processor until very finely ground.

Refrigerate any unused sauce in an airtight container for up to 2 days.

Ice cream maker

Sauce

1 1/2 cups	packed light brown sugar	375 mL
1 cup	unsweetened Dutch-process cocoa powder, sifted	250 mL
2 tsp	vanilla	10 mL

Sorbet

3 cups	pomegranate juice, chilled	750 mL
1/2 cup	superfine sugar (see Tip, at left)	125 mL

1. *Sauce:* In a large saucepan over medium–high heat, whisk together 2 cups (500 mL) water and brown sugar. Cook, whisking occasionally, for 5 minutes or until hot and sugar is dissolved. Whisk in cocoa powder. Simmer for 2 minutes. Remove from heat and whisk in vanilla. Let sauce cool to room temperature.

2. *Sorbet:* While sauce is cooling, in a bowl, whisk together pomegranate juice and sugar. Pour mixture into an ice cream maker and freeze according to manufacturer's directions. Freeze until sorbet is very thick and frozen.

3. Scoop sorbet into dishes and drizzle with sauce.

Mocha Ice

SERVES 4

This is a great dessert to serve when you want something delectable but light. You can top this with a dollop of whipped cream or serve it alongside a scoop of vanilla ice cream. Basically, it's delicious any way you serve it!

TIPS

To make strong brewed coffee, use a heaping 2 tbsp (25 mL) finely ground coffee, such as espresso roast, French roast or other dark roasted strong coffee, for every 3/4 cup (175 mL) water.

If you want to make this dessert ahead of time, place frozen cubes in a resealable plastic bag. They will keep, frozen, for several days. Remove from freezer and process right before serving.

This is fabulous drizzled with store-bought chocolate sauce.

2 plastic ice cube trays

2 cups	hot freshly brewed strong coffee (see Tip, at left)	500 mL
1/3 cup	packed light brown sugar	75 mL
1/4 cup	unsweetened Dutch-process cocoa powder, sifted	50 mL
2 oz	bittersweet chocolate, chopped	60 g
3 tbsp	superfine sugar (see Tip, page 308)	45 mL
1 tbsp	dark rum	15 mL
1/2 tsp	ground cinnamon	2 mL

1. Pour hot coffee into a large bowl. Whisk in brown sugar, cocoa powder, chocolate, sugar, rum and cinnamon until smooth.

2. Pour chocolate mixture into ice cube trays. Freeze ice cube trays overnight or until solid.

3. In a food processor fitted with a metal blade, pulse frozen cubes until finely chopped with a texture like snow.

4. Scoop ice into cups and serve immediately.

Chocolate Chai Snow Cones

**MAKES 4
SNOW CONES**

I have always loved snow cones, but as an adult, the super-sweet syrup, brightly colored with dye, has lost much of its appeal. So I have taken what I love most about snow cones — the crushed ice and silky syrup — and turned it into an adult treat. Here we have a light chai-flavored ice drizzled with chocolate syrup. You can serve it in small glass bowls, paper cones or wineglasses.

TIPS

You can make the chai ice cubes several days in advance. Make sure to cover the ice cube trays with plastic wrap or remove the cubes from the molds and place in a resealable plastic freezer bag. Chop in a food processor right before serving.

To use loose chai tea, substitute 2 tbsp (25 mL) loose tea for the tea bags.

Ice cube trays

2 cups	boiling water	500 mL
6	chai spice tea bags (see Tips, at left)	6
1/2 cup	whipping (35%) cream	125 mL
1/3 cup	liquid honey	75 mL
1 cup	store-bought or homemade Chocolate Syrup (see recipe, page 333) or more to taste	250 mL

1. In a heatproof bowl or glass measuring cup, combine boiling water and tea bags. Let stand for 15 minutes. Remove tea bags and discard. Stir in cream and honey.

2. Pour mixture into ice cube trays and freeze overnight or until solid.

3. In a food processor fitted with a metal blade, pulse chai ice cubes until finely chopped with a texture like snow.

4. Scoop into four bowls and drizzle with chocolate sauce. Serve immediately.

Chocolate Bonbons

Remember a time when bonbons were as much a part of going to the movies as the film itself? Bonbons are very easy to make and are fabulously fun to serve for dessert. Children love them, and bonbons will keep in the freezer for several weeks.

TIPS

If making these on a hot day, make them in three batches. If you can't fit the baking sheets in your freezer, use sturdy paper plates that are lined with parchment or waxed paper.

I like to use my very small ice cream scoop when making this recipe.

2 baking sheets, lined with parchment paper

2 cups	ice cream, any flavor	500 mL
7 oz	bittersweet or semisweet chocolate, chopped	210 g

1. Using a heaping tablespoon (15 mL) or a small ice cream scoop and working quickly, scoop 16 small mounds of ice cream, placing 8 on each prepared baking sheet. Place baking sheets in freezer until ice cream is very hard and frozen.

2. When ice cream is hard, place chopped chocolate in a microwave-safe bowl. Microwave, uncovered, on Medium (50%) for 1 to 2 minutes, stirring every 30 seconds, or until chocolate is soft and almost melted. Stir until completely melted and smooth.

3. Remove one baking sheet at a time from freezer. Quickly dip each ice cream scoop in melted chocolate. Place dipped bonbons back on prepared baking sheet and place in freezer. Repeat with remaining baking sheet. When chocolate is hardened, bonbons are ready to serve.

Variation
This recipe is great with many different ice cream flavors. Some good ones to try are coffee, mint chip, chocolate, cherry, banana and raspberry sorbet.

Chocolate Cherry Bombs

My daughter thought that these should be called cherry bombs as they have a hidden center of brandied cherries. They have also been proclaimed a "10" on the dessert scale.

Baking sheet, lined with parchment paper

6	whole maraschino cherries, drained	6
2 tbsp	brandy	25 mL
2 cups	chocolate ice cream	500 mL
2 cups	semisweet chocolate chips	500 mL
3 tbsp	shortening	45 mL

1. In a small dish, combine cherries and brandy. Set aside for 15 minutes to macerate. Drain cherries and pat dry.

2. Scoop ice cream into six balls, placing on prepared baking sheet. Push a macerated cherry into center of each ice cream ball. Freeze until solid.

3. In a microwave-safe bowl, combine chocolate chips and shortening. Microwave on High for 2 minutes, stirring every 30 seconds, until chocolate is shiny and almost melted. Stir until smooth.

4. Remove ice cream balls from freezer and quickly dip into melted chocolate to coat. Return to pan. Freeze until chocolate is hardened, about 1 hour, or for up to several hours. Serve directly from the freezer.

Variation
Omit the brandy, if desired.

Chocolate Pudding Pops

I love frozen pops, especially in the hot summer months (they make me feel like a kid again). After making these, you'll see that homemade pops are always much tastier than store-bought and very quick to prepare. This recipe calls for grocery store ingredients, which really makes it go together quickly. Feel free to substitute homemade chocolate pudding and chocolate milk, should you desire.

TIP

If you don't have ice pop molds, you can substitute small paper cups. Fill cups almost to the top and freeze for 1 hour or until partially frozen. Poke ice pop sticks into pudding and continue freezing until solid. Peel paper cup off frozen pop before eating.

Ice pop molds

1½ cups	chocolate pudding	375 mL
¾ cup	chocolate milk	175 mL

1. In a medium bowl, whisk together chocolate pudding and chocolate milk until smooth.
2. Spoon pudding into ice pop molds. Freeze overnight until solid or for up to 1 week.

Chocolate Banana Pops

MAKES 6 POPS

Remember the chocolate banana pops from county fairs, amusement parks and carnivals? Well, now you don't have to wait for the next time a fair comes through your town to get one. Roll the pops in nuts, candy sprinkles or whatever else strikes your fancy.

TIP

Do not use overripe bananas for this dessert.

Six wooden Popsicle sticks
Baking sheet, lined with parchment paper

3	large bananas (see Tip, at left)	3
2 cups	semisweet chocolate chips	500 mL
3 tbsp	shortening	45 mL

1. Slice bananas in half lengthwise, preferably at an angle. Push a Popsicle stick halfway into cut side of bananas. Place on prepared baking sheet and freeze until frozen solid.

2. In a microwave-safe dish, combine chocolate chips and shortening. Microwave on High for 2 minutes, stirring every 30 seconds, until chocolate is shiny and almost melted. Stir until smooth.

3. Dip frozen bananas into melted chocolate. Return dipped bananas to baking sheet and freeze until chocolate is hardened, about 1 hour. Store in freezer in a resealable freezer bag until ready to serve.

Variation
Sprinkle dipped bananas with chopped nuts or candy sprinkles before freezing.

Orange Fudge Pops

MAKES ABOUT
8 POPS

Pops are super-refreshing on hot days. You can usually find ice pop molds in late spring and early summer at grocery stores. I have even spotted them at discount stores. The inspiration for this recipe came from Natalie Haughton's Mandarin Sherbet recipe.

TIPS

There may be some leftover pop mixture after filling the molds (or not quite enough). This is because ice pop molds often vary in size. To freeze any extra mixture in paper cups, see Tip, page 313.

If you prefer your pops less sweet, you can decrease the sugar to ³/₄ cup (175 mL).

Ice pop molds

1¹/₂ cups	milk	375 mL
1 cup	granulated sugar	250 mL
²/₃ cup	unsweetened Dutch-process cocoa powder, sifted	150 mL
¹/₂ cup	orange juice concentrate	125 mL
2 oz	bittersweet chocolate, chopped	60 g

1. In a microwave-safe bowl, heat milk, uncovered, on High for 1 to 2 minutes or until steaming. Whisk in sugar, cocoa powder and orange juice concentrate until smooth. Add chocolate.

2. Pour mixture into ice pop molds. Freeze overnight until solid or for up to 1 week.

> **Variation**
> Substitute semisweet chocolate for the bittersweet.

Sauces, Syrups, Frostings and Spreads

Chocolate Fondue *318*

Chocolate Honey Sauce *319*

Chocolate Caramel Sauce *320*

Toffee Chocolate Sauce *321*

Sticky Chocolate Raisin Sauce *322*

Milk Chocolate Banana Sauce *323*

Black Forest Sauce *324*

Raspberry Chocolate Sauce *325*

Bittersweet Chocolate Mint
Sauce *326*

Chocolate Merlot Sauce *327*

Mocha Fudge Sauce *328*

Bourbon Fudge Sauce *329*

Walnut Whiskey Fudge Sauce *330*

White Chocolate Rum Raisin
Sauce *331*

White Chocolate Mocha Sauce *332*

Chocolate Syrup *333*

Dark Chocolate Syrup *334*

Chocolate Strawberry Syrup *335*

Chocolate Glaze *336*

Chocolate Fudge Frosting *337*

Peanut Butter Fudge Frosting *338*

Killer Mocha Frosting *339*

Chocolate Almond Bread
Spread *340*

Warm Raspberry Chocolate
Chip Spread *341*

Chocolate Fondue

Chocolate fondue is a very elegant dessert. It is so easy to make that you shouldn't let others know exactly how easy. It is a very special dessert for a child's birthday when made without the liqueur; you can substitute decaf coffee instead.

TIPS

Leftover fondue can be refrigerated overnight. Warm in microwave before serving.

Try to use a fondue pot with a tea light that is made for chocolate fondue so that the chocolate won't burn.

Ceramic fondue pot or medium ceramic dish

³/₄ cup	whipping (35%) cream	175 mL
1 cup	semisweet chocolate chips	250 mL
2 tbsp	liqueur such as hazelnut or Galliano	25 mL

Suggested Dipping Items

Cubes of loaf or pound cake

Strawberries

Banana chunks

Orange segments

Pretzels

Large marshmallows

Small cookies

Dried fruit

1. In a microwave-safe bowl, combine cream and chocolate chips. Microwave on High for 1 to 2 minutes, stirring every 30 seconds, until chocolate is shiny and almost melted. Stir until smooth.

2. Whisk liqueur into chocolate mixture. Transfer to fondue pot.

3. Arrange dipping items on a platter and serve.

Chocolate Honey Sauce

**MAKES
ABOUT 1⅓ CUPS
(325 ML)**

The honey provides a mild sweetness to this divine chocolate sauce. Winnie the Pooh would be proud to call this sauce his own. It's delicious over ice cream.

TIP

This sauce can be made ahead and stored for several days in an airtight container in the refrigerator.

¼ cup	salted butter	50 mL
¾ cup	liquid honey	175 mL
½ cup	unsweetened Dutch-process cocoa powder, sifted	125 mL
⅓ cup	whipping (35%) cream	75 mL

1. In a saucepan, melt butter over medium heat. Whisk in honey, cocoa powder and cream. Bring mixture to a boil. Reduce heat to medium–low and simmer for 3 minutes.

2. Remove saucepan from heat. Let stand for 10 minutes or until slightly thickened. Pour sauce over ice cream.

Chocolate Caramel Sauce

This decadent sauce goes together in a snap. From beginning to end, it takes only 5 minutes to prepare (quicker than running to the store). It's great served warm over ice cream.

TIPS

For a fun fondue, serve this sauce warm with fruit, small cookies and cake cubes.

Store in a covered container in the refrigerator for up to 1 week.

¼ cup	unsalted butter	50 mL
¾ cup	packed light brown sugar	175 mL
⅓ cup	light corn syrup	75 mL
¼ tsp	salt	1 mL
⅓ cup	whipping (35%) cream	75 mL
⅓ cup	semisweet chocolate chips	75 mL

1. In a medium saucepan, melt butter over medium heat. Add brown sugar, corn syrup and salt. Increase heat to medium–high and bring mixture to a boil, stirring constantly. Once boiling, it will look like bubbling lava. Boil for 1 minute and remove from heat.

2. Whisk in cream. Add chocolate chips, whisking until smooth. The sauce will look as if it's separating but will smooth out after a minute or so of whisking. Sauce will thicken as it cools.

Variation
You can omit the chocolate chips for an equally delicious caramel sauce. Use in recipes that call for caramel sauce.

Toffee Chocolate Sauce

Chocolate and toffee make beautiful music together. Try this sauce warm drizzled over slices of cake, ice cream or whatever suits your fancy. You can even dip shortbread cookies into it.

TIP

This sauce keeps very well, covered and refrigerated, for at least 1 week. Let sauce cool and store in a glass canning jar. When ready to reheat, remove the metal lid and reheat in the microwave until warm.

1 cup	whipping (35%) cream	250 mL
¾ cup	packed dark brown sugar	175 mL
2 oz	unsweetened chocolate, chopped	60 g
2 tbsp	salted butter	25 mL

1. In a saucepan over medium–high heat, whisk together cream and brown sugar. Bring to a boil. Reduce heat to medium and simmer for 5 minutes, whisking continuously, until sauce is darker and somewhat thickened.

2. Remove from heat and whisk in chocolate and butter until smooth. The sauce will thicken as it cools.

3. Let sauce cool slightly before serving over ice cream, sorbet or other dessert.

Sticky Chocolate Raisin Sauce

**MAKES
ABOUT 1⅓ CUPS
(325 ML)**

This sauce is what dreams are made of! It's almost like candy — sweet, chocolaty, sticky and chewy. It's practically a meal in itself.

TIP

This sauce keeps very well, covered and refrigerated, for up to 2 days. Let sauce cool and store in a glass canning jar. When ready to reheat (the sauce will be very thick), remove the metal lid and reheat in the microwave until warm.

6 tbsp	salted butter	90 mL
1 cup	packed light brown sugar	250 mL
⅓ cup	unsweetened Dutch-process cocoa powder, sifted	75 mL
⅓ cup	raisins	75 mL
⅓ cup	whipping (35%) cream	75 mL
2 tbsp	light corn syrup	25 mL

1. Melt butter in a saucepan over medium–high heat. Whisk in brown sugar, cocoa powder, raisins, cream and corn syrup. Bring to a boil. Reduce heat to medium and simmer for 3 minutes or until thickened.

2. Serve warm over ice cream or sorbet.

Variation
You can omit the raisins altogether or substitute ⅓ cup (75 mL) dried cherries for them.

Milk Chocolate Banana Sauce

MAKES
ABOUT 1¼ CUPS
(300 ML)

Something about the flavor of bananas caramelized in butter and brown sugar and then mixed with a touch of cream and milk chocolate is utterly irresistible to me. Needless to say, I can forgo the ice cream altogether and eat this sauce with a spoon. Dieters, beware!

TIP

This sauce is best eaten warm when it is first made.

2 tbsp	salted butter	25 mL
¼ cup	packed light brown sugar	50 mL
1	large banana, sliced	1
¾ cup	whipping (35%) cream	175 mL
2 oz	milk chocolate, chopped	60 g

1. Melt butter in a nonstick skillet over medium–high heat. Stir in brown sugar until melted.

2. Add bananas and cook, stirring as needed, until the bananas are soft and caramelized and the mixture starts to thicken. Stir in cream and cook, stirring continuously, for 2 to 3 minutes longer or until sauce is smooth and thickened.

3. Remove from heat and stir in chopped chocolate until smooth. Spoon warm sauce over ice cream and serve immediately.

Variation

If you love bananas, use 2 medium bananas instead of 1 large.

Black Forest Sauce

**MAKES ABOUT
3 CUPS (750 ML)**

By now I'm sure that everyone knows I love chocolate and cherries together. The combo is truly a match made in heaven. I love this sauce spooned over chocolate ice cream.

TIPS

This sauce can be cooled, covered and refrigerated for up to 3 days. When ready to serve, reheat, uncovered, in the microwave until warm.

Sour cherries don't work too well in this recipe. Make sure the sweet cherries are packed in water or juice, not a thick cherry sauce. A 14- or 15-oz (398 or 425 mL) can will yield a little more than 1 cup (250 mL) of drained cherries. Feel free to add the extras to the sauce, if desired. Pitted fresh dark cherries will work beautifully, too. Simmer about 5 minutes longer.

1 cup	unsweetened Dutch-process cocoa powder, sifted	250 mL
1 cup	whipping (35%) cream	250 mL
6 tbsp	unsalted butter, cut into pieces	90 mL
3/4 cup	packed dark brown sugar	175 mL
1/3 cup	light corn syrup	75 mL
1 cup	drained canned pitted dark or Bing cherries (see Tips, left)	250 mL
1 tbsp	dark rum	15 mL

1. Place cocoa powder in a bowl. In a saucepan over medium–high heat, heat cream and butter until butter is melted. When mixture is gently simmering (light bubbling), whisk into cocoa powder until smooth.

2. Return cocoa mixture to saucepan and whisk in brown sugar and corn syrup. Bring to a boil, whisking. Reduce heat to medium. Stir in cherries and simmer, stirring, for 2 minutes.

3. Remove from heat and stir in rum. Let stand until thickened, stirring as necessary to keep cherries submerged in sauce. Spoon warm sauce over ice cream.

Variation
Substitute cherry liqueur for the rum in this recipe.

Raspberry Chocolate Sauce

**MAKES ABOUT
2 CUPS (500 ML)**

Raspberry sauce is a great way to fancy up a dessert. It goes beautifully with chocolate cake, ice cream, sorbet and soufflé. It's even great over yogurt.

TIPS

If you prefer a more pronounced chocolate flavor, add an additional 1 oz (30 g) chocolate. If you prefer the sauce a bit sweeter, you can add additional sugar to taste. If you prefer your sauce a bit tangier, reduce the sugar to taste.

This sauce keeps very well, covered and refrigerated, for up to 2 days. Let sauce cool and store in a glass canning jar. When ready to reheat, remove the metal lid and reheat in the microwave until warm.

1	bag (12 oz/375 g) unsweetened frozen raspberries, thawed	1
$1/2$ cup	superfine sugar, or to taste (see Tip, page 308)	125 mL
3 oz	bittersweet chocolate, chopped	90 g

1. In a food processor fitted with a metal blade, process raspberries, $1/2$ cup (125 mL) water and sugar until blended and smooth.

2. Strain raspberry mixture into a small saucepan over medium heat. Bring to a simmer. Remove saucepan from heat and stir in chocolate until smooth.

3. Sauce can be served warm or cold.

Variation
Raspberry Sauce: If you need a plain raspberry sauce to serve with a chocolate dessert, you can omit the chocolate from the sauce and reduce the sugar to 6 tbsp (90 mL), or to taste.

Bittersweet Chocolate Mint Sauce

If you like thick, rich, bittersweet chocolate sauces, then don't let this recipe pass you by. It's fast to make and even faster to eat.

TIP

This sauce keeps very well, covered and refrigerated, for up to 2 days. Let sauce cool and store in a glass canning jar. When ready to reheat, remove the metal lid and reheat in the microwave until warm.

1 cup	whipping (35%) cream	250 mL
¹/₂ cup	light corn syrup	125 mL
4 oz	unsweetened chocolate, chopped	125 g
2 oz	bittersweet chocolate, chopped	60 g
2 tbsp	superfine sugar (see Tip, page 308)	25 mL
1 tsp	peppermint extract	5 mL

1. In a saucepan over medium heat, combine cream and corn syrup. Bring to a simmer.

2. Remove from heat and whisk in unsweetened and bittersweet chocolates, sugar and peppermint extract until smooth.

3. Spoon warm sauce over ice cream or use as a dipping sauce for fruit.

Chocolate Merlot Sauce

**MAKES
ABOUT 1⅓ CUPS
(325 ML)**

This is an outrageous sauce. Complex and simple at the same time, it takes only a couple of minutes to prepare. You will want to use this on everything you eat — although I wouldn't necessarily recommend it!

TIP

Serve drizzled over ice cream, sorbet or chocolate cake.

1 cup	semisweet chocolate chips	250 mL
½ cup	Merlot wine	125 mL
⅓ cup	light corn syrup	75 mL

1. In a medium saucepan, combine chocolate chips, wine and corn syrup. Warm over medium heat, whisking constantly, just until chocolate is melted. Remove from heat and whisk until smooth.

Variation
Substitute Cabernet Sauvignon for the Merlot.

Mocha Fudge Sauce

This beats store-bought fudge sauce any day! I thought that a coffee-based sauce with a chewy fudge flavor would be dynamite over ice cream. I realized that I was on to something when my husband started eating the sauce with a spoon.

TIP

This sauce can be made ahead. Simply cover and refrigerate cooled sauce for up to 2 days. Reheat in the microwave until warm and melted.

1 cup	unsweetened Dutch-process cocoa powder, sifted	250 mL
½ cup	packed light brown sugar	125 mL
1 cup	hot freshly brewed coffee	250 mL
½ cup	whipping (35%) cream	125 mL
½ cup	light corn syrup	125 mL
2 cups	semisweet chocolate chips	500 mL
2 tbsp	dark rum	25 mL

1. In a large saucepan, whisk together cocoa powder and brown sugar. Add coffee, cream and corn syrup, whisking until smooth.
2. Bring to a boil over medium–high heat, whisking continuously. Remove from heat and whisk in chocolate chips and rum.
3. Let cool and thicken slightly before serving over ice cream.

Variation
Use a flavored liqueur in place of the rum. Kirsch or crème de menthe work well.

Bourbon Fudge Sauce

When you're in the mood for a grown-up dark chocolate sauce, this is it. Don't be surprised if this sauce brings on marriage proposals.

TIP

This sauce keeps very well, covered and refrigerated, for up to 2 days. Let sauce cool and store in a glass canning jar. When ready to reheat, remove the metal lid and reheat in the microwave until warm.

¾ cup	whipping (35%) cream	175 mL
6 oz	bittersweet chocolate, chopped	175 g
2 tbsp	bourbon	25 mL

1. In a saucepan over medium-high heat, bring cream to a boil.
2. Remove from heat and whisk in chocolate and bourbon until smooth.
3. Let sauce cool for 5 minutes to thicken before using. Serve over ice cream.

Variation
Omit the bourbon for a G rating, adding 2 tsp (10 mL) vanilla.

Walnut Whiskey Fudge Sauce

MAKES
ABOUT 1½ CUPS
(375 ML)

This fudge sauce is a favorite of my husband, Jay. You can omit the nuts altogether or substitute almonds or pecans for the walnuts. You can also substitute rum or your favorite liqueur for the whiskey, as this sauce lends itself well to many flavors. Go ahead and have some fun!

TIP

This sauce keeps very well, covered and refrigerated, for at least 1 week. Let sauce cool and store in a glass canning jar. When ready to reheat (the sauce will be very thick), remove the metal lid and reheat in the microwave until warm.

½ cup	unsweetened Dutch-process cocoa powder, sifted	125 mL
½ cup	whipping (35%) cream	125 mL
3 tbsp	unsalted butter	45 mL
½ cup	packed dark brown sugar	125 mL
¼ cup	light corn syrup	50 mL
½ cup	coarsely chopped walnuts, toasted (see Tip, page 218)	125 mL
2 tbsp	whiskey	25 mL

1. Place cocoa powder in a bowl. In a saucepan over medium–high heat, heat cream and butter until butter is melted. When mixture is gently simmering (lightly bubbling), whisk into cocoa powder until smooth.

2. Return cocoa mixture to saucepan and whisk in brown sugar and corn syrup. Bring to a simmer over medium-high heat, whisking continuously.

3. Remove from heat and whisk in walnuts and whiskey. Let sauce cool slightly before serving over ice cream.

White Chocolate Rum Raisin Sauce

Traditional ice cream sauces have needed a facelift for quite a while, so I went to work to see what I could do. This is one dynamite sauce! It's creamy and luscious, with a little spice. Rum-raisin never tasted so good.

TIPS

Try it over chocolate ice cream.

This sauce keeps very well, covered and refrigerated, for up to 2 days. Let sauce cool and store in a glass canning jar. When ready to reheat, remove the metal lid and reheat in the microwave until warm.

1 cup	whipping (35%) cream	250 mL
¼ cup	raisins	50 mL
5 oz	white chocolate, chopped	150 g
2 tsp	dark rum	10 mL
¼ tsp	ground cinnamon	1 mL

1. In a small saucepan over medium-low heat, combine cream and raisins. Bring to a simmer.

2. Remove from heat and stir in white chocolate, rum and cinnamon until smooth. Let stand for 15 minutes to thicken slightly before serving.

3. Serve over ice cream.

White Chocolate Mocha Sauce

What do you get when you cross coffee, white chocolate and cream? You get a most irresistible, silky sauce that tastes as amazing on ice cream as it does stirred into hot milk.

TIP

This sauce keeps very well, covered and refrigerated, for up to 2 days. You can reheat the sauce in the microwave, but white chocolate is more temperamental than dark chocolate and needs to be reheated carefully to avoid burning.

¾ cup	whipping (35%) cream	175 mL
1 tbsp	instant coffee granules	15 mL
5 oz	white chocolate, chopped	150 g

1. In a microwave-safe bowl, mix together cream and instant coffee. Microwave, uncovered, on High for about 80 seconds or until steaming. Whisk in white chocolate until melted and smooth.

2. Let mixture stand for 10 minutes to thicken slightly before serving over ice cream.

Variation
Omit the instant coffee for a plain white chocolate version.

Chocolate Syrup

MAKES ABOUT 3 CUPS (750 ML)

For an out-of-this-world taste, whip up a batch of chocolate syrup from scratch. One taste and you will see why. This dark and delicious syrup goes together in a flash and will satisfy your deepest chocoholic tendencies.

TIPS

This sauce is delish stirred into milk, soymilk or hot coffee. It also tastes great drizzled over ice cream.

To prevent refrigerated chocolate syrup from tasting grainy, warm it briefly in the microwave before using. I like to store any leftover sauce in a wide-mouth glass canning jar.

2 cups	water	500 mL
1¾ cups	granulated sugar	425 mL
1 cup	unsweetened Dutch-process cocoa powder, sifted	250 mL
2 oz	unsweetened chocolate, chopped	60 g
2 tsp	vanilla	10 mL

1. In a large saucepan over medium-high heat, mix together water and sugar, whisking occasionally until water is hot and sugar is dissolved. Whisk in cocoa powder and chocolate. Bring mixture to a simmer. Reduce heat slightly to maintain a low simmer and, whisking continuously, simmer for 2 minutes. Remove from heat and whisk in vanilla.

2. Let syrup cool to room temperature. Use immediately or store in the refrigerator for up to 1 week (for reheating directions, see Tip, at left).

Variation
Stir 2 tsp (10 mL) instant coffee granules into the hot syrup.

Dark Chocolate Syrup

**MAKES
ABOUT 3¼ CUPS
(800 ML)**

Since most of us probably have a can or two of chocolate syrup in our fridge, you might think it crazy to make it from scratch. But after just one taste, you will be convinced.

TIP

The syrup is fabulous stirred into milk, soy milk or hot coffee. It also tastes great drizzled over ice cream. It will keep, refrigerated, for at least 1 week. If refrigerated chocolate syrup becomes slightly grainy, warm briefly in microwave before using.

2 cups	water	500 mL
1½ cups	granulated sugar	375 mL
1 cup	unsweetened Dutch-process cocoa powder, sifted	250 mL
2 tsp	instant coffee granules	10 mL
½ cup	semisweet chocolate chips	125 mL
2 tsp	vanilla	10 mL

1. In a large saucepan over medium–high heat, whisk together water and sugar. Heat mixture for about 5 minutes, whisking occasionally, until hot and sugar is dissolved. Whisk in cocoa powder and instant coffee. Simmer for 2 minutes. Remove from heat.

2. Add chocolate chips to saucepan, whisking until smooth. Whisk in vanilla.

3. Let syrup cool to room temperature. Use immediately or store in refrigerator until ready to use.

Variation
Stir 1 tsp (5 mL) orange zest into the hot syrup for a fantastic flavor.

Chocolate Strawberry Syrup

MAKES ABOUT 2 CUPS (500 ML)

This quick sauce is great drizzled on pancakes or French toast or spooned over vanilla ice cream. Served warm or cold, this is a winner.

TIP

This syrup is best served the day it is made.

10 oz	frozen unsweetened strawberries, thawed and including juice (about $2\frac{1}{2}$ cups/625 mL)	300 g
$\frac{1}{3}$ cup	superfine sugar (see Tip, page 308)	75 mL
1 cup	semisweet chocolate chips	250 mL
$\frac{1}{3}$ cup	water	75 mL
2 tsp	Triple Sec or other orange-flavored liqueur	10 mL

1. In a processor fitted with a metal blade, pulse strawberries and sugar until smooth. Pour blended strawberries into a microwave-safe bowl. Add chocolate chips and microwave on High for 1 to 2 minutes, stirring every 30 seconds, until chocolate is shiny and almost melted. Stir until smooth.
2. Whisk sauce until smooth. If chocolate isn't completely melted, microwave for 20 seconds longer. Whisk in water and liqueur.

Chocolate Glaze

MAKES ABOUT
1/2 CUP (125 ML),
ENOUGH TO
GLAZE ABOUT
12 CUPCAKES

This is a very quick and chocolaty topping for cupcakes when you don't have time to make a buttercream. This glaze, also known as a ganache, gives an elegant look to your homemade cupcakes.

1/2 cup	semisweet chocolate chips	125 mL
1/3 cup	whipping (35%) cream	75 mL

1. In a microwave-safe bowl, combine chocolate chips and cream. Microwave, uncovered, on High for 30 to 60 seconds or until cream is hot and chocolate starts to melt. Stir until chocolate is melted and mixture is thick and smooth.

2. If chocolate is not completely melted, return to microwave for another 10 to 20 seconds or until chocolate is soft and melted. Stir well. Let glaze sit for a few minutes to thicken slightly. Pour glaze over tops of cooled cupcakes.

3. Refrigerate cupcakes until glaze is firm.

Variation
Substitute chopped semisweet chocolate for the chocolate chips.

Chocolate Fondue (page 318)

Almond Chocolate Ginger Bark (page 251)

Chocolate Caramel Sauce (page 320)

Chocolate Malted (page 349)

Frozen Cappuccino (page 307)

Morning Mocha (page 359)

Chocolate Fudge Frosting

· ·

**MAKES ABOUT
1½ CUPS (375 ML),
ENOUGH TO
FROST 12 TO
18 CUPCAKES**

As far as chocolate frostings go, this is one of my all-time, hands-down favorites. My mom made this frosting all the time when I was growing up. It goes together quickly and is outrageously chocolaty.

TIP

Extra frosting will keep in an airtight container in the refrigerator for several days. Let soften and stir until smooth before spreading.

1½ cups	confectioner's (icing) sugar	375 mL
¾ cup	unsweetened Dutch-process cocoa powder, sifted	175 mL
½ cup	unsalted butter, at room temperature	125 mL
2 tbsp	chocolate cream liqueur	25 mL
1 tbsp	strong brewed coffee or milk	15 mL
Pinch	salt	Pinch

1. In a food processor fitted with a metal blade, process confectioner's sugar, cocoa powder, butter, chocolate liqueur, coffee and salt until smooth, scraping down sides as necessary.

2. Spread frosting on cooled cupcakes.

Variations

If you prefer your frosting a little less sweet, you can reduce the confectioner's sugar by ½ cup (125 mL) for the full recipe or ¼ cup (50 mL) for half the recipe.

To make this frosting vegan, substitute margarine for the butter and replace the chocolate cream liqueur with chocolate liqueur or rum.

Peanut Butter Fudge Frosting

Here's a frosting that's almost like candy. You've got your chocolate fudge and your peanut butter, blended together into an outstanding topping for chocolate cupcakes (or peanut butter cupcakes). It's delicious on almost anything.

TIPS

Store frosting in an airtight container and refrigerate until ready to use or for up to 2 days. Let soften at room temperature before using.

Regular peanut butter rather than natural-style peanut butter works best in this recipe.

³/₄ cup	unsalted butter, at room temperature	175 mL
¹/₂ cup	creamy peanut butter	125 mL
Pinch	salt	Pinch
2 cups	confectioner's (icing) sugar	500 mL
³/₄ cup	unsweetened Dutch-process cocoa powder, sifted	175 mL

1. In a large bowl, beat together butter, peanut butter and salt until creamy. With mixer on low speed, beat in confectioner's sugar, ¹/₂ cup (125 mL) at a time so that the sugar doesn't fly all over the place. Add cocoa powder, beating until very smooth and creamy.

2. Spread frosting on cooled cupcakes.

Variation
Use crunchy peanut butter instead of creamy.

Killer Mocha Frosting

I love this frosting so much that I make it all the time. It's really easy to whip together quickly in the food processor and tastes amazing. I've even caught my husband eating it with a spoon.

TIPS

Extra frosting will keep in a covered container in the refrigerator for up to 2 days. Let it soften before spreading.

Be sure to use salted butter in this recipe because it needs the slight saltiness to enhance the chocolate flavor.

2$\frac{1}{2}$ cups	confectioner's (icing) sugar	625 mL
1$\frac{1}{2}$ cups	unsweetened Dutch-process cocoa powder	375 mL
1 cup	salted butter, at room temperature (see Tips, left)	250 mL
$\frac{1}{4}$ cup	strong brewed coffee, cooled to room temperature (see Tip, page 309)	50 mL
1 tbsp	dark rum	15 mL

1. In a food processor fitted with a metal blade, process confectioner's sugar, cocoa powder, butter, coffee and rum until smooth, scraping down sides as necessary.
2. Spread frosting on cake or cupcakes.

Variation
If you prefer your frosting a little less sweet, you can reduce the confectioner's sugar by $\frac{1}{2}$ cup (125 mL).

Chocolate Almond Bread Spread

· ·

This is a delectable breakfast spread and dessert rolled into one. A protein and chocolate combination is a wonderful way to jump-start your day. Serve with bagels, scones or even on bread as a breakfast sandwich.

TIPS

To toast almonds: Preheat oven to 350°F (180°C). Spread nuts on a baking sheet lined with foil or parchment. Bake for 5 to 7 minutes or until light brown and fragrant.

If you want to decrease the oil in this recipe, you can cut it down to 1 tsp (5 mL). Note, though, that the spread will be very thick and somewhat difficult to spread.

1 cup	whole almonds, toasted (see Tips, left)	250 mL
3/4 cup	semisweet chocolate chips	175 mL
4 tsp	canola oil (see Tips, left)	20 mL
2 tsp	light corn syrup	10 mL
1/4 tsp	salt	1 mL

1. In a food processor fitted with a metal blade, combine almonds and chocolate chips. Process for about 4 minutes (this will be very loud for the first minute or so), until mixture becomes smooth and almost forms a ball. With motor running, add oil, corn syrup and salt through the feed tube.

2. Transfer to a microwave-safe bowl. Cover and refrigerate for up to 2 days. Just before serving, warm spread in microwave on High for about 20 seconds, until spreadable.

Warm Raspberry Chocolate Chip Spread

**MAKES ABOUT
¾ CUP (175 ML)**

Here's a new way to enjoy jam, with the addition of melted chocolate. Try this spread warm on everything from scones and toast to pancakes and waffles. You'll wonder why no one has thought of this before.

TIP

When chilled, this spread will get thick and fudge-like (it's delicious eaten right from the spoon). It is divine this way as well, but feel free to warm it slightly in the microwave until spreadable. Just be careful not to reheat for too long or the chocolate could burn.

½ cup	raspberry jam (with or without seeds)	125 mL
½ cup	semisweet chocolate chips	125 mL

1. In a microwave-safe bowl, combine jam and chocolate chips. Microwave on High for 2 minutes, stirring every 30 seconds, until jam is warm and chocolate is shiny and almost melted. Stir until smooth.

2. Let cool for 10 minutes. (The mixture will thicken as it cools.)

Beverages

Quick and Easy Chocolate Milk *344*

Hot White Chocolate Milk *345*

Cookies-and-Cream Shake *346*

Chocolate Caramel Cream Shake *347*

Strawberry Chips "Moo-thie" *348*

Chocolate Malted *349*

Very Cherry Chocolate Float *350*

Dark Chocolate Ginger Fizz *351*

Blended Mocha Frappé *352*

Milk Chocolate Caramel Cream *353*

Hot Spiced Chocolate *354*

Spicy Haute Chocolate *355*

Mexican Cocoa *356*

Chocolate No Egg Nog *357*

Chocolate Tea *358*

Morning Mocha *359*

Hot Chocolate Chai Latte *360*

Cosmic Coffee with Chocolate Chips
and Chantilly Cream *361*

Chocolatini *362*

Chocolate Dream *363*

Chocolate Peppermint Stick *364*

Chocolate Liqueur *365*

Chocolate Snow *366*

Orange Chocolate Cup *367*

Quick and Easy Chocolate Milk

Store-bought chocolate milk is convenient, but you can't compare it to the taste of homemade. For chocolate lovers, it's chocolate nirvana! This is quick as a wink, and there are several variations to boot.

TIP

Mix up a pitcher of chocolate milk before bed and awaken to a delicious morning treat. Make sure that the milk is really hot when you add the chocolate or else you'll wind up with little flecks of unmelted chocolate in your milk (still tasty but not smooth). Chocolate milk is super-delicious in coffee or blended into a smoothie.

1 1/2 cups	milk, divided	375 mL
1/4 cup	unsweetened Dutch-process cocoa powder, sifted	50 mL
1/4 cup	granulated sugar	50 mL
1 oz	bittersweet chocolate, chopped	30 g

1. In a microwave-safe bowl, microwave 1/2 cup (125 mL) milk, uncovered, on High for 1 minute or until steaming and bubbles appear around edge.

2. Whisk in cocoa powder, sugar and chocolate until smooth.

3. Add remaining milk, whisking well. Serve right away or refrigerate until ready to drink.

Variations

You can double or triple the recipe for a crowd.

Add a pinch of ground cinnamon for a spiced version.

Whisk in 1 tbsp (15 mL) malted milk powder, or to taste, if you want a chocolate malted version.

For an adult treat, stir in 1/4 cup (50 mL) Irish cream liqueur, or more to taste.

Hot White Chocolate Milk

Here's a nice change of pace from hot chocolate. My kids love a steamy hot mug on chilly mornings.

TIP
Garnish with a dollop of whipped cream and a sprinkle of ground cinnamon or nutmeg.

1 cup	milk	250 mL
1/2 cup	whipping (35%) cream	125 mL
3 oz	white chocolate, chopped	90 g
1/2 tsp	vanilla	2 mL

1. In a small saucepan over medium heat, bring milk and cream to a simmer.

2. Reduce heat to low. Add white chocolate and vanilla, whisking until melted and smooth and mixture is steaming hot.

3. Pour into mugs. Serve immediately.

Variation
Flavor the white chocolate milk with 1 tbsp (15 mL) flavored syrup, such as almond, hazelnut or caramel.

Cookies-and-Cream Shake

SERVES 2 TO 3

This is a fun shake, especially for those diehard fans of cookies and milk. And when they're served this way, you won't be chasing broken cookie pieces around the cup of milk.

6	scoops vanilla ice cream	6
1 cup	milk	250 mL
$\frac{1}{4}$ cup	semisweet chocolate chips	50 mL
4	cream-filled chocolate sandwich cookies	4
	Whipped cream (optional)	

1. In a blender, combine ice cream, milk, chocolate chips and chocolate sandwich cookies. Blend until frothy.

2. Pour into glasses and serve immediately with straws. Garnish with a dollop of whipped cream, if desired.

Variation
Substitute chocolate chip cookies for the chocolate sandwich cookies.

Chocolate Caramel Cream Shake

I am a huge fan of caramel. The combination of caramel, Irish cream and chocolate makes this shake one of my faves.

TIP
For a thicker shake, add additional ice cream.

8	large scoops vanilla ice cream	8
3/4 cup	milk	175 mL
1/4 cup	Chocolate Caramel Sauce (see recipe, page 320) or store-bought caramel sauce	50 mL
1/4 cup	semisweet chocolate chips	50 mL
1 tbsp	Irish cream liqueur	15 mL
	Whipped cream (optional)	

1. In a blender, combine ice cream, milk, chocolate caramel sauce, chocolate chips and liqueur. Blend until smooth.

2. Pour into glasses and serve immediately with straws. Garnish with a dollop of whipped cream, if desired.

Variation
Substitute Irish cream syrup for the liqueur.

Strawberry Chip "Moo-thie"

Smoothies have been around for many years but recently have become very popular. This delicious version combines strawberries, banana and, of course, chocolate chips.

TIPS

Superfine sugar dissolves very quickly in liquid. It is sometimes labeled as "instant dissolving fruit powdered sugar." If you can't find it in your grocery store, make your own: Process granulated sugar in a food processor until very finely ground.

If you prefer a sweeter smoothie, add more sugar to taste.

1 1/4 cups	milk	300 mL
5 oz	frozen unsweetened strawberries (about 1 1/3 cups/325 mL)	150 g
1/2	banana	1/2
2	scoops vanilla ice cream	2
1/4 cup	semisweet chocolate chips	50 mL
3 tbsp	superfine sugar (see Tip, at left)	45 mL
	Fresh strawberries (optional)	

1. In a blender, combine milk, strawberries, banana, ice cream, chocolate chips and sugar. Blend until smooth.

2. Pour into glasses and serve immediately with straws. Garnish with a fresh strawberry, if desired.

Chocolate Malted

When you're in the mood for something sweet and creamy, give this beverage a try. It's a smooth drink of malted milk powder, ice cream and chocolate chips.

6	scoops vanilla ice cream	6
3/4 cup	milk	175 mL
1/2 cup	semisweet chocolate chips	125 mL
3 tbsp	malted milk powder	45 mL
	Whipped cream (optional)	

1. In a blender, combine ice cream, milk, chocolate chips and malted milk powder. Blend until smooth.

2. Pour into glasses and serve immediately with straws. Garnish the shake with a dollop of whipped cream, if desired.

Very Cherry Chocolate Float

My children love floats, so I find myself getting very creative in the summer months. Here is an unbelievably delicious twist, using cherry vanilla soda, vanilla extract and chocolate ice cream. It tastes like chocolate-dipped cherries!

TIP

Make sure to have extra soda and ice cream on hand — you'll hear loud screams for seconds.

1	can (12 oz/355 mL) cherry vanilla soda, chilled	1
4 tbsp	whipping (35%) cream	60 mL
1/2 tsp	vanilla	2 mL
4	scoops chocolate ice cream	4

1. Fill two tall glasses with soda.
2. Stir 2 tbsp (25 mL) cream and 1/4 tsp (1 mL) vanilla into each glass.
3. Top each glass with two scoops of chocolate ice cream. Serve immediately.

Variation
Substitute dark cherry soda for the cherry vanilla.

Dark Chocolate Ginger Fizz

Double yum! Ginger and chocolate make a tongue-tantalizing team. Try this on a hot day, as it is delectable and refreshing.

1	can (12 oz/355 mL) ginger ale, chilled	1
2 tbsp	store-bought or homemade Chocolate Syrup (see recipe, page 333)	25 mL
6 tbsp	whipping (35%) cream	90 mL
4	scoops store-bought chocolate sorbet	4

1. Fill two tall glasses with ginger ale.
2. Stir 1 tbsp (15 mL) chocolate syrup and 3 tbsp (45 mL) cream into each glass.
3. Top each glass with two scoops of chocolate sorbet. Serve immediately.

Variation
Substitute chocolate ice cream for the sorbet.

Blended Mocha Frappé

Here is your chance to be your own barista. I live on these frosty coffee-flavored shakes during the hot summer months. You can make this blended coffee creation — found at coffeehouses around the globe — at home for a fraction of the cost.

TIPS

A great ratio for strong brewed coffee is 2 tbsp (25 mL) finely ground French-roast coffee or espresso for every $3/4$ cup (175 mL) water.

Superfine sugar dissolves very quickly in liquid. It is sometimes labeled as "instant dissolving fruit powdered sugar." If you can't find it in your grocery store, make your own: Process granulated sugar in a food processor until very finely ground.

2 cups	ice cubes	500 mL
1 cup	milk	250 mL
$1/2$ cup	strong brewed coffee, chilled (see Tip, at left)	125 mL
$1/3$ cup	superfine sugar (see Tip, at left)	75 mL
$1/3$ cup	table (18%) cream	75 mL
$1/3$ cup	semisweet chocolate chips	75 mL
2 tbsp	instant coffee granules	25 mL

1. In a blender, combine ice, milk, chilled coffee, sugar, cream, chocolate chips and instant coffee granules. Blend until smooth and frothy.

2. Pour into glasses and serve immediately.

Variation
Reduce sugar and add your choice of flavored syrups, such as hazelnut, almond or caramel, to taste.

Milk Chocolate Caramel Cream

Remove the chill of that cold winter's day with this steamy, dreamy chocolate drink. This recipe can be whipped together quickly and is a welcome treat after a day playing in the snow.

TIPS

Do not substitute nonfat or low-fat milk in this recipe.

Look for caramel sauce in the ice cream aisle in grocery stores or coffee bars.

1 $\frac{1}{2}$ cups	whole milk (see Tips, left)	375 mL
$\frac{1}{2}$ cup	whipping (35%) cream	125 mL
4 oz	milk chocolate, finely chopped	125 g
$\frac{1}{2}$ cup	caramel sauce, divided (see Tips, left)	125 mL
	Whipped cream	

1. In a saucepan over medium-low heat, combine milk, cream, chocolate and $\frac{1}{4}$ cup (50 mL) caramel sauce. Bring to a simmer, whisking continuously, for 5 minutes or until chocolate and caramel are melted and mixture is smooth.

2. Pour into four mugs and garnish with whipped cream.

3. Drizzle remaining caramel sauce over whipped cream. Serve immediately.

Hot Spiced Chocolate

Hot chocolate has never tasted so good. Honest! Four little ingredients combine in this recipe to concoct one powerhouse beverage.

TIP

You can garnish this steaming hot chocolate with marshmallows or a dollop of whipped cream. Personally, I love it just the way it is.

3 cups	milk	750 mL
1/2 cup	whipping (35%) cream	125 mL
1 cup	semisweet chocolate chips	250 mL
1/4 tsp	ground cinnamon	1 mL

1. In a medium saucepan over medium-high heat, bring milk and cream to a simmer.

2. Remove saucepan from heat and whisk in chocolate chips and cinnamon until smooth.

3. Serve hot chocolate in mugs.

Spicy Haute Chocolate

Add a bit of spice to your life. Inspired by the movie *Chocolat*, this rich and chocolaty recipe uses a dash of smoked chili powder. Turn up the heat and find yourself in a spicy mood! Everyone will be trying to guess the "secret" ingredient.

TIP

Chipotles are smoked jalapeño peppers. You can vary the amount of chipotle powder to taste ($1/8$ tsp/0.5 mL gives you a nice little kick, which balances well with the chocolate flavor). But if you love things really spicy, try adding an additional $1/8$ tsp (0.5 mL). Look for chipotle powder in well-stocked grocery and health food stores.

1 cup	milk	250 mL
$3/4$ cup	whipping (35%) cream	175 mL
3 oz	bittersweet chocolate, chopped	90 g
$1/4$ cup	granulated sugar	50 mL
1 tsp	vanilla	5 mL
$1/2$ tsp	ground cinnamon	2 mL
$1/8$ tsp	ground chipotle powder (see Tip, at left)	0.5 mL

1. In a small saucepan over medium heat, bring milk and cream to a simmer.

2. Remove from heat and add chocolate and sugar to saucepan, whisking until chocolate is melted and mixture is smooth. Whisk in vanilla, cinnamon and chipotle powder.

3. Pour into mugs and serve immediately.

Variation

If you don't have chipotle powder, you can substitute $1/2$ tsp (2 mL) ancho chili powder, or more to taste.

Mexican Cocoa

SERVES 4

Come taste a delicious rendition of Mexican chocolate. You can buy discs of Mexican chocolate in some well-stocked grocery stores, but this is an even easier way to make it. I've added a touch of cornstarch, which gives the cocoa a silky texture. Muy delicioso!

TIP

You'll want to make this recipe right before serving, as it won't keep well.

1/2 cup	unsweetened Dutch-process cocoa powder, sifted	125 mL
1/3 cup plus 2 tbsp	granulated sugar	100 mL
1 tbsp	cornstarch	15 mL
3/4 tsp	ground cinnamon	4 mL
2 cups	milk	500 mL
1/2 cup	whipping (35%) cream	125 mL
1/4 tsp	almond extract	1 mL

1. In a saucepan, whisk together cocoa powder, sugar, cornstarch and cinnamon. Whisk in milk and cream.
2. Place saucepan over medium heat and bring to a simmer, whisking continuously, until chocolate mixture is slightly thickened.
3. Remove from heat and whisk in almond extract. Serve immediately.

Variation
For a lower-fat version, you can omit the cream and increase the milk to 3 cups (750 mL).

Chocolate No Egg Nog

This is a satisfying, soul-warming hot chocolate recipe. Quick, chocolaty and creamy, store-bought chocolate milk is my choice for speed and ease. There is a touch of ground nutmeg, which gives it a hint of eggnog flavor (without the eggs).

TIP

Serve with whipped cream and cinnamon sticks, if desired.

2 cups	store-bought chocolate milk	500 mL
1/2 cup	whipping (35%) cream	125 mL
1/2 tsp	ground nutmeg	2 mL
3 oz	milk chocolate, chopped	90 g
1 tsp	vanilla	5 mL

1. In a small saucepan over medium heat, whisk together milk, cream and nutmeg. Bring mixture to a simmer, stirring constantly. Remove from heat and whisk in chocolate and vanilla.

2. Whisk hot chocolate until foamy (this is a great time to use a hand rotary beater, hand blender or latte whip).

3. Pour into four cups or mugs.

Variation

Substitute bittersweet or semisweet chocolate for the milk chocolate.

Chocolate Tea

SERVES 2

If you love tea, don't pass this one by! The tea lends a very subtle yet exotic note to the bittersweet chocolate flavor. Quick, easy and satisfying, this tea is heartwarming.

1½ cups	milk	375 mL
2 tbsp	granulated sugar, or to taste	25 mL
4	Earl Grey tea bags	4
2 oz	bittersweet chocolate, finely chopped	60 g
	Whipped cream (optional)	

1. In a small saucepan over medium heat, bring milk and sugar to a simmer. Remove from heat and add tea bags. Let stand, covered, for 10 minutes to steep.

2. Remove tea bags from milk, pressing them with the back of a spoon to extract last bit of flavor.

3. Add chocolate to hot tea mixture, whisking until smooth. Sweeten to taste with more sugar, if desired. Serve hot or cold. Garnish with a dollop of whipped cream, if using.

Morning Mocha

SERVES 2

What do you call a mug of your favorite coffee with a scoop of chocolate ice cream and a drizzle of chocolate sauce? I call it breakfast, but you can enjoy it any time of the day. This treat won't be found at your neighborhood coffee house.

TIP

This recipe can be doubled.

1½ cups	hot freshly brewed coffee	375 mL
2 tbsp	store-bought or homemade Chocolate Syrup (see recipe, page 333)	25 mL
2	scoops chocolate ice cream	2
	Whipped cream	
	Ground cinnamon	

1. Pour coffee into two mugs or glasses. Stir 1 tbsp (15 mL) chocolate syrup into each mug.

2. Place one scoop of chocolate ice cream on top of coffee. Top with whipped cream and a sprinkle of ground cinnamon. Serve immediately.

Variation

Substitute chilled strong brewed coffee for the hot coffee. Serve in tall glasses.

Hot Chocolate Chai Latte

I love to pack a Thermos of this creamy tea for winter picnics or early morning outings. It's a fun alternative to coffee or hot chocolate.

2 cups	water	500 mL
1/4 cup	loose-leaf black tea	50 mL
2 cups	milk	500 mL
1/3 cup	granulated sugar	75 mL
1 tsp	ground cinnamon	5 mL
1/2 tsp	ground allspice	2 mL
1/2 tsp	ground cardamom	2 mL
1/2 cup	semisweet chocolate chips	125 mL
	Whipped cream (optional)	

1. In a large saucepan over medium heat, bring water to a simmer. Remove from heat and add loose tea. Let steep for 5 minutes.

2. Add milk, sugar, cinnamon, allspice and cardamom. Return saucepan to medium heat and bring to a simmer for several minutes or until steaming. Remove from heat and strain into a measuring cup with spout.

3. Whisk in chocolate chips and serve at once in mugs. Garnish with whipped cream, if desired.

Cosmic Coffee with Chocolate Chips and Chantilly Cream

SERVES 4

This is a really fun way to end a dinner. Just make sure you save some room. Once you have tried this beverage, you will never want plain, boring coffee again.

TIPS

Garnish each mug of coffee with a cinnamon stick. It adds a great flavor to the coffee. Another fun way to serve this coffee is to offer flavored coffee syrups in addition to the whipped cream and chocolate chips. Hazelnut, peppermint, vanilla and almond would all be equally delicious.

This recipe can be doubled.

1 cup	whipping (35%) cream	250 mL
2 tsp	confectioner's (icing) sugar, sifted	10 mL
1/2 tsp	vanilla	2 mL
4 cups	strong brewed coffee (see Tip, page 352)	1 L
1/3 cup	semisweet chocolate chips	75 mL

1. In a small bowl, combine cream, confectioner's sugar and vanilla. Beat until soft peaks form.

2. Pour the hot coffee into mugs. Dollop with whipped cream. Top with chocolate chips.

Variation
Substitute espresso for the brewed coffee.

Chocolatini

SERVES 2

This is a really fun cocktail to serve — decadent and equally delicious to drink. Not too sweet, even with the chocolate touch, this is the queen of cocktails. I dedicate this recipe to my sister-in-law Randie, who, like this drink, is always the "belle of the ball."

TIP

Store vodka in the freezer to keep it cold and ready for perfect martinis.

2 martini glasses
Cocktail shaker

2 tbsp	confectioner's (icing) sugar, sifted	25 mL
	Ice cubes	
3 oz	cold vodka	90 mL
1 tbsp	chocolate syrup	15 mL
1 tbsp	crème de cassis liqueur	15 mL
10	semisweet chocolate chips	10

1. Place martini glasses in the freezer for 10 minutes to chill. Spread confectioner's sugar on a small saucer. Dip the rims of the chilled glasses in the confectioner's sugar to coat lightly.

2. Fill a cocktail shaker with ice cubes. Pour vodka, chocolate syrup and crème de cassis over the ice.

3. Shake mixture until cocktail shaker becomes frosty. Strain into prepared glasses. Garnish each drink with 5 chocolate chips.

Variation
Substitute raspberry liqueur for the crème de cassis.

Chocolate Dream

SERVES 2

It's always fun to have a surprise drink up your sleeve for unsuspecting guests. Even better is the fact that this sophisticated drink is creamy and chocolaty. Drink up!

TIP

If possible, use good-quality vodka and chocolate liqueur for this recipe. If you can't find a chocolate cream liqueur, you can use a non-creamy, full-flavored chocolate liqueur.

Cocktail shaker
2 martini glasses

	Ice cubes	
1/3 cup	vanilla vodka	75 mL
1/4 cup	chocolate cream liqueur (see Tip, at left)	50 mL
2 tbsp	store-bought or homemade Chocolate Syrup (see recipe, page 333)	25 mL
2	large marshmallows	2

1. Fill cocktail shaker half full of ice cubes. Pour vodka, chocolate liqueur and chocolate syrup over ice.

2. Shake mixture until cocktail shaker becomes frosty. Strain into glasses.

3. Place each marshmallow on a short skewer. Place in drink for garnish and serve.

Variation
Substitute 2 tbsp (25 mL) miniature marshmallows for the large marshmallows. Instead of skewering the marshmallows, float 1 tbsp (15 mL) in each drink.

Chocolate Peppermint Stick

SERVES 2

Here's a great winter drink that will warm you from the inside out. I like to serve it martini-style, in a chilled martini glass, garnished with a small candy cane.

TIP

Store your vodka in the freezer so that it's always ready at a moment's notice.

2 martini glasses
Cocktail shaker

2 tbsp	granulated sugar	25 mL
	Ice cubes	
1/3 cup	vanilla vodka, chilled	75 mL
1/4 cup	crème de cacao	50 mL
1/4 cup	store-bought or homemade Chocolate Syrup (see recipe, page 333)	50 mL
1 1/2 tsp	peppermint schnapps	7 mL
	Whipped cream	
2	small candy canes	2

1. Place martini glasses in freezer for 10 minutes to chill. Spread granulated sugar on a small saucer. Lightly moisten the very top of chilled glass rims with water and dip into sugar to coat lightly.

2. Fill cocktail shaker half full of ice cubes. Pour vodka, crème de cacao, chocolate syrup and peppermint schnapps over ice.

3. Shake mixture until cocktail shaker becomes frosty. Strain into glasses.

4. Top each drink with a dollop or swirl of whipped cream and garnish with one candy cane. Serve immediately.

Variation
Substitute a round peppermint candy on top of the whipped cream instead of a candy cane for garnish.

Chocolate Liqueur

**MAKES 2³/₄
CUPS (675 ML)**

I consider this drink the "Nectar of the Gods." No one will believe that you made it from scratch. It literally takes 10 minutes to prepare and will keep, refrigerated, for up to a week.

TIPS

Stir liqueur well before serving.

Liqueur will keep, refrigerated, for up to 1 week.

1¹/₂ cups	whipping (35%) cream	375 mL
7 oz	milk chocolate, chopped	210 g
3 tbsp	granulated sugar, or to taste	45 mL
1 tbsp	instant coffee granules	15 mL
¹/₂ cup	light (5%) or half-and-half (10%) cream	125 mL
³/₄ cup	whiskey	175 mL

1. In a small saucepan over medium–high heat, bring cream to a simmer.

2. Remove from heat and whisk in chocolate, sugar and instant coffee until chocolate is melted and mixture is smooth. Whisk in light cream.

3. Let cool to lukewarm. Stir in whiskey and refrigerate until chilled and ready to serve.

Variation
Substitute bittersweet or semisweet chocolate for the milk chocolate.

Chocolate Snow

SERVES 4

This is what snow would be like if you lived in heaven. It has a pure milk chocolate flavor with a pinch of coffee liqueur. While making this recipe, I poured the shake into two very tall glasses and placed one in the freezer for my husband to enjoy later. Several hours later, it was almost like gelato.

TIPS

This drink freezes well. After removing from the freezer, let stand at room temperature for about 10 minutes.

The size of actual scoops of ice cream can differ somewhat, so if the shake is too thick, add a touch more milk or coffee liqueur to thin slightly. If the shake is too runny, add a bit more ice cream.

4 oz	milk chocolate, chopped	125 g
1 cup	milk	250 mL
1/4 cup	coffee liqueur	50 mL
6	large scoops vanilla ice cream	6
6	large scoops chocolate ice cream	6

1. In a microwave-safe bowl, microwave chocolate, uncovered, on Medium (50%) for 1 to $1\frac{1}{2}$ minutes, stirring every 30 seconds, or until chocolate is soft and almost melted. Stir until completely melted and smooth. Let cool slightly.

2. In a blender, combine milk, melted chocolate, coffee liqueur and vanilla and chocolate ice creams. Blend mixture until smooth.

3. Pour into glasses and serve immediately.

Variations

The liqueur can be omitted or you can substitute dark rum.

You can also substitute all chocolate or all vanilla ice cream in this recipe, should you desire. But the addition of both ice creams adds a deep milk chocolate flavor.

Orange Chocolate Cup

Hot chocolate with a twist of orange, orange zest, coffee and orange liqueur. Sounds tantalizing, doesn't it? This cocoa is just the thing to warm the cockles of your heart on a chilly evening. Try packing a Thermos of this on your next winter outing.

TIPS

Do not substitute nonfat or low-fat milk in this recipe.

Garnish with a dollop of whipped cream and a twist of orange peel, if desired.

2 cups	whole milk (see Tips, left)	500 mL
1/4 cup	packed light brown sugar	50 mL
	Grated zest of 1 orange	
1 tbsp	instant coffee granules	15 mL
4 oz	bittersweet chocolate, finely chopped	125 g
1/4 cup	orange-flavored liqueur	50 mL

1. In a small saucepan over medium heat, bring milk, brown sugar and orange zest to a simmer.

2. Strain mixture into a pitcher. Discard orange zest.

3. Add instant coffee and chocolate, whisking until smooth. Whisk in orange liqueur and serve.

Variation
Omit the orange liqueur, if desired.

Library and Archives Canada Cataloguing in Publication

Hasson, Julie
    300 best chocolate recipes / Julie Hasson.

A collection of recipes, some already published in 125 best chocolate chip recipes
and 125 best chocolate recipes.

ISBN-13: 978-0-7788-0144-3
ISBN-10: 0-7788-0144-6

1. Cookery (Chocolate). I. Title. II. Title: Three hundred best chocolate recipes.

TX767.C5H39 2006   641.6'374   C2006-902498-7

Sources

Bernard Callebaut
(800) 661-8367
www.bernardcallebaut.com
Fine Belgian chocolate. Retail stores throughout Canada and the United States. (Operates under the trade name Chocolaterie Bernard C in the U.S.)

Boyajian
(800) 965-0665 or (781) 828-9966
www.boyajianinc.com
Citrus oils and flavorings.

Charles H. Baldwin & Sons
(413) 232-7785
www.baldwinextracts.com
Pure extracts from anise to peppermint.

Dagoba Organic Chocolate
(541) 482-2001
www.dagobachocolate.com
All products Certified Organic.

Demarle At Home
(888) 838-1998 or (310) 568-1731
www.demarleathome.com
Silpat® pan liners, silicone baking pans and specialty cookware.

Ener-G Foods, Inc.
(800) 331-5222
www.ener-g.com
Egg replacer.

Julie Hasson
www.juliehasson.com
Author's website with recipes and a free monthly newsletter.

King Arthur Flour
(800) 827-6836
www.kingarthurflour.com
An amazing selection of baking and cooking tools, appliances, specialty flours, chocolates, hard-to-find ingredients and more.

Lindt
(800) 701-8489
www.lindt.com
Swiss chocolate. Shop online and order catalogue.

Qualifirst
(416) 244-1177
www.qualifirst.com
Canadian distributor for Boyajian, including citrus oils. Also fine chocolate and much more.

Select Appliance
(888) 235-0431
www.selectappliance.com
A great selection of ChocoVision® chocolate tempering machines and accessories.

Surfas
(310) 559-4770
www.surfasonline.com
Restaurant supply and gourmet
food, including Callebaut and
Valrhona chocolates.

Sur La Table
(800) 243-0852
www.surlatable.com
Specialty bakeware, cookware,
utensils and Guittard and
Scharffen Berger chocolates.

Williams Sonoma
(877) 812-6235 (U.S.)
(866) 753-1350 (Canada)
www.williams-sonoma.com
Specialty bakeware, cookware,
utensils and gourmet food.

Index

Affogato, 296
almond paste
  Chocolate Almond Chews,
    191
  Chocolate-Dipped Fruit
    Skewers (variation), 253
  Chocolate-Drizzled Almond
    Cake, 93
almond syrup
  Affogato, 296
  Blended Mocha Frappé
    (variation), 352
  Chocolate Chip Trifle, 280
  Hot White Chocolate Milk
    (variation), 345
almonds
  Almond and Coconut
    Chocolate Chip Tart, 161
  Almond Caramel Bars, 228
  Almond Chocolate Coconut
    Torte, 94
  Almond Chocolate Ginger
    Bark, 251
  Almond Poppy Seed
    Chocolate Chip Muffins, 76
  Chocolate Almond Bars, 227
  Chocolate Almond Bread
    Spread, 340
  Chocolate Almond Drops, 190
  Chocolate Almond Graham
    Bars, 229
  Chocolate Brittle Bars, 220
  Chocolate Caramel Bars
    (variation), 230
  Chocolate Cherry Biscotti
    (variation), 210
  Chocolate Cherry Drops, 246
  Chocolate Chip Cherry
    Granola, 26
  Chocolate Club, 48
  Chocolate-Dipped Sesame
    Almond Candy, 250
  Chocolate Macaroon Bars, 232
  Chocolate Matzo, 260
  Chocolate Salami (variation),
    252
  Chocolate Tea Cakes
    (variation), 206
  Double Chocolate Dips, 204
  Hip Chip Trail Mix, 255

Mississippi Mud Pie, 298
Raspberry Chocolate Chip
  Bars (variation), 223
Rocky Roads, 248
Six-Layer Bars, 233
Slice-and-Bake Chocolate
  Chip Almond Cookies, 186
Vancouver Bars, 234
White Chocolate Almond
  Chunk Biscotti, 213
White Chocolate Almond
  Rice Pudding, 270
White Chocolate Macadamia
  Cupcakes (variation), 140
apricots
  Apricot Chip Scones, 57
  Apricot Chocolate Chip
    Cheesecake Muffins, 68
  Chocolate Cherry Drops
    (variation), 246
  Chocolate Chip Cherry
    Granola, 26
  Chocolate-Dipped Fruit
    Skewers, 253
  Chocolate Fruit Tarts, 168
  Chocolate Rum Balls, 244
  Double Chocolate Apricot
    Muffins, 79
  Hip Chip Trail Mix, 255
  Matzo Pizza (variation), 261
  Raspberry Chocolate Chip
    Cookies (variation), 180

Baklava with Chocolate, Walnuts
  and Honey Syrup, 172
bananas
  Banana Blondies with
    Chocolate Chips and
    Walnuts, 218
  Banana Caramel Terrine, 294
  Banana Chip Foster, 295
  Banana Chocolate Breads, 43
  Banana Chocolate Cake, 90
  Banana Chocolate Chip Cake,
    91
  Banana Chocolate Ice Cream,
    289
  Banana Fanna Pie, 150
  Chocolate Banana Bread
    Pudding, 272

Chocolate Banana Pops, 314
Chocolate Chip Hotcakes
  (variation), 32
Chocolate Club, 48
Chocolate Fondue, 318
Chocolate Fruit Tarts, 168
Milk Chocolate Banana Sauce,
  323
Strawberry Chip "Moo-thie,"
  348
bars, 220–33
Better-Than-Store-Bought
  Chocolate Pudding Mix,
  264
beverage recipes, 344–67
beverages, alcoholic (as
  ingredient). See also specific
  types of liquor; liqueur; wine
Chocolate Butterscotch
  Pudding, 268
Chocolate Chip Trifle, 280
Chocolate Dream, 363
Chocolate Liqueur, 365
Chocolate Peppermint Stick,
  364
Chocolatini, 362
Mud Cake, 86
Walnut Whiskey Fudge Sauce,
  330
Whiskey Fudge, 240
biscuits, 28–30
Bittersweet Chocolate Mint
  Sauce, 326
Black Forest Sauce, 324
Blended Mocha Frappé, 352
bourbon
  Bourbon Fudge Sauce, 329
  Chocolate Banana Bread
    Pudding, 272
  Mud Cake, 86
  Sweet Potato Pie with White
    Chocolate Chunks, 154
brandy
  Chocolate Cherry Bombs, 312
  Little Chocolate Cakes, 127
bread and bun recipes, 38–47
bread (as ingredient)
  Chocolate Banana Bread
    Pudding, 272
  Chocolate Buns, 47

bread (as ingredient) *(continued)*
    Chocolate Chip Bread Pudding
        with Irish Cream, 271
    Chocolate Club, 48
    Chocolate Orange French
        Toast, 34
    Cinnamon Toast with Milk
        Chocolate, 27
    Grilled Chocolate, 49
    Pumpkin Chip Bread
        Pudding, 273
Brown Sugar Chocolate Chunk
    Pound Cake, 112
Brown Sugar Shortbread, 208
Brownie Pie, 159
brownies/blondies, 214–19
buttermilk, 12
    Apricot Chip Scones, 57
    Café Mocha Cake, 116
    Chocolate Chili Cupcakes, 144
    Chocolate Chip Chai Cake,
        122
    Chocolate Chip Hotcakes, 32
    Chocolate Chip Jammer
        Scones, 54
    Chocolate Chip Pecan Waffles,
        33
    Chocolate Potato Cake, 102
    Chocolate-Stuffed Scones, 52
    Chocolate Surprise Cupcakes,
        138
    Coconut Chocolate Chip
        Bundt Cake, 110
    Coconut Cupcakes, 134
    Cookies and Cream Cake, 82
    Rich Lemon Chocolate Chip
        Bundt Cake, 108
Butterscotch Pecan Chocolate
    Chip Blondies, 219

Café au Lait Pudding, 267
Café Mocha Cake, 116
cake (as ingredient)
    Chocolate Chip Trifle, 280
    Chocolate Fondue, 318
cake recipes, 82–128. *See also*
    cupcakes
caramel
    Banana Caramel Terrine, 294
    Blended Mocha Frappé
        (variation), 352
    Chocolate Caramel Cream
        Shake, 347
    Hot White Chocolate Milk
        (variation), 345

Milk Chocolate Caramel
    Cream, 353
Mississippi Mud Pie, 298
cereal (as ingredient)
    Chocolate Almond Graham
        Bars, 229
    Cowgirl Cookies, 187
    Crispy Chocolate Drops, 245
chai tea
    Chocolate Chai Snow Cones,
        310
    Chocolate Chip Chai Cake, 122
    Hot Chocolate Chai Latte, 360
cherries
    Apricot Chocolate Chip
        Cheesecake Muffins
        (variation), 68
    Black Forest Sauce, 324
    Cherry Chocolate Chunk Ice
        Cream, 290
    Chocolate Challah, 44
    Chocolate Cherry Biscotti, 210
    Chocolate Cherry Bombs, 312
    Chocolate Cherry Bundt
        Cake, 104
    Chocolate Cherry Drops, 246
    Chocolate Cherry Rum
        Cakes, 128
    Chocolate Cherry Terrine, 281
    Chocolate Cherry Truffles, 243
    Chocolate Chip Cherry Bars,
        222
    Chocolate Chip Cherry
        Breakfast Biscuits, 28
    Chocolate Chip Cherry
        Granola, 26
    Chocolate Chip Jammer
        Scones (variation), 54
    Chocolate Salami, 252
    Double Chocolate Apricot
        Muffins, 79
    Double Fudge Espresso
        Brownies (variation), 216
    Raspberry Dutch Baby with
        Chocolate Chips
        (variation), 35
    Ricotta Puddings (variation),
        274
    Rocky Roads (variation), 248
    Sticky Chocolate Raisin Sauce
        (variation), 322
chips, baking, 14. *See also*
    chocolate chips
    Chocolate Chip Butterscotch
        Cookies, 183

Chocolate Mint Cupcakes, 145
Double Chocolate Mint
    Chunkers, 182
Chipwiches, 297
chocolate, 10–12, 11. *See also*
    chocolate, white; chocolate
    chips; chocolate sauce/syrup;
    cocoa powder
    Almond Chocolate Coconut
        Torte, 94
    Almond Chocolate Ginger
        Bark, 251
    Banana Chocolate Breads, 43
    Banana Chocolate Cake, 90
    Banana Chocolate Ice Cream,
        289
    Bittersweet Chocolate Mint
        Sauce, 326
    Bourbon Fudge Sauce, 329
    Brown Sugar Chocolate
        Chunk Pound Cake, 112
    Café au Lait Pudding
        (variation), 267
    Café Mocha Cake, 116
    Cherry Chocolate Chunk Ice
        Cream, 290
    Chocolate Almond Chews,
        191
    Chocolate Almond Graham
        Bars, 229
    Chocolate Bonbons, 311
    Chocolate Brownie Baby
        Cakes, 126
    Chocolate Buns, 47
    Chocolate Butter Cookies, 176
    Chocolate Butterscotch
        Pudding, 268
    Chocolate Caramel Bars, 230
    Chocolate Cheesecake
        Cupcakes, 146
    Chocolate Cherry Bundt
        Cake, 104
    Chocolate Cherry Drops, 246
    Chocolate Cherry Terrine, 281
    Chocolate Chip Brownie Tart,
        160
    Chocolate Chip Espresso
        Cookies, Julie's, 184
    Chocolate Club, 48
    Chocolate Coconut Clouds,
        197
    Chocolate-Dipped Coconut
        Macaroons, 198
    Chocolate-Dipped Fruit
        Skewers, 253

Chocolate-Dipped Sesame Almond Candy, 250
Chocolate Espresso Cake, 118
Chocolate Espresso Cups, 275
Chocolate Fruit Tarts, 168
Chocolate Glaze (variation), 336
Chocolate Halvah Mounds, 249
Chocolate Liqueur, 365
Chocolate Macaroon Bars, 232
Chocolate Macaroon Tarts, 170
Chocolate Matzo, 260
Chocolate Mints, 246
Chocolate Muffins, 60
Chocolate No Egg Nog, 357
Chocolate Port Torte, 98
Chocolate Potato Chips, 256
Chocolate Quesadillas, 50
Chocolate Raisin Scones, 56
Chocolate Salami, 252
Chocolate Snow, 366
Chocolate Soup, 283
Chocolate Surprise Cupcakes, 138
Chocolate Syrup, 333
Chocolate Tea, 358
Chocolate Tea Cakes, 206
Chocolate Truffle Tart, 162
Cinnamon Chocolate Crisps, 193
Cinnamon Toast with Milk Chocolate, 27
Cookie Tarts, 166
Crispy Chocolate Drops, 245
Dark Chocolate Mousse, 278
Dark Chocolate Sorbet in Frozen Orange Cups, 304
Dark Chocolate Truffles, 242
Date Flapjack Cake, Tish's, 97
Double Chocolate Apricot Muffins, 79
Double Chocolate Cheesecake Ice Cream, 286
Double Chocolate Dips, 204
Double Chocolate Lollipops, 241
Espresso Dark Brownie Cupcakes, 142
Frozen Chocolate Malt Yogurt, 303
Frozen Chocolate Mousse, 300
Ginger Chocolate Molasses Cookies, 194
Grilled Chocolate, 49

Hazelnut Chocolate Cookies, 192
Ice Cream Cookie Cups, 200
Little Chocolate Cakes, 127
Matzo Pizza, 261
Milk Chocolate Banana Sauce, 323
Milk Chocolate Caramel Cream, 353
Milk Chocolate Latte Scones, 51
Milk Chocolate S'mores, 254
Mocha Ice, 309
Mud Cake, 86
Orange Chocolate Cup, 367
Orange Fudge Pops, 315
Pumpkin Chocolate Chip Ice Cream, 292
Quick and Easy Chocolate Milk, 344
Quick Chocolate Pudding, 265
Quick-Mix Chocolate Fudge, 238
Raspberry Chocolate Ice Cream (variation), 291
Raspberry Chocolate Sauce, 325
Ricotta Puddings, 274
Rum Raisin Spoon Brownies, 217
Spicy Haute Chocolate, 355
Toffee Chocolate Sauce, 321
Triple Chocolate Chip Cookies, 179
Vancouver Bars, 234
Vegan Chocolate Espresso Brownies, 214
Whiskey Fudge, 240
White Chocolate Chunk Fudge Cookies, 188
White Chocolate Sesame Shortbread Bars (variation), 226
chocolate, white, 11
Banana Chocolate Ice Cream (variation), 289
Café au Lait Pudding, 267
Chocolate Matzo, 260
Double Chocolate Cheesecake Ice Cream, 286
Double Chocolate Dips (variation), 204
Double Chocolate Lollipops, 241

Espresso Dark Brownie Cupcakes (variation), 142
Green Tea White Chocolate Chip ice Cream, 293
Hot White Chocolate Milk, 345
Sweet Potato Pie with White Chocolate Chunks, 154
Triple Chocolate Chip Cookies, 179
White Chocolate Almond Chunk Biscotti, 213
White Chocolate Almond Rice Pudding, 270
White Chocolate Chunk Fudge Cookies, 188
White Chocolate Key Lime Pie, 156
White Chocolate Lemon Fudge, 239
White Chocolate Mocha Sauce, 332
White Chocolate Rum Raisin Sauce, 331
White Chocolate Sesame Shortbread Bars, 226
chocolate chips, 11. See also chips, baking
Affogato, 296
Almond and Coconut Chocolate Chip Tart, 161
Almond Caramel Bars, 228
Almond Poppy Seed Chocolate Chip Muffins, 76
Apricot Chip Scones, 57
Apricot Chocolate Chip Cheesecake Muffins, 68
Baklava with Chocolate, Walnuts and Honey Syrup, 172
Banana Blondies with Chocolate Chips and Walnuts, 218
Banana Caramel Terrine, 294
Banana Chip Foster, 295
Banana Chocolate Chip Cake, 91
Banana Fanna Pie, 150
Better-Than-Store-Bought Chocolate Pudding Mix, 264
Blended Mocha Frappé, 352
Brown Sugar Shortbread, 208
Brownie Pie, 159

chocolate chips *(continued)*
Butterscotch Pecan Chocolate Chip Blondies, 219
Chipwiches, 297
Chocolate Almond Bars, 227
Chocolate Almond Bread Spread, 340
Chocolate Almond Drops, 190
Chocolate Almond Graham Bars, 229
Chocolate Banana Bread Pudding, 272
Chocolate Banana Pops, 314
Chocolate Brittle Bars, 220
Chocolate Butter Cookies, 176
Chocolate Cappuccino Chip Cookies, 185
Chocolate Caramel Cream Shake, 347
Chocolate Caramel Sauce, 320
Chocolate Challah, 44
Chocolate Cherry Biscotti, 210
Chocolate Cherry Bombs, 312
Chocolate Cherry Bundt Cake, 104
Chocolate Cherry Rum Cakes, 128
Chocolate Cherry Terrine, 281
Chocolate Cherry Truffles, 243
Chocolate Chili Cupcakes, 144
Chocolate Chip Bread Pudding with Irish Cream, 271
Chocolate Chip Brownie Tart, 160
Chocolate Chip Butterscotch Cookies, 183
Chocolate Chip Calypso Cake, 120
Chocolate Chip Chai Cake, 122
Chocolate Chip Cheese Tart, 164
Chocolate Chip Cherry Bars, 222
Chocolate Chip Cherry Breakfast Biscuits, 28
Chocolate Chip Cherry Granola, 26
Chocolate Chip Coconut Pie, 157

Chocolate Chip Cranberry Muffins, 70
Chocolate Chip Cream Cheese Pound Cake, 113
Chocolate Chip Dream Cream, 287
Chocolate Chip Eggnog Muffins, 67
Chocolate Chip Espresso Cookies, Julie's, 184
Chocolate Chip Hotcakes, 32
Chocolate Chip Jammer Scones, 54
Chocolate Chip Lemon Muffins, 73
Chocolate Chip Madeleines, 205
Chocolate Chip Meringues, 207
Chocolate Chip Oat Breakfast Biscuits, 29
Chocolate Chip Orange Biscotti, 211
Chocolate Chip Orange Muffins, 74
Chocolate Chip Pecan Pie, 158
Chocolate Chip Pecan Waffles, 33
Chocolate Chip Pumpkin Muffins, 75
Chocolate Chip Raspberry Clafouti, 279
Chocolate Chip Spice Bars with Maple Glaze, 224
Chocolate Chip Trifle, 280
Chocolate Cinnamon Cupcakes, 139
Chocolate Crunchies, 259
Chocolate Cupcakes with Mocha Frosting, 136
Chocolate-Dipped Coconut Macaroons, 198
Chocolate-Dipped Pretzels, 257
Chocolate-Drizzled Almond Cake, 93
Chocolate Espresso Lava Cakes, 125
Chocolate Fondue, 318
Chocolate Glaze, 336
Chocolate Macaroon Bars, 232
Chocolate Malted, 349
Chocolate Merlot Sauce, 327

Chocolate Midnight Cake, 92
Chocolate Mint Cupcakes, 145
Chocolate Mint Sandwich Cookies, 199
Chocolate Mousse Cake, 88
Chocolate Mousse–Filled Cupcakes, 132
Chocolate Orange French Toast, 34
Chocolate Peanut Butter Cupcakes, 137
Chocolate Port Torte, 98
Chocolate Rum Balls, 244
Chocolate Rum Raisin Ice Cream, 288
Chocolate Salt and Pepper Cookies, 196
Chocolate Strawberry Syrup, 335
Chocolate-Stuffed Scones, 52
Chocolate Swirl Bread, 38
Chocolate Tapioca for Grown-ups, 269
Chocolate Tiramisu, 282
Chocolate Toffee Crackers, 258
Chocolatini, 362
Coconut Chip Sorbet, 306
Coconut Chocolate Chip Bundt Cake, 110
Coconut Cupcakes, 134
Cookie Tarts (variation), 166
Cookies and Cream Cake, 82
Cookies-and-Cream Shake, 346
Cosmic Coffee with Chocolate Chips and Chantilly Cream, 361
Cowgirl Cookies, 187
Cranberry Sour Cream Bundt Cake, 106
Crumbcake Muffins, 62
Dark Chocolate Syrup, 334
Donut Muffins, 63
Double Chocolate Chip Muffins, 61
Double Chocolate Chunkies, 178
Double Chocolate Cinnamon Bread, Jay's, 40
Double Chocolate Mint Chunkers, 182
Double Chocolate Zucchini Cake, 103

Double Fudge Espresso
Brownies, 216

Eggnog Chocolate Chip Tea
Cake, 124

Frozen Cappuccino, 307

Frozen Chocolate Malt Yogurt
(variation), 303

Ginger Chocolate Shortbread,
209

Ginger Muffins, 66

High-Octane Espresso Chip
Morning Muffins, 64

Hip Chip Trail Mix, 255

Hot Chocolate Chai Latte,
360

Hot Spiced Chocolate, 354

Irish Cream Cake (variation),
99

Little Chocolate Cakes, 127

Lone Star Double Chocolate
Chip Cake, 84

Maple-Glazed Chocolate
Walnut Breakfast Biscuits,
30

Maple Pecan Muffins with
Chocolate Chips, 77

Matzo Pizza, 261

Mississippi Mud Pie, 298

Mocha Chocolate Chip Cake,
117

Mocha Fudge Sauce, 328

Oat Bars, 221

Old-Fashioned Chocolate
Orange Pie, 152

Old-Fashioned Dark
Chocolate Pudding, 266

Peppermint Chip Gelato, 302

Pumpkin Chip Bread
Pudding, 273

Pumpkin Chocolate Chip
Cookies, 181

Pumpkin Chocolate Chip
Loaves, 46

Quick Cinnamon Chocolate
Pastries, 171

Quick-Mix Chocolate Fudge,
238

The Quintessential Chocolate
Chip Cookie, 177

Raspberry Chocolate Chip
Bars, 223

Raspberry Chocolate Chip
Cookies, 180

Raspberry Chocolate Chip
Muffins, 71

Raspberry Chocolate Chip
Sorbet, 305

Raspberry Dutch Baby with
Chocolate Chips, 35

Rich Lemon Chocolate Chip
Bundt Cake, 108

Rocky Roads, 248

Rum Raisin Spoon Brownies,
217

Six-Layer Bars, 233

Slice-and-Bake Chocolate
Chip Almond Cookies, 186

Snickerdoodle Chip Biscotti,
212

Sour Cream Coffee Cake
Muffins, 78

Sour Cream Coffee Cake with
Chocolate Pecan Streusel,
114

Strawberry Cheesecake
Mousse Parfaits, 276

Strawberry Chip "Moo-thie,"
348

Strawberry Chocolate Chip
Muffins, 72

Tiramisu Chip Gelato, 301

Triple Chocolate Chip
Cookies, 179

24 Carrot Cake, 100

Vegan Chocolate Espresso
Brownies, 214

Walnut Chocolate Chip Cake,
96

Warm Raspberry Chocolate
Chip Spread, 341

White Chocolate Macadamia
Cupcakes, 140

chocolate sauce/syrup
Chocolate Chai Snow Cones,
310

Chocolate Dream, 363

Chocolate Peppermint Stick,
364

Chocolatini, 362

Dark Chocolate Ginger Fizz,
351

Mississippi Mud Pie, 298

Morning Mocha, 359

Chocolatini, 362

Cinnamon Chocolate Crisps,
193

Cinnamon Chocolate Pastries,
Quick, 171

Cinnamon Toast with Milk
Chocolate, 27

cocoa powder, unsweetened, 11,
12

Banana Chocolate Ice Cream,
289

Better-Than-Store-Bought
Chocolate Pudding Mix,
264

Black Forest Sauce, 324

Brownie Pie, 159

Chocolate Almond Bars, 227

Chocolate Butter Cookies,
176

Chocolate Cappuccino Chip
Cookies, 185

Chocolate Cappuccino
Creams, 202

Chocolate Challah, 44

Chocolate Cherry Truffles, 243

Chocolate Chili Cupcakes,
144

Chocolate Cinnamon
Cupcakes, 139

Chocolate Cupcakes with
Mocha Frosting, 136

Chocolate Espresso Cake, 118

Chocolate Espresso Lava
Cakes, 125

Chocolate Fudge Frosting,
337

Chocolate Honey Sauce, 319

Chocolate Midnight Cake, 92

Chocolate Mint Cupcakes,
145

Chocolate Mint Sandwich
Cookies, 199

Chocolate Mousse–Filled
Cupcakes, 132

Chocolate Muffins, 60

Chocolate Orange French
Toast, 34

Chocolate Peanut Butter
Cupcakes, 137

Chocolate Potato Cake, 102

Chocolate Raisin Scones, 56

Chocolate Rum Balls, 244

Chocolate Salt and Pepper
Cookies, 196

Chocolate-Stuffed Scones, 52

Chocolate Syrup, 333

Cinnamon Chocolate Crisps,
193

Cookie Tarts, 166

Cookies and Cream Cake, 82

Dark Chocolate Sorbet in
Frozen Orange Cups, 304

cocoa powder, unsweetened, *(continued)*
Dark Chocolate Syrup, 334
Dark Chocolate Truffles, 242
Double Chocolate Chip Muffins, 61
Double Chocolate Chunkies, 178
Double Chocolate Cinnamon Bread, Jay's, 40
Double Chocolate Mint Chunkers, 182
Double Chocolate Zucchini Cake, 103
Double Fudge Espresso Brownies, 216
Espresso Dark Brownie Cupcakes, 142
Frozen Cappuccino, 307
Irish Cream Cake, 99
Killer Mocha Frosting, 339
Little Chocolate Cakes, 127
Lone Star Double Chocolate Chip Cake, 84
Mexican Cocoa, 356
Mocha Fudge Sauce, 328
Mocha Ice, 309
Mud Cake, 86
Old-Fashioned Dark Chocolate Pudding, 266
Orange Fudge Pops, 315
Peanut Butter Fudge Frosting, 338
Pomegranate Ice with Dark Chocolate Sauce, 308
Quick and Easy Chocolate Milk, 344
Sticky Chocolate Raisin Sauce, 322
24 Carrot Cake, 100
Walnut Whiskey Fudge Sauce, 330
White Chocolate Chunk Fudge Cookies, 188
coconut
Almond and Coconut Chocolate Chip Tart, 161
Almond Chocolate Coconut Torte, 94
Chocolate Chip Cheese Tart, 164
Chocolate Chip Coconut Pie, 157
Chocolate Coconut Clouds, 197

Chocolate-Dipped Coconut Macaroons, 198
Chocolate Macaroon Bars, 232
Chocolate Macaroon Tarts, 170
Coconut Chip Sorbet, 306
Coconut Chocolate Chip Bundt Cake, 110
Coconut Cupcakes, 134
Quick Chocolate Pudding, 265
Six-Layer Bars, 233
Slice-and-Bake Chocolate Chip Almond Cookies, 186
24 Carrot Cake, 100
White Chocolate Almond Chunk Biscotti, 213
coffee, 12
Affogato, 296
Blended Mocha Frappé, 352
Café au Lait Pudding, 267
Café Mocha Cake, 116
Chocolate Cappuccino Chip Cookies, 185
Chocolate Cappuccino Creams, 202
Chocolate Chili Cupcakes, 144
Chocolate Chip Espresso Cookies, Julie's, 184
Chocolate Chip Spice Bars with Maple Glaze, 224
Chocolate Cinnamon Cupcakes, 139
Chocolate Cupcakes with Mocha Frosting, 136
Chocolate Espresso Cake, 118
Chocolate Espresso Cups, 275
Chocolate Espresso Lava Cakes, 125
Chocolate Fudge Frosting, 337
Chocolate Liqueur, 365
Chocolate Midnight Cake, 92
Chocolate Mousse–Filled Cupcakes, 132
Chocolate Muffins, 60
Chocolate Syrup (variation), 333
Chocolate Tiramisu, 282
Cosmic Coffee with Chocolate Chips and Chantilly Cream, 361
Dark Chocolate Syrup, 334
Double Fudge Espresso Brownies, 216

Espresso Dark Brownie Cupcakes, 142
Frozen Cappuccino, 307
Frozen Chocolate Mousse, 300
High-Octane Espresso Chip Morning Muffins, 64
Killer Mocha Frosting, 339
Lone Star Double Chocolate Chip Cake, 84
Milk Chocolate Latte Scones, 51
Mocha Chocolate Chip Cake, 117
Mocha Fudge Sauce, 328
Mocha Ice, 309
Morning Mocha, 359
Orange Chocolate Cup, 367
Ricotta Puddings, 274
Tiramisu Chip Gelato, 301
Vancouver Bars, 234
Vegan Chocolate Espresso Brownies, 214
White Chocolate Chunk Fudge Cookies, 188
White Chocolate Mocha Sauce, 332
cookie recipes, 176–213
Cookie Tarts, 166
cookies and crackers (as ingredient). *See also* cookies, chocolate sandwich
Chipwiches, 297
Chocolate Chip Mocha Tarts, 165
Chocolate Fondue, 318
Chocolate Rum Balls, 244
Chocolate Salami, 252
Chocolate Tiramisu, 282
Chocolate Toffee Crackers, 258
Cookie Parfaits, 277
cookies, chocolate sandwich (Oreo-type)
Brownie Pie (variation), 159
Chocolate Cheesecake Cupcakes, 146
Chocolate Mousse Cake, 88
Cookie Parfaits (variation), 277
Cookies and Cream Cake, 82
Cookies-and-Cream Shake, 346
Double Chocolate Dips, 204
Mississippi Mud Pie, 298

Strawberry Cheesecake Mousse
  Parfaits (variation), 276
cooking spray, nonstick, 14
Cosmic Coffee with Chocolate
  Chips and Chantilly Cream,
  361
Cowgirl Cookies, 187
cranberries
  Apricot Chocolate Chip
    Cheesecake Muffins
    (variation), 68
  Chocolate Cherry Biscotti
    (variation), 210
  Chocolate Cherry Rum Cakes
    (variation), 128
  Chocolate Chip Cherry Bars
    (variation), 222
  Chocolate Chip Cherry
    Breakfast Biscuits
    (variation), 28
  Chocolate Chip Cherry
    Granola (variation), 26
  Chocolate Chip Cranberry
    Muffins, 70
  Chocolate Rum Balls
    (variation), 244
  Chocolate Salami (variation),
    252
  Cowgirl Cookies (variation),
    187
  Cranberry Sour Cream Bundt
    Cake, 106
  Raspberry Dutch Baby with
    Chocolate Chips
    (variation), 35
cream cheese, 13
  Apricot Chocolate Chip
    Cheesecake Muffins, 68
  Chocolate Cheesecake
    Cupcakes, 146
  Chocolate Chip Cheese Tart,
    164
  Chocolate Chip Cream
    Cheese Pound Cake, 113
  Chocolate Tiramisu, 282
  Coconut Chocolate Chip
    Bundt Cake, 110
  Coconut Cupcakes, 134
  Cream Cheese Icing, 141
  Double Chocolate Cheesecake
    Ice Cream, 286
  Rich Lemon Chocolate Chip
    Bundt Cake, 108
  Strawberry Cheesecake
    Mousse Parfaits, 276

Tiramisu Chip Gelato, 301
24 Carrot Cake, 100
White Chocolate Key Lime
  Pie, 156
White Chocolate Lemon
  Fudge, 239
Crispy Chocolate Drops, 245
Crumbcake Muffins, 62
cupcakes, 132–46. See also cake
  recipes

dairy-free recipes
  Lone Star Double Chocolate
    Chip Cake (variation), 84
  Vegan Chocolate Espresso
    Brownies (variation), 214
Dark Chocolate Ginger Fizz, 351
Dark Chocolate Mousse, 278
Dark Chocolate Pudding,
  Old-Fashioned, 266
Dark Chocolate Sorbet in Frozen
  Orange Cups, 304
Dark Chocolate Syrup, 334
Dark Chocolate Truffles, 242
Date Flapjack Cake, Tish's, 97
Donut Muffins, 63
Double Chocolate Apricot
  Muffins, 79
Double Chocolate Cheesecake
  Ice Cream, 286
Double Chocolate Chip Muffins,
  61
Double Chocolate Chunkies, 178
Double Chocolate Cinnamon
  Bread, Jay's, 40
Double Chocolate Dips, 204
Double Chocolate Lollipops, 241
Double Chocolate Mint
  Chunkers, 182
Double Chocolate Zucchini
  Cake, 103
Double Fudge Espresso
  Brownies, 216

egg replacements, 215 (tip)
eggnog
  Chocolate Chip Eggnog
    Muffins, 67
  Eggnog Chocolate Chip Tea
    Cake, 124
eggs, 13
  Brown Sugar Chocolate
    Chunk Pound Cake, 112
  Chocolate Banana Bread
    Pudding, 272

Chocolate Chip Bread Pudding
  with Irish Cream, 271
Chocolate Chip Cream
  Cheese Pound Cake, 113
Chocolate Chip Meringues,
  207
Chocolate Chip Raspberry
  Clafouti, 279
Chocolate Coconut Clouds,
  197
Chocolate-Dipped Coconut
  Macaroons, 198
Chocolate Macaroon Bars, 232
Chocolate Macaroon Tarts,
  170
Chocolate Orange French
  Toast, 34
Chocolate Port Torte, 98
Cranberry Sour Cream Bundt
  Cake, 106
Little Chocolate Cakes, 127
Pumpkin Chip Bread
  Pudding, 273
Raspberry Dutch Baby with
  Chocolate Chips, 35
espresso. See coffee
Espresso Dark Brownie Cupcakes,
  142

floats
  Dark Chocolate Ginger Fizz,
    351
  Very Cherry Chocolate Float,
    350
Frozen Cappuccino, 307
Frozen Chocolate Malt Yogurt,
  303
Frozen Chocolate Mousse, 300
fruit, 13. See also specific types of
    fruit
  Chocolate-Dipped Fruit
    Skewers, 253
  Chocolate-Dipped Pretzels
    (variation), 257
  Chocolate Fondue, 318
  Chocolate Fruit Tarts, 168
  Tish's Date Flapjack Cake, 97
  24 Carrot Cake, 100
fudge, 238–40

ginger, candied
  Almond Chocolate Ginger
    Bark, 251
  Chocolate Chip Calypso
    Cake, 120

ginger, candied *(continued)*
  Ginger Chocolate Molasses
    Cookies, 194
  Ginger Chocolate Shortbread,
    209
  Ginger Muffins, 66
  Pumpkin Chocolate Chip Ice
    Cream (variation), 292
  White Chocolate Almond Rice
    Pudding (variation), 270
glazes and frostings, 336–39
  eggnog glaze, 124
graham crackers and crumbs
  Chocolate Chip Cheese Tart,
    164
  Milk Chocolate S'mores, 254
  Six-Layer Bars, 233
  Strawberry Cheesecake
    Mousse Parfaits, 276
  Green Tea White Chocolate Chip
    ice Cream, 293
  Grilled Chocolate, 49

hazelnut syrup
  Blended Mocha Frappé
    (variation), 352
  Hot White Chocolate Milk
    (variation), 345
hazelnuts
  Chocolate Cherry Drops
    (variation), 246
  Chocolate Club, 48
  Chocolate Matzo, 260
  Chocolate Salami (variation),
    252
  Chocolate Tea Cakes, 206
  Hazelnut Chocolate Cookies,
    192
  Rocky Roads (variation),
    248
High-Octane Espresso Chip
  Morning Muffins, 64
Hip Chip Trail Mix, 255
honey, 16
  Baklava with Chocolate,
    Walnuts and Honey Syrup,
    172
  Chocolate Chai Snow Cones,
    310
  Chocolate Chip Cherry
    Granola, 26
  Chocolate Chip Dream
    Cream, 287
  Chocolate-Dipped Sesame
    Almond Candy, 250

Chocolate Honey Sauce, 319
Ricotta Puddings, 274
Hot Chocolate Chai Latte, 360
Hot Spiced Chocolate, 354
Hot White Chocolate Milk, 345

ice cream and gelato recipes,
  286–93, 301–2
ice cream and sorbet (as
  ingredient)
Affogato, 296
Banana Caramel Terrine, 294
Banana Chip Foster, 295
Cherry Chocolate Float, 350
Chipwiches, 297
Chocolate Bonbons, 311
Chocolate Caramel Cream
  Shake, 347
Chocolate Cherry Bombs, 312
Chocolate Chip Mocha Tarts,
  165
Chocolate Malted, 349
Chocolate Snow, 366
Cookies-and-Cream Shake,
  346
Dark Chocolate Ginger Fizz,
  351
Ice Cream Cookie Cups, 200
Mississippi Mud Pie, 298
Morning Mocha, 359
Strawberry Chip "Moo-thie,"
  348
Irish Cream Cake, 99

Jay's Double Chocolate
  Cinnamon Bread, 40
Julie's Chocolate Chip Espresso
  Cookies, 184

Killer Mocha Frosting, 339
kirsch
  Affogato, 296
  Chocolate Cherry Truffles,
    243
  Chocolate Mousse Cake, 88

lemon and lime, 13
  Chocolate Chip Lemon
    Muffins, 73
  Rich Lemon Chocolate Chip
    Bundt Cake, 108
  White Chocolate Key Lime
    Pie, 156
  White Chocolate Lemon
    Fudge, 239

liqueurs. *See also* kirsch
  Black Forest Sauce (variation),
    324
  Cherry Chocolate Chunk Ice
    Cream, 290
  Chocolate Caramel Cream
    Shake, 347
  Chocolate Cheesecake
    Cupcakes, 146
  Chocolate Chip Bread
    Pudding with Irish Cream,
    271
  Chocolate Dream, 363
  Chocolate Fondue, 318
  Chocolate Fudge Frosting, 337
  Chocolate Mousse Cake
    (variation), 88
  Chocolate Orange French
    Toast, 34
  Chocolate Peppermint Stick,
    364
  Chocolate Snow, 366
  Chocolate Strawberry Syrup,
    335
  Chocolate Surprise Cupcakes,
    138
  Chocolate Tapioca for
    Grown-ups, 269
  Chocolatini, 362
  Cranberry Sour Cream Bundt
    Cake, 106
  Dark Chocolate Mousse, 278
  Frozen Chocolate Mousse, 300
  Irish Cream Cake, 99
  Mocha Fudge Sauce
    (variation), 328
  Orange Chocolate Cup, 367
  Quick and Easy Chocolate
    Milk (variation), 344
  Quick-Mix Chocolate Fudge,
    238
  Tiramisu Chip Gelato, 301
  Vancouver Bars, 234
Little Chocolate Cakes, 127
Lone Star Double Chocolate
  Chip Cake, 84

macadamia nuts
  Almond Caramel Bars
    (variation), 228
  Almond Chocolate Ginger
    Bark (variation), 251
  The Quintessential Chocolate
    Chip Cookie (variation),
    177

Six-Layer Bars (variation), 233
Slice-and-Bake Chocolate
    Chip Almond Cookies
    (variation), 186
White Chocolate Macadamia
    Cupcakes, 140
malted milk powder
    Chocolate Malted, 349
    Frozen Chocolate Malt Yogurt,
    303
    Quick and Easy Chocolate
    Milk (variation), 344
Maple-Glazed Chocolate Walnut
    Breakfast Biscuits, 30
Maple Pecan Muffins with
    Chocolate Chips, 77
marshmallow
    Chocolate Almond Graham
    Bars, 229
    Chocolate Dream, 363
    Chocolate Fondue, 318
    Chocolate Surprise Cupcakes,
    138
    Grilled Chocolate, 49
    Milk Chocolate S'mores, 254
    Mud Cake, 86
    Rocky Roads, 248
marzipan. See almond paste
matzo
    Chocolate Matzo, 260
    Matzo Pizza, 261
Mexican Cocoa, 356
milk, 12. See also ice cream and
    gelato recipes; milk,
    chocolate; milk, condensed
milk, chocolate
    Chocolate No Egg Nog, 357
    Chocolate Pudding Pops,
    313
    Chocolate Soup, 283
    Cookie Tarts, 166
    Quick Chocolate Pudding,
    265
milk, condensed (sweetened), 13
    Quick-Mix Chocolate Fudge,
    238
    Six-Layer Bars, 233
    Whiskey Fudge, 240
    White Chocolate Key Lime
    Pie, 156
Milk Chocolate Banana Sauce,
    323
Milk Chocolate Caramel Cream,
    353
Milk Chocolate Latte Scones, 51

Milk Chocolate S'mores, 254
Mississippi Mud Pie, 298
Mocha Chocolate Chip Cake,
    117
Mocha Fudge Sauce, 328
Mocha Ice, 309
molasses, 16
    Chocolate Chip Calypso
    Cake, 120
    Ginger Chocolate Molasses
    Cookies, 194
    Ginger Muffins, 66
Morning Mocha, 359
Mud Cake, 86
muffins, 60–79

nuts, 14. See also specific types of
    nuts
    Chocolate Banana Pops
    (variation), 314
    Chocolate Toffee Crackers
    (variation), 258

oats (rolled), 15
    Chocolate Caramel Bars, 230
    Chocolate Chip Cherry Bars,
    222
    Chocolate Chip Cherry
    Granola, 26
    Chocolate Chip Oat Breakfast
    Biscuits, 29
    Cowgirl Cookies, 187
    Date Flapjack Cake, Tish's, 97
    Oat Bars, 221
    Raspberry Chocolate Chip
    Bars, 223
Old-Fashioned Chocolate
    Orange Pie, 152
Old-Fashioned Dark Chocolate
    Pudding, 266
oranges and orange juice
    Chocolate Chip Orange
    Biscotti, 211
    Chocolate Chip Orange
    Muffins, 74
    Chocolate Fondue, 318
    Chocolate Orange French
    Toast, 34
    Dark Chocolate Sorbet in
    Frozen Orange Cups, 304
    Dark Chocolate Syrup
    (variation), 334
    Old-Fashioned Chocolate
    Orange Pie, 152
    Orange Chocolate Cup, 367

Orange Fudge Pops, 315
Rich Lemon Chocolate Chip
    Bundt Cake (variation),
    108
Sour Cream Coffee Cake with
    Chocolate Pecan Streusel,
    114
Oreo cookies. See cookies,
    chocolate sandwich

pastries, 170–72
pastry, prepared
    Baklava with Chocolate,
    Walnuts and Honey Syrup,
    172
    Quick Cinnamon Chocolate
    Pastries, 171
peanut butter
    Chocolate Club, 48
    Chocolate Crunchies
    (variation), 259
    Chocolate Peanut Butter
    Cupcakes, 137
    Grilled Chocolate (variation),
    49
    Peanut Butter Fudge Frosting,
    338
pecans
    Banana Blondies with
    Chocolate Chips and
    Walnuts (variation), 218
    Brown Sugar Shortbread
    (variation), 208
    Butterscotch Pecan Chocolate
    Chip Blondies, 219
    Chocolate Chip Pecan Pie,
    158
    Chocolate Chip Pecan Waffles,
    33
    Chocolate Quesadillas, 50
    Chocolate Rum Balls
    (variation), 244
    Double Chocolate Chunkies,
    178
    High-Octane Espresso Chip
    Morning Muffins
    (variation), 64
    Hip Chip Trail Mix, 255
    Maple-Glazed Chocolate
    Walnut Breakfast Biscuits
    (variation), 30
    Maple Pecan Muffins with
    Chocolate Chips, 77
    Pumpkin Chocolate Chip
    Loaves (variation), 46

pecans *(continued)*
    Sour Cream Coffee Cake with
      Chocolate Pecan Streusel,
      114
    Walnut Chocolate Chip Cake
      (variation), 96
    Whiskey Fudge (variation), 240
Peppermint Chip Gelato, 302
pies, 150–59
pistachios
    Chocolate Brittle Bars
      (variation), 220
    Chocolate Halvah Mounds,
      249
Pomegranate Ice with Dark
    Chocolate Sauce, 308
potato chips
    Chocolate-Dipped Pretzels
      (variation), 257
    Chocolate Potato Chips, 256
pretzels and Chinese noodles
    Chocolate Crunchies, 259
    Chocolate-Dipped Pretzels,
      257
    Chocolate Fondue, 318
pudding and mousse recipes,
    264–83
pudding (as ingredient)
    Better-Than-Store-Bought
      Chocolate Pudding Mix,
      264
    Chocolate Chip Trifle, 280
    Chocolate Pudding Pops, 313
    Cookie Parfaits, 277
pumpkin purée
    Chocolate Chip Pumpkin
      Muffins, 75
    Pumpkin Chip Bread
      Pudding, 273
    Pumpkin Chocolate Chip
      Cookies, 181
    Pumpkin Chocolate Chip Ice
      Cream, 292
    Pumpkin Chocolate Chip
      Loaves, 46

Quick and Easy Chocolate Milk,
    344
Quick Chocolate Pudding, 265
Quick Cinnamon Chocolate
    Pastries, 171
Quick-Mix Chocolate Fudge,
    238
The Quintessential Chocolate
    Chip Cookie, 177

raisins
    Chocolate Challah (variation),
      44
    Chocolate Chip Cherry Bars
      (variation), 222
    Chocolate Chip Spice Bars
      with Maple Glaze, 224
    Chocolate Crunchies, 259
    Chocolate Raisin Scones, 56
    Chocolate Rum Raisin Ice
      Cream, 288
    Cowgirl Cookies, 187
    Double Chocolate Chunkies,
      178
    Rum Raisin Spoon Brownies,
      217
    Sticky Chocolate Raisin
      Sauce, 322
    White Chocolate Rum Raisin
      Sauce, 331
raspberries
    Chocolate Chip Jammer
      Scones, 54
    Chocolate Chip Raspberry
      Clafouti, 279
    Chocolate Chip Trifle, 280
    Raspberry Chocolate Chip
      Bars, 223
    Raspberry Chocolate Chip
      Cookies, 180
    Raspberry Chocolate Chip
      Muffins, 71
    Raspberry Chocolate Chip
      Sorbet, 305
    Raspberry Chocolate Sauce,
      325
    Raspberry Dutch Baby with
      Chocolate Chips, 35
    Warm Raspberry Chocolate
      Chip Spread, 341
Rich Lemon Chocolate Chip
    Bundt Cake, 108
Ricotta Puddings, 274
Rocky Roads, 248
rum
    Banana Chip Foster, 295
    Black Forest Sauce, 324
    Cherry Chocolate Chunk Ice
      Cream, 290
    Chocolate Cherry Rum
      Cakes, 128
    Chocolate Chip Cheese Tart,
      164
    Chocolate Fudge Frosting
      (variation), 337

Chocolate Midnight Cake, 92
Chocolate Rum Balls, 244
Chocolate Rum Raisin Ice
    Cream, 288
Chocolate Salami, 252
Chocolate Snow (variation),
    366
Chocolate Tiramisu, 282
Chocolate Truffle Tart, 162
Coconut Chip Sorbet, 306
Coconut Chocolate Chip
    Bundt Cake, 110
Dark Chocolate Sorbet in
    Frozen Orange Cups, 304
Eggnog Chocolate Chip Tea
    Cake, 124
Frozen Cappuccino, 307
Irish Cream Cake (variation),
    99
Killer Mocha Frosting, 339
Mocha Fudge Sauce, 328
Mocha Ice, 309
Mud Cake, 86
Rum Raisin Spoon Brownies,
    217
Strawberry Cheesecake
    Mousse Parfaits, 276
Sweet Potato Pie with White
    Chocolate Chunks, 154
White Chocolate Rum Raisin
    Sauce, 331

sandwiches and wraps, 48–50
sauces, 318–32
scones, 51–57
sesame seed
    Chocolate-Dipped Sesame
      Almond Candy, 250
    Chocolate Halvah Mounds,
      249
    White Chocolate Sesame
      Shortbread Bars, 226
Six-Layer Bars, 233
Slice-and-Bake Chocolate Chip
    Almond Cookies, 186
Snickerdoodle Chip Biscotti, 212
sorbet and ice recipes, 301–9
sour cream, 13
    Banana Chocolate Breads, 43
    Banana Chocolate Cake, 90
    Banana Chocolate Ice Cream,
      289
    Café Mocha Cake, 116
    Chocolate Cheesecake
      Cupcakes, 146

Chocolate Quesadillas, 50
Cranberry Sour Cream Bundt
Cake, 106
Sour Cream Coffee Cake
Muffins, 78
Sour Cream Coffee Cake with
Chocolate Pecan Streusel,
114
Strawberry Chocolate Chip
Muffins, 72
Walnut Chocolate Chip Cake,
96
Spicy Haute Chocolate, 355
spreads, 340–41
Sticky Chocolate Raisin Sauce,
322
strawberries
Chocolate Chip Jammer
Scones (variation), 54
Chocolate Fondue, 318
Chocolate Strawberry Syrup,
335
Strawberry Cheesecake
Mousse Parfaits, 276
Strawberry Chip "Moo-thie,"
348
Strawberry Chocolate Chip
Muffins, 72
sugar, 15–16
Sweet Potato Pie with White
Chocolate Chunks, 154
syrups, 333–35

tarts, 160–69
tea
Chocolate Chai Snow Cones,
310
Chocolate Chip Calypso
Cake, 120
Chocolate Chip Chai Cake,
122
Chocolate Tea, 358
Green Tea White Chocolate
Chip ice Cream, 293
Hot Chocolate Chai Latte,
360
Tiramisu Chip Gelato, 301
Tish's Date Flapjack Cake, 97
toffee
Chocolate Brittle Bars, 220
Chocolate Crunchies, 259

Toffee Chocolate Sauce, 321
tools and equipment, 17–21
Triple Chocolate Chip Cookies,
179
24 Carrot Cake, 100

Vancouver Bars, 234
vegan recipes
Chocolate Fudge Frosting
(variation), 337
Vegan Chocolate Espresso
Brownies, 214
vegetables
Chocolate Potato Cake, 102
Double Chocolate Zucchini
Cake, 103
24 Carrot Cake, 100
Very Cherry Chocolate Float,
350

walnuts
Almond Caramel Bars
(variation), 228
Baklava with Chocolate,
Walnuts and Honey Syrup,
172
Banana Blondies with
Chocolate Chips and
Walnuts, 218
Banana Caramel Terrine, 294
Banana Chocolate Breads, 43
Banana Chocolate Cake, 90
Banana Chocolate Chip Cake,
91
Banana Chocolate Ice Cream,
289
Brown Sugar Chocolate
Chunk Pound Cake, 112
Brown Sugar Shortbread, 208
Butterscotch Pecan Chocolate
Chip Blondies (variation),
219
Chocolate Caramel Bars, 230
Chocolate Chip Coconut Pie
(variation), 157
Chocolate Chip Pecan Pie
(variation), 158
Chocolate Rum Balls, 244
Chocolate Swirl Bread, 38
Maple-Glazed Chocolate
Walnut Breakfast Biscuits, 30

Pumpkin Chocolate Chip
Cookies (variation), 181
Pumpkin Chocolate Chip
Loaves (variation), 46
The Quintessential Chocolate
Chip Cookie, 177
Sour Cream Coffee Cake
Muffins, 78
Sour Cream Coffee Cake with
Chocolate Pecan Streusel
(variation), 114
Vegan Chocolate Espresso
Brownies (variation), 214
Walnut Chocolate Chip Cake,
96
Walnut Whiskey Fudge Sauce,
330
Whiskey Fudge (variation),
240
Warm Raspberry Chocolate
Chip Spread, 341
White Chocolate Almond
Chunk Biscotti, 213
White Chocolate Almond Rice
Pudding, 270
White Chocolate Chunk Fudge
Cookies, 188
White Chocolate Key Lime Pie,
156
White Chocolate Lemon Fudge,
239
White Chocolate Macadamia
Cupcakes, 140
White Chocolate Mocha Sauce,
332
White Chocolate Rum Raisin
Sauce, 331
White Chocolate Sesame
Shortbread Bars, 226
wine
Chocolate Merlot Sauce, 327
Chocolate Port Torte, 98
Dark Chocolate Truffles, 242
Date Flapjack Cake, Tish's,
97
Raspberry Chocolate Chip
Sorbet, 305

yogurt
Frozen Chocolate Malt
Yogurt, 303

More Great Books from Robert Rose

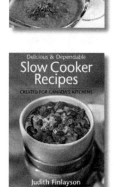

Appliance Cooking

- 125 Best Microwave Oven Recipes
  by Johanna Burkhard

- The Blender Bible
  by Andrew Chase and Nicole Young

- The Mixer Bible
  by Meredith Deeds and Carla Snyder

- The 150 Best Slow Cooker Recipes
  by Judith Finlayson

- Delicious & Dependable Slow Cooker Recipes
  by Judith Finlayson

- 125 Best Vegetarian Slow Cooker Recipes
  by Judith Finlayson

- 125 Best Rotisserie Oven Recipes
  by Judith Finlayson

- 125 Best Food Processor Recipes
  by George Geary

- The Best Family Slow Cooker Recipes
  by Donna-Marie Pye

- The Best Convection Oven Cookbook
  by Linda Stephen

- 125 Best Toaster Oven Recipes
  by Linda Stephen

- 250 Best American Bread Machine Baking Recipes
  by Donna Washburn and Heather Butt

- 250 Best Canadian Bread Machine Baking Recipes
  by Donna Washburn and Heather Butt

Baking

- 250 Best Cakes & Pies
  by Esther Brody

- 500 Best Cookies, Bars & Squares
  by Esther Brody

- 500 Best Muffin Recipes
  by Esther Brody

- 125 Best Cheesecake Recipes
  by George Geary

- 125 Best Chocolate Recipes
  by Julie Hasson

- 125 Best Chocolate Chip Recipes
  by Julie Hasson

- 125 Best Cupcake Recipes
  by Julie Hasson

- Complete Cake Mix Magic
  by Jill Snider

Healthy Cooking

- 125 Best Vegetarian Recipes
  by Byron Ayanoglu with contributions from Algis Kemezys

- America's Best Cookbook for Kids with Diabetes
  by Colleen Bartley

- Canada's Best Cookbook for Kids with Diabetes
  by Colleen Bartley

- The Juicing Bible
  by Pat Crocker and Susan Eagles

- The Smoothies Bible
  by Pat Crocker

125 best vegan recipes

500 best Healthy recipes

Lynn Roblin, RD
NUTRITION EDITOR

125 Best Gluten-Free Recipes

Donna Washburn and Heather Butt

125 Best ICE CREAM Recipes

Marilyn Linton and Tanya Linton

- 125 Best Vegan Recipes
  by Maxine Effenson Chuck and Beth Gurney

- 500 Best Healthy Recipes
  Edited by Lynn Roblin, RD

- 125 Best Gluten-Free Recipes
  by Donna Washburn and Heather Butt

- The Best Gluten-Free Family Cookbook
  by Donna Washburn and Heather Butt

- America's Everyday Diabetes Cookbook
  Edited by Katherine E. Younker, MBA, RD

- Canada's Everyday Diabetes Choice Recipes
  Edited by Katherine E. Younker, MBA, RD

- Canada's Complete Diabetes Cookbook
  Edited by Katherine E. Younker, MBA, RD

- The Best Diabetes Cookbook (U.S.)
  Edited by Katherine E. Younker, MBA, RD

- The Best Low-Carb Cookbook
  from Robert Rose

Recent Bestsellers

- 125 Best Soup Recipes
  by Marylin Crowley and Joan Mackie

- The Convenience Cook
  by Judith Finlayson

- 125 Best Ice Cream Recipes
  by Marilyn Linton and Tanya Linton

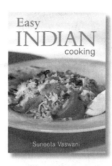

Easy INDIAN cooking

Suneeta Vaswani

THE HOSPITAL FOR SICK CHILDREN

THE COMPLETE Kid's ALLERGY AND ASTHMA GUIDE

THE PARENT'S HANDBOOK FOR CHILDREN OF ALL AGES
GENERAL EDITOR, DR. MILTON GOLD

The Complete Natural Medicine Guide to BREAST CANCER

A Practical Manual for Understanding, Prevention & Care

SAT DHARAM KAUR
Preface by Dr. Carolyn Dean, ND, MD

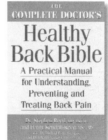

THE COMPLETE DOCTOR'S Healthy Back Bible

A Practical Manual for Understanding, Preventing and Treating Back Pain

Dr. Stephen Reed, MD and Penny Kendall-Reed, MS

- Easy Indian Cooking
  by Suneeta Vaswani

- Simply Thai Cooking
  by Wandee Young and Byron Ayanoglu

Health

- The Complete Natural Medicine Guide to the 50 Most Common Medicinal Herbs
  by Dr. Heather Boon, B.Sc.Phm., Ph.D. and Michael Smith, B.Pharm, M.R.Pharm.S., ND

- The Complete Kid's Allergy and Asthma Guide
  Edited by Dr. Milton Gold

- The Complete Natural Medicine Guide to Breast Cancer
  by Sat Dharam Kaur, ND

- The Complete Doctor's Stress Solution
  by Penny Kendall-Reed, MSc, ND and Dr. Stephen Reed, MD, FRCSC

- The Complete Doctor's Healthy Back Bible
  by Dr. Stephen Reed, MD and Penny Kendall-Reed, MSc, ND with Dr. Michael Ford, MD, FRCSC and Dr. Charles Gregory, MD, ChB, FRCP(C)

- Everyday Risks in Pregnancy & Breastfeeding
  by Dr. Gideon Koren, MD, FRCP(C), ND

- Help for Eating Disorders
  by Dr. Debra Katzman, MD, FRCP(C), and Dr. Leora Pinhas, MD

Also Available
from Robert Rose

125 best
Cupcake
recipes

Julie Hasson

125 Best Cupcake Recipes

ISBN 0-7788-0112-8 13-Digit ISBN 978-0-7788-0112-2
$19.95 Canada/$18.95 U.S.

For more great books, see previous pages